The Fountain
Nation Building with Econometric Representation

By Jordan David Weisinger

CONTENTS

FORWORD

The most important property of econometric representation is its ability to extend the life of democracy by emphasizing the representation of wealthier districts and increasing the adjusted per capita income of voting residents. Higher per capita incomes are associated with states prolonging their status as a democracy. This could be a critical component of nation building exercises after occupation. If a one nation could better guarantee success after installing democratic entitlements in an occupied nation, it could justify the large amount of labor and capital spent on the effort. Anything that makes it more likely the nation will preserve the democratic status of the target of the nation building should be considered a viable option or strategy.

The second most important property of Econometric representation based on GDP is that it permits one state to incorporate another state with little change to overall representation in the short term with expectations that the new state gains proportional representation in the long term. Therefore, a state will accept an initial inferior position in expectation of realizing the promise of an equal position in the future. The independent variable is GDP and the dependent variable is political representation. However, there are two important intervening variables.

The first and most important intervening variable is the rate of federal tax subsidy provided to less developed states in a political union. The premise is federal tax subsidies will improve a low GDP state's rate of GDP growth and thus accelerate the rate of normalization in representation. The next most important intervening variable is the quality of economic reforms passed on regional level and federal level. Fiscal policy and labor laws can have a dramatic impact on GDP growth rates between states. The expected tendency or direction of the relationship is positive; the GDP of the developing nation will increase at a faster rate than that of the developed nation as thus eventually achieve a more proportional form of representation. The faster the GDP growth rate is the greater the representation gained.

This book uses a comparison of means (roughly equated to the interval measurements of GDP/population) across two or more states/nations over time to look at representational changes in demographics and econometrics. However, this book does not offer a comparison of means for GDP/population across multiple developing nations. Developing nations might have a competitive relationship with different GDP growth rates producing much bigger changes in net representation. An interaction relationship exists. States that receive more federal tax subsidy should acquire faster rates of GDP growth regardless of developmental stage. More importantly, a less developed nation may have faster GDP growth rates, but this is may be offset by the GDP advantage in the more developed nation. A nation with a smaller economy and faster GDP growth may never reach parity with a nation with a slower growth rate but much larger economy. The last effect to be measured is the difference in population growth between the more developed nation and the less developed nation. Growth in demographic representation may be faster than growth in econometric representation

The interaction relationship suggests mixed outcomes; different states will have different outcomes based on GDP growth and population growth, especially when the intervening variable of federal subsidies and economic reforms are present. Both the null hypothesis and alternative hypothesis have strategic value when used in a mixed representation system combining both demographics and econometrics. It is possible that developing states acquire adequate GDP growth to acquire proportional representation using demographic representation as normative standard. However, contrary to the stated hypothesis, Econometric Representation often concentrates majority political power in the developed nation providing a buffer against significant changes in demographic representation. Thus, econometric representation will be more often a strategy for developed nations to retain majority political control when incorporating less developed states with faster population growth rates.

Larger wealthier states will have several incentives to expand their territorial boundaries and their electorate. The evidence suggests that developed economies can incorporate smaller and poorer states into their political unions without significant long-term risk in transferring political majorities. Imposing democracy on formerly despotic nations may be improved if they are incorporated into larger more established democracies who make long term commitments to economic stimulus through federal subsidies and improved security by a permanent presence. This could promote an environment of democratic imperialism that will offset the increased risk from climate change, wealth inequality, and the rise in economic power of despotic nations like China.

Most political systems are imposed when movements form around unsubstantiated ideologies like economic opportunity or equality. Most of the contemporary democracies were founded on the twin virtues of hope and faith. It must inspire confidence without the evidence. This book plays on those tendencies. It attempts to provide a reasonable alternative to conventional demographic based democracy. None of these purported political systems current exists. The lack of concrete examples makes rigorous testing of the hypothesis impossible. Claims are made but the actual GDP data and demographic data to support the conclusions are missing. However, with a little imagination and confidence the evidence can be conjured up and examples of econometric representation will thrive in a more competitive environment for democracy.

1 ECONOMETRIC REPRESENTATION

It is human nature to reorganize our environment in a manner that produces more security and more order. One of our greatest tools in this endeavor is the state. States allow us to marshal our productivity and harness our resources. They provide a common defense against those external persons that would exploit us or harm us. They also provide for law and order to protect us against those internal persons who would exploit or marginalize us. However, for all their self-evident benefits, we continue to succumb to ancient tribalism and partisan belief systems when it comes to immigration and expansionism. This is especially true, when democratic representation is intimately connected to demographics.

Econometric representation is a major innovation in disentangling representation from the arbitrary representation of senates. The Senate is a regressive form of representation that overtly contradicts the tenants of self-governance and majority rule (*i.e., consensus*). Senates distribute an equal number of representatives to each state regardless of their populations or other attributes. Therefore, arbitrary representation is essentially an inverse of demographic based representation. The two tend to cancel each other out resulting in increased stagnation and obstruction. Bicameral legislatures rely on cooperation between two chambers to pass economic regulations and fully fund the government. Decoupling representation from majority consent introduces political instability and the possibility of catastrophe or conflict.

The use of Gross Domestic Product (GDP) as a representational coefficient is a less extreme option than the arbitrary representation of a senate. Political unions predicated on a combination of Gross Domestic Product and demographics will help insulate representation from demographic changes. This is a significant improvement for political unions which helps dispels fears of coercion when integrating two large populations with different cultures or economic prospects. Gross Domestic Product is a simple measurement that occurs over a district or state jurisdiction. It is an aggregate measurement of economic activity for a large and diverse community. This helps distances it from a single ethnicity, tribe, or religion in more open societies. More specifically, GDP is the total dollar value of all goods and services produced over a specific period of time [1].

GDP isn't an accurate measure of individual wealth and it is only weakly correlated to population in nations with high variance between aggregate economic activity. However, the value in using GDP for a representational coefficient is that it is standardized and denominated in a common currency. Standardization is the key property to consider. A nation can reasonably calculate its current GDP in relation to another nation's GDP. It can examine its trajectory for growth in comparison to another countries comparison to growth. Current options are constrained by current theory, and GDP is easily translated into representational coefficients for use in class-based systems of representation. All of the calculations in this book use GDP as the baseline, but GDP can be easily substituted with Gross National Income (GNP). GNP is "the total income earned by the nation's permanent residents"[2]. The difference and their uses can be debated.

There are two primary methods to allocate GDP based representation among participating nations and states. The first method is the straight method and it assigns a number of representatives to each state in accord with the proportional value of GDP compared to other states in the Union. The second method is called a median partition and is more complicated. The districts or states are ordered according to GDP and split into two equal parts by the median GDP value. Both methods conform to the standards of universal suffrage but the median partition preserves majority rule. They offer excellent alternatives for demographic representation when nation building or forming political unions. Each has its own advantages depending on the circumstances.

Straight GDP based representation allows a nation to incorporate new states without dramatically changing the disposition of their own legislative chambers in the near term. The assuming nation can expand its population base for consumption or

---

[1] Gregory N. Mankiw, The Essentials of Economics (6th ed.) (Stanford: CT Cengage Learning, 2015), page 309.
[2] Gregory N. Mankiw, The Essentials of Economics (6th ed.) (Stanford: CT Cengage Learning, 2015), page 313.

conscription. It can gain access to natural resources and geo-spatial advantages. The recently incorporated state gains some potent benefits. In the near term, the state gains access to tax subsidies and investment revenues for faster economic growth. More importantly, it also receives martial support to protect voting rights and ensure the new republican form of government has an opportunity to root in culture and expectations. In the long run, GDP based representation will provide an opportunity for the state to acquire full representation in a stable democracy with a mature economy. All participating states will benefit from the new relationship, albeit at different times during the re-organization. This is the promise made. Sacrifice now for a future benefit of improved security and increased equity.

Straight GDP based representation will result in a concentration of representatives in wealthier states. This isn't representative of population but many institutions in contemporary democracies aren't either. Senates are notorious for over-representing rural states and smaller states. Those states are often poorer with fewer residents. This allows exploitative economic policies to propagate through the nation despite the majority objecting to them. It allows corporations to deregulate labor markets and obstruct environmental laws. It reinforces counterproductive policies like austerity measures and regressive taxes. Arbitrary representation is often a deficiency, but it should conform to contemporary standards for representation in systems aspiring for Universal Suffrage.

The imbalance in representation within econometric systems is purposefully engineered; it allows the more successful partners it to project their financial management expertise and culture the other states within the Union. The single market and single currency zone will promote investment and trade within the less developed economy and eventually the currency exchange rates will equilibrate. More importantly, the lower GDP states should receive a larger proportion of federal tax subsidies promoting faster GDP growth with the economic stimulus and engineering. When parity in per capita GDP is earned, the state will receive proportional representation and acquire equal status with the other states. This is the promise of economic integration. This is the promise of citizenship and union.

Econometric representation should improve outcomes in nation building when the wealthier cities and regions earn proportionally more representation in the fledgling democracy. The ability to maintain democracy is dependent on the nation's ability to acquire economic security for its citizens. "The expected life of democracy in a country with per capita income under $1,000 is about eight years. Between $1,001 and $2,000, an average democracy can expect to endure 18 years. But above $6,000, democracy lasts forever"[3]. Econometric Representation emphasizes the political will of the regions with higher per capita incomes over those regions with lower per capita income presenting an opportunity to capture outcomes usually associated with higher economic output.

For example, a per capita income of $900 might include regions with per capita incomes of $1200 and $600. If the regions with per capita incomes of $1200 earned more proportional representation, it could effectively prolong the life of the democracy from 8 years to 18 years. The additional 10 years may give a fledgling democracy an opportunity to pass economic reforms raising the average per capita income passed the $1000 threshold and extend state longevity. In order to test this hypothesis, a nation must first accept the use of GDP as a representational coefficient in their legislature. This requires trust and trust is hard earned.

Administrations should examine econometric representation as an option for nation building after occupations. Econometric representation can produce a per capita income that is much higher when adjusted in proportion of net representation in the union. The first step in the calculation is taking the number of representatives from the demographic representational coefficient and multiplying the figure by the per capita income for the state. These values are summed and divided by the total number of representatives. The modified per capita income uses a number of representatives based on a GDP based representational coefficient. The GDP for each state is tallied and divided by the pre-determined number of representatives. The GDP of each state is then divided by this number with all non-whole numbers rounded down except those less than 1. All values less than one are rounded up to one. The new number of representatives is multiplied by the per capita income. These figures are tallied and divided by the total number of representatives producing the modified per capita income.

The hypothesis that a modified per capita income will result in greater longevity will remain untested until an occupying nation or rebel group agree to the terms of GDP-based representational coefficients in a democracy. Most democracies have a second

---

[3]   Adam Przeworski, Minimalist Conception of Democracy: A Defense." In Democracy's Value edited by Shapiro, I. and Hacker-Cordon, C. (Cambridge: Cambridge University), page 16.

chamber to their legislatures introducing an intervening variable in most experiments. The rational is GDP-based representational coefficient emphasize states with higher GDP simulating a state with a higher per capita income. Each state will include an electorate that incorporates residents of all income brackets with diversity in ethnicity and religion. This helps justify the emphasis of wealthier states with in the political union. These wealthier states will in turn pursue sounder economic policies that contribute to wage growth and economic stability.

Take India as another example. India had a per capita income of $1627 in 2015[4]. If GDP was used as a representational coefficient in India instead of population, the modified per capita income increases to $1929[5]. This 18.58%[6] increase in per capita GDP could be meaningful in terms of state longevity. This could effectively double the expected period for preserving democratic entitlements passed the 18 years predicted at $1627[7]. Increasing per capita to over $2000 is suddenly a short term goal when viewed through the prism of a modified per capita income of $1929. Other nations like Iraq may have more profound outcomes. It has a current per capita income of $5695 and a GDP-based representational coefficient might easily inflate the figure above the $6000 threshold for permanent democracy[8]. This is an important strategic goal of the occupying force from 2004. If econometric representation makes success more likely than it will be viewed as a viable option during other nation building efforts.

The impact of econometric representation on democratic longevity may be more important for less developed nations. Take for example Afghanistan with a per capita GDP of $590[9] and the tentative grasp it has on democracy. If the lifespan of a democracy with $590 GDP is only 8 years, then raising it passed $1000 could be a critical

---

[4] "GDP per capita India", StatisticsTimes.com, accessed on April 2nd, 2018 at http://statisticstimes.com/economy/gdp-capita-of-india.php

[5] "Indian states by GDP", Worldatlas.com, accessed on April 2nd, 2018 at https://www.worldatlas.com/articles/indian-states-by-gdp.html

[6] This is an imperfect translation. It does not include the 12 nominated representatives in the lower house. The GDP-based representational coefficient produced 228 base representatives rather than the current 233 without the nominated representatives

[7] Adam Przeworski, Minimalist Conception of Democracy: A Defense." In Democracy's Value edited by Shapiro, I. and Hacker-Cordon, C. (Cambridge: Cambridge University), page 16.

[8] "Iraq: GDP per capita", Trading Economics, accessed on April 2nd, 018 from https://tradingeconomics.com/iraq/gdp-per-capita

[9] Accessed on 4/2/2018 at https://www.worldatlas.com/finance/afghanistan/gdp.html

strategy for preserving democracy. If Afghanistan's modified per capita income could be raised above $1000 it could extend the timeframe for achieving durable democracy from just 8 years to 18 years or more. Afghanistan is America's longest war with nearly 17 years of active combat[10]. If Afghanistan accepted the use of GDP-based representational coefficients, its legislature would emphasize the wealthier states over the poorer and more rural states providing an arc to more stability and more equitable economic reforms. These reforms can include minimum wage laws, union protections, progressive taxes and other simple reforms. Accelerated GDP growth over 17 years may have pushed its modified per capita income passed the $1000 threshold helping suppress support for the Taliban. The higher modified per capita income could extend the life of the democracy until it acquired enough wealth to perpetuate itself indefinitely. This is the promise of GDP-based representational coefficients for nation building. However, without a controlled experiment this speculation will remain unproven.

Representational coefficients also offer more potential for peaceful integration of nations and states. The promise of one person and one vote is a powerful inducement for Union. The assimilated states will likely have less developed economies limiting their GDP based representation on the federal tier. Larger populations will have less net representation in the initial union. However, as the economy matures, the currency will gain value and the region's GDP will grow in value along with the number of representatives apportioned to the state. It permits the assuming nation to take on a new state without necessarily disrupting its current fragile balance in leadership and political representation.

In peacetimes, these political unions will be cooperative efforts. They will be negotiated by lawyers and economists in the bureaucracy of government. The process will be metered out over years or decades with several generations participating in the process. Trade negotiations will expand into currency zones. Uninhibited travel and labor movement will follow. Eventually, the nations' will agree to share political representation and modest regulatory control. Each phase is a step towards complete integration as a single economic and political union.

---

[10] Accessed on 4/4/2018 from http://abcnews.go.com/Politics/afghanistan-americas-longest-war/story?id=10770029

History doesn't always move so slowly. In war time, these political unions will be part of expansionist designs for democratic empire. The premise of imperial democracy is a notion that is anchored in history. The Romans forged for themselves an empire that stretched across hundreds of thousands of square miles. It bestowed citizenship on the elite within the conquered cities and nations. This allowed them to pacify populations that would otherwise persist in turmoil and pursue revolt at every opportunity. Contemporary econometric systems have this capacity too.

GDP based representation distributes universal suffrage among the newly incorporated people that is nearly indistinguishable to the quality of suffrage provided to the other citizens. Net Representation is still a function of wealth, with the federal level while each eligible citizen continues to receive one full vote (one person one vote). Within the region, the citizens will continue to benefit from proportional representation on the local and state level. Legislators within the GDP based chamber will represent only a small portion of the total number of elections. Most of their representatives will be elected on a local level, producing equivalency between the voters of that city or region. The integrated nation will preserve a large part of their independence despite losing sovereignty to the larger nation with more mature economy. Often, national elections for Presidents are based on majority rule or popular votes. This will offset the non-proportional representation found within the bicameral legislature.

One person one vote qualifies as universal suffrage even if the tenant of majority rule is violated. Majority rule is assumed to be a core component of democracy, but the earliest versions of democracy all included restricted electorates. People only assume democracy is predicated on majority rule. This is the promise of demographic chambers of representation. However, claims of majority rule can easily be disputed by the incorporation of the Senate based on arbitrary representation. All arbitrary systems of representation actively counteract or mitigate the majority rule provided by demographic chambers. In this respect, econometric representation based on GDP can be declared as high quality democratic entitlements despite relying more on universal suffrage than majority rule.

Political Unions with non-proportional representation will rely on marketing their Constitutions and civil liberties when trying to strike a deal. A strong Constitution can fill the vacuum when a low GDP doesn't provide substantial and reciprocal upfront representation.

A strong Constitution gives a new state an immediate benefit rather than a future benefit. The people will still expect economic development and a substantial improvement in GDP and representation, but the Democratic institutions protecting civil liberties from a Constitution will imbue patience and discipline in the electorate. This is significantly more important, if the assume nation was previously despotic or totalitarian where citizens were routinely tortured, imprisoned, or murdered for free speech or political activism.

Civil liberties promote non-violent protest and they have demonstrated to be nearly twice as effective as armed insurrection or riot. A stable democracy with strong civil rights agencies and other Democratic institutions will help ensure the new population inculcates into the culture of peaceful civil disobedience and faith in the due process of democracy. These virtues make it more likely that the new state adopts the culture of democracy and its positive institutions. This will improve outcomes in nation building with special emphasis on the democratization movement.

GDP based representation helps diffuse tensions from changes in the demographics of a union. This should make it possible to avoid demographic based violence. If representation isn't completely predicated on demographics there is very little fear in losing political power to an emergent population with a growth rate larger than the current majority population. Demographic fears are an overarching concern in many democracies where nativism and populism can cause social upheaval, unrest, riots, and civil wars. Worse, it can result in direct and imminent threat to democracy and due process in the nation.

GDP representation continues to rely on personal voting, but it disrupts the direct translation of political power from population size. GDP carries some parity with demographic based systems of representation when located within the same nation, but it has a weak association with populations between nations split by mature economy or developing economy status. This makes political unions between states of different population and wealth to coordinate their political and economic activity while preserving universal suffrage. It is intended to limit the severity of demographic shifts by diffusing the magnitude of political power transferred when one demographic group loses majority status and another gain's it. If the representational coefficients were never exclusively based on population, the fear of loss is ablated by the uncertainty in representational outcomes.

The primary role of GDP based representation is to minimize the correlation of population with political power but there is no legitimate way to disentangle individual votes from political outcomes. This makes all political systems vulnerable to political instability resulting from demographic shifts. Nothing will change the fact that another demographic group acquires majority status within a state, but if that state doesn't receive a number of representatives equal to its population, the perceived risk to other demographic groups is lessened. A higher variance in representation between states undergoing demographic shifts reduces the risk of loss of political power. The loss of power is moderated by the variance between states and this obfuscates the risk.

This sounds like an affront on the very nature of democracy, but the purpose of the senate and a bicameral process was to insulate the nation from animal spirits in the population. Arbitrary representation is an inverse to population which takes the power away from the majority demographic group. However, senates are not always effective in this respect. A senate creates the opportunity for a minority to monopolize the legislative process and completely obstruct due process and reform. Although, senates were intended to be the bulwark against nativism and populism, their design has aided it. It is often the less densely populated and poorer states, with less educated residents and more homogenous electorates, that benefit from the inverse of demographic political representation Most nativist and populist movements come from these regions creating a dangerous trend in national sentiments and public policy.

GDP based representation is intended to achieve the same goals without this increased risk from minority political party control. GDP typically favors more diverse regions with more educated residents. This implicitly checks the momentum of a populist movement. Not only are wealthier states less prone to nativist tendencies but they will have significantly more political power. States with larger metropolitan areas and more educated workforces will have more GDP and more representatives in the federal legislature. This is true in systems that utilize a straight GDP representational coefficient and those that use a median partition.

Econometric representation may make class tensions worse with the possibility of substituting wealth-based conflict. However, class-based tensions are safer and more productive than demographic based tensions. Most class-based tensions can be addressed by economic reforms and tax reform. Institutions like Unions can reduce poverty and improve wealth equality. Most demographic attributes are fixed and permanent over a lifetime. The only solution is anti-democratic policies limiting voting rights and election. Obviously, this a terrible response and counter-productive in every aspect. This makes demographic shifts intrinsically more dangerous than periods of wealth inequality

Civil disobedience through peaceful protest would be successful at earning economic reforms. This is not true for demographic instability. Nothing will satisfy the growing anger in a population that fears it is being crowded out by another population. Democracy is a terrifying process as it peacefully transfers majority political power from one majority demographic group to another. It is even more terrifying when one majority group has been responsible for exploiting or oppressing the other for generations with austerity measures and deregulated labor laws. The majority demographic group would have to permanently alter the trajectory of the nation with mass incarcerations, mass murders, or anti-democratic measures like voter suppression or voter fraud. Class tensions are far easy to mitigate, with progressive taxes, minimum wage laws, and unionization rights. Class based representation increases the odds a nation will identify the issues or policies that will address the instability and then more easily pass them. Nations can't completely exclude the possibility for riots, violence, or civil war as it is often a mix of both demographic and class-based tensions, but they can reduce the frequency and magnitude with GDP based representation.

The alternative to straight GDP representation is the median partition. Median partitions are primarily class-based systems that separate above median GDP states or districts from below median GDP states or districts. Two co-equal chambers are created, with all citizens retaining one person one vote and the legitimacy of majority rule. Class based representation helps the electorate align their public policy to their interests and then facilitate bargaining and negotiation between the above median GDP class and the below median GDP class. The bicameral legislature will require each class to barter and compromise on legislation resulting in higher quality laws containing benefits for both classes.

There are three types of median partitions. A standard median partition uses a demographic representational coefficient to determine the number of representatives each state receives, but it then arranges the individual districts from highest GDP to lowest GDP and splits them in half at the median value. There are an equal number of districts in the above median GDP chamber and the below median GDP chamber. A biaxial median partition allocates states to above median GDP and below median GDP chambers with the larger more populous states concentrated in one chamber. The states are arranged by GDP from highest to lowest and split between the two chambers. The third variety is Senatorial. It continues to divide the states between the above median and below median chambers, but this version drops the demographic representational coefficient and allocates an arbitrary number of senators per state.

A median partition concentrates districts with similar median incomes into similar representational regions. Districts with lower GDP will belong within a legislative chamber with other low GDP districts. Higher GDP districts will participate in a legislative chamber with higher GDP districts. This makes it more likely that the wealthiest citizens will vote in elections with other wealthy citizens. It also makes it more likely that poorer citizens vote for candidates representing poor jurisdictions. They will form more accurate class identities within their respective chambers helping facilitate more informed debate between the above median GDP and below median GDP chambers.

Within state wide jurisdictions, the variance between incomes within the population is significantly higher. Greater variance produces less homogenous electorates and less predictable outcomes. However, a more diverse electorate has other advantages. Its lack of homogeny is built on different perspectives and economic outcomes. This should contribute to debate on policy options. More importantly, less predictable electoral outcomes keep political parties more honest and makes the political system more competitive. Dividing states by median GDP will help shape the political preference of their residents and the class identity. This is a small concession, but it does make the conditions more acceptable for developing nations when they are integrating unto political unions with more mature economies. They will find solace in caucusing with states of similar economic status.

The intersection of states and districts by GDP forms classes of governments. It splits the nation into "haves" and "have nots". The class division will aid in issue identity and then conflict resolution. High GDP regions will have different concerns than low GDP regions. Labor laws, federal tax policy, education, and healthcare issues may be viewed differently by the two competing classes. It also splits the nation into urban districts and rural classes. The role specialization within the chambers should allow them to negotiate more effectively. It is simply a higher form of organization for democratic representation. Class based representation will significantly improve the deliberative process by focusing the interests of the two groups.

The median partition avoids many of the pitfalls of wealth-based representation calculated by weakly correlated or poorly defined econometric figures. Median partition often uses demographic representational coefficients reaffirming majority control over a political system. GDP is used as a means of separating the electorate by class rather than assigning political power to the wealth attribute. In a median partition, poor districts or states have just as much political representation and power as wealthy districts or states. This is not true in straight GDP representation that assigns a number of representatives based on its comparative economic activity. It is easier for persons to object to a straight GDP based system of representation based on the over representation of the wealthier communities.

2 DEMOCRATIC IMPERIALISM

Democracy inhibits imperial expansion in two major ways. When a population has access to due process and can self-regulate, they are far less interested in waging war for territorial gain. Peace is the best means to improve economy in an efficiently regulated and adequately taxed economy. This was not true in the age of mercantilism and monarchy. In those conditions, economy suffered under a zero percent growth rate. For a nation to expand its economy, it had to expand into other markets, most often by violence or subversion. This was not productive. Worse, monarchs were loath to extend any representational rights to the conquered cities or states. Large empires were formed with weak associations and no loyalty. The instability eventually produced a democratic revolution and the start of a new era in history. It was an improvement on the Magna Carta and resurrected the democratic policies of the Greek and Roman eras.

However, the emergence of democracy didn't end Imperialism. Imperialism continued even during periods where major reform movements towards democracy were rooted in the Americas and common in Europe. The United States maintained several possessions despite its status as the progenitor contemporary democracy. Great Britain maintained most of its territorial possessions until the end of World War II – and that accounted for nearly 25% of the world's landmass[11]. France preserved its territorial possession in South East Asia until roughly 20 years after the conclusion of World War II[12]. Many of the nation's still retain small islands as protectorates or territories with special rights but the

---

[11] Richard Halloran, "The Sad, Dark End of the British Empire", Politico.com, last modified on August 26, 2014. http://www.politico.com/magazine/story/ 2014/08/the-sad-end-of-the-british-empire-110362

[12] "Battlefield Vietnam", PBS.org, accessed on June 24th, 2017. http://www.pbs.org/battlefieldvietnam/

movement is almost exhausted. Imperialism appears to be a dead movement. However, climate change may produce instability and opportunity to resurrect the old science of imperialism.

There is another risk. The world is watching the emergence of China as the next dominant economic superpower and it is uncertain if the old habits of colonialism and imperialism won't creep back into the domain of acceptable behavior. The financial influence of a despotic economic superpower may imbalance the current ecology of low quality democracies. Wealth inequality is present making them more susceptible to regime change and revolution. Economy was a powerful inducement towards democracy, when democracies commanded the majority of GDP. Now that China is emergent, the world may slip back into a period of sustained imperialism as the moral framework in the world's democracies buckles under the compromise of despotic commerce.

To counter-act these dangerous conditions, democracies may seek to expand their political boundaries through negotiated treaty or force. Each time they incorporate a new territory, they increase the population that can be enlisted into their armed forces, they improve access to natural resources, and they gain access to new economic markets for profit and government revenues. More importantly, nations can spread the culture of democracy and self-determination. The more people participating in democracy, the more likely it is to survive global pandemics, world wars, or economic collapses. This is especially important, in an environment seeing the rise of despotism and climate related instability. Democratic nations will need to defend themselves by scaling up their resources and eliminating threats as they are encountered. A larger number of conflicts increases the number of opportunities for democratic expansion helping to mitigate the increased environmental risks.

The core principle of self-rule in democracy is not always contradictory to expansionary policies. The most successful democratic empires all extend citizenship voting rights to conquered people. However, this expansion of the electorate is often the most dangerous consequence of imperial democracy. Incorporating a larger population into the electorate might change it. Expanding the electorate is also the momentum behind its success. Otherwise, conquered nations require too much labor and capital to continue to oppress. The act breeds contempt and suspicion in its own public and outright hatred in the occupied territory. This doesn't only drain treasuries; it also destroys labor. It demoralizes the soldiers and increasing the numbers of disabled and wounded warriors. Worse, it is a vector for antidemocratic tendencies in the population of the conquering nation. The soldiers and the public internalize the violence, and this can negative impact their expectations, their ambitions, or their intentions.

The imperial democracies of history didn't distribute voting rights to all people equally. They didn't conform to contemporary standards of universal suffrage and equality. Restrictive electorates allow nations to expand their borders by acquiring new territory and then providing a voter entitlement to a select group within the conquered people. Distributing votes exclusively to the aristocracy will elicit support from the wealthiest citizens and help quell any dissent from the lower classes. It was the wealth and power of the landed aristocracy that allowed the assuming nations to maintain power in the newly acquired state. They would regularly put down uprisings and riots to maintain the status quo. This facilitated a quicker integration into the imperial democracy despite the fact a large majority of the public remained subjects rather than citizens.

If a democratic nation conquers another nation with the intent to expand its territory and impart voting rights to the entire population, it would quickly lose its national character. The conquered populations could easily vote in their own leaders and possibly assume control over the entire republic. A conquering nation could be dominated by a larger and more homogenous population within the assumed territory. The Conservative populations that were most inclined to imperialism were the most discouraged by expanding the electorate to include newly conquered people. For this reason, democratic empire was never pursued. In the few examples of expansion available, the conquering nation usually exhausted the host population or native population or denied them due process and voting rights in the republic.

GDP based representation accommodates these defects by establishing a variable rate of representation that increases over time. At first, the new territory may have abridged rights but after a few decades of economic reforms they should acquire more proportional representation within the empire or the union. Developing economies integrated into political unions with mature economies, should get more tax support in addition from the combined benefits of pro-growth policies on the local or state level and more investment from allied states. This should improve the rate at which they assume mature market attributes with more equitable GDP distribution between the states of the new union. The assuming nation (or conquering nation) can therefore expand it borders and economy without fear of losing its mandate in the electorate, at least until the new states are inculcated into the culture and establish firm business and personal relationships within the greater population.

Predicating representation on GDP allows a host nation to incorporate another nation into its political union without excluding any persons from the electorate. Unlike the Imperial Democracies of ancient history, the new democracy need not rely on just the aristocracy. When GDP is used as an index for representation, the integrity of universal suffrage is preserved but the aggregate voting power of the new electorate is diminished. This isn't optimal from an ideological perspective, but there is no perfect solution when expanding political unions between mature economies and developing economics. The lower quality representation should conform to more situations and satisfy more conditions for political union. The greater frequency of unionization will the efficiency in the political markets even if the equity is not perfect.

The expectation is the two economies will eventually reach equilibrium and provide more proportional representation to all the citizens in the Union. Most unions already accept representational deficiencies between states. This was the original intention of the Senate in the United States. Only the idealization of a more representative system can be achieved with expansion. It is doubtful that two already incorporated states will agree to perfectly representative systems during unionization negotiations. However, the promise of nearly perfect representation creates a compact between the newly incorporated states and the host nation. Every time a new state is incorporated into the empire, or political union, it has an opportunity to acquire full citizenship status with proportional representation. It will be an equal among the other states when all accept the variable representation based on Gross Domestic Product. This is the promise made.

In 1776, the original framers of United States were not too concerned with the legitimacy of a democracy based on majority rule. When the United States was first incorporated, it was an aristocratic slave state that required nearly 250 years of reforms to make it compliant with universal suffrage and the due process we now associate with contemporary democracy. Not only had they installed a Senate with nonproportional representation but they also advocated for the Electoral college. They organized a restricted electorate that excluded the poor, women, and minorities, with only a small proportion of the total body politic retained the right to vote. Under different conditions, our revolutionary leaders might have come to alternative conclusions and made different decisions. The founding fathers were elitists and might have had affinities for a wealth-based system of representation. If the founding fathers had GDP data to draw from, they may have substituted GDP based representation for demographic representation. They may have also substituted GDP representation for Senatorial representation.

The Senate was a compromise to smaller states for accepting the House, which was predicated on demographic representation. The House provided proportional representation based on population. Thus, the more populous states would have proportionally more representation. Smaller states feared this arrangement. They thought they would be overwhelmed and dominated by the larger states. Senates operate as an inverse to demographic representation. The smaller a state is in terms of population, the greater its proportional representation in the Senate. Most contemporary democracies rely on Senatorial representation.

The Senate serves the same purpose in a political system that utilizes GDP for representational coefficients. The senate will favor the underrepresented new state by reducing the proportional representation afforded to states with higher GDP and more mature economies. Each new state can be provided the typical number of senators thus increasing their total net representation. Senates served the same purpose by enticing poorer states into unions with wealthier states when an exclusively demographic based representation was used while still maintaining a more favorable ratio for older more established states. This is a basis for more equal representation at the onset, which isn't conditional on economic performance or currency exchange rates. The senate will be an inducement towards unionization that all new states will see as favorable.

The imbalance of representation usually found in the Senate is an upfront payment on the promise of full citizenship in the future. As the new state's economy improves with a stronger economic performance and currency exchange rate, it will rely less on the senate and more on the more proportional GDP based representation. Arbitrary representation from the Senate is also a guarantee on continued representation despite economic performance. If GDP growth should falter in the developing economy, the new state will have already acquired representational parity with the richer states in that institution. States with excessively high GDP will receive as much representation in the Senate as states with very low GDP. The Senate splits the difference in possible outcomes, averaging out the product of population and GDP.

GDP based representation is a reasonable substitute for the Senate too. Outside of being an inducement to unionization, it is almost completely counterproductive. If one is to accept the legitimacy of demographic representation due to the innate authority of the majority population, then senatorial representation is entirely unacceptable. A nation could employ both a demographic system of representation and a GDP based system of representation. This would eliminate the arbitrary representation and substitute it with coefficients correlated with education and population density. This combination respects the implicit authority of majority rule and consensus by affording it more representational power. It is not a perfect ratio, but a meritocracy that rewards improved economic performance may outperform those nations still relying on arbitrary representation in bicameral legislatures.

If states and nations are willing to accept the high representational ratios in arbitrary systems like the Senate, they may also be willing to accept the terms for GDP representation. This is especially true in cases where a demographic chamber is also present, providing a gradient towards proportional representation. The poorer nation or state can continue to rely on its numerical parity or superiority with population even if it suffers deficits in economic activity. If one looks at the least populated state in the United States it is Wyoming with 579,679 persons projected in 2015[13]. The most populated state is California with 38,421,464 persons[14]. If both states are apportioned 2 Senators each regardless of the population, Wyoming has nearly 66x as much proportional representation than California[15]. If one looks at New York, 19,673,174[16] (2015), and Florida, 19,645,772[17] (2015) the leverage is a little more than 34x[18],

---

[13] "Wyoming, Community Facts", Census.gov, accessed on July 1st, 2017.
https://factfinder.census.gov/faces/nav/jsf/pages/index.xhtml

[14] "California, Community Facts", Census.gov, accessed on July 1st, 2017 at
https://factfinder.census.gov/faces/nav/jsf/pages/index.xhtml

[15] Derivative of California 2015 population estimate / Wyoming 2015 population estimate

[16] "New York, Community Facts", Cenus.gov, accessed on July 1st, 2017.
https://factfinder.census.gov/faces/nav/jsf/pages/index.xhtml

[17] "Florida, Community Facts", Cenus.gov, accessed on July 1st, 2017.

and the differential in Texas, 26,538,614[19] (2015) at nearly 46x[20]. It is obvious that the residents and citizens of states within the same union are comfortable with different ratios of representation, despite the fact it is not correlated to population, GDP, or taxes remitted back to the federal government.

This presents an opportunity to legitimize GDP based representation by relating the differential in Senatorial representation back to the differential in Gross Domestic Product. Let us examine the GDP of Mexico versus the United States. In 2015, Mexico had a 1.151T[21] dollar economy compared to the 18.037T dollar GDP of the United States[22]. This is only a ratio of nearly 16x[23]. This representational ratio is nearly one third that of the difference between Senatorial representation between the state of Texas and Wyoming[24]. The representational ratio for Canada with a GDP of 1.553T[25] is nearly 12x[26] which is only a fifth of the nearly 66x ratio between the largest state, California, and the smallest state Wyoming, within the US Senate[27]. The 66x ratio is maintained precisely when a comparison between California's \$2,531,304B GDP and Wyoming's \$38,357B GDP is made[28].

For better comparisons of representational ratios between Mexico, Canada, and the United States examine the 2015 GDP of California at 2.531T, Texas at 1.592T, New York at 1.447T, and Florida at 0.903T[29]. Mexico has a population of close to 125.9m[30]

---

https://factfinder.census.gov/faces/nav/jsf/pages/index.xhtml

[18] Derivative of New York and Florida 2015 population estimates / Wyoming 2015 population estimate (individual)

[19] "Texas, Community Facts", Cenus.gov accessed on July 1st, 2017. https://factfinder.census.gov/faces/nav/jsf/pages/index.xhtml

[20] Derivative of Texas 2015 population estimates / Wyoming 2015 population estimate

[21] "Mexico GDP", worldbank.org, accessed on July 1st, 2017. http://data.worldbank.org/indicator/NY.GDP.MKTP.CD?locations=MX

[22] "United States GDP", worldbank.org, accessed on July 1st, 2017. http://data.worldbank.org/indicator/NY.GDP.MKTP.CD?locations=US&view=chart

[23] Derivative of US 2015 GDP estimates / Mexico 2015 GDP estimate

[24] Representational ratio of Texas/Wyoming and US/Mexico, or 46/16 = 2.875

[25] "California GDP", worldbank.org, accessed on July 1st, 2017. http://data.worldbank.org/indicator/NY.GDP.MKTP.CD?locations=CA

[26] Derivative of GDP estimate for Canada/ GDP estimate of U.S.

[27] Derivative of California 2015 population estimate / Wyoming 2015 population estimate

[28] "News Releases, Regional GDP by State", bea.gov, accessed on July 1st, 2017. https://bea.gov/newsreleases/regional/gdp_state/qgsp_newsrelease.htm

persons and Canada has 35.84m[31] persons in 2015. In 2015, California had a population of 38.42m[32], Texas has 26.54m[33], Florida has 19.65m[34], and New York has 19.67m[35]. All of the representational ratios fall within reasonable expectation when compared to the U.S. Senate. Canada falls in line with the largest states in the Union presenting no significant deviation in population or GDP. Mexico has a population of nearly 3x that of California[36] and 5x that of Texas[37]. This is high, but Mexico might be split into multiple states to lower the representation ratio. The limited statistical analysis presents a solid argument that GDP is a valid index to base representational coefficients on if one already approves of the differentials in ratios present in Senatorial representation.

Contemporary democracies reliance on senatorial representation opens the rhetorical door for GDP based representation, as it is an arbitrary form of representation not correlated to population on the individual basis but earning an inverse relationship on the aggregate. This is a direct contrast to the positive aspects of representation based on GDP. Gross Domestic Product is a function of the capacity for production in the nation, the availability natural resources, and the quality of industrial organization. These are critical components in modern society and economy. If legitimate governments are already predicated on the arbitrary representation found in a Senate, then a GDP based system of representation already has enough precedent to make a warrant of legitimacy.

It is far more effective to develop representational coefficients which moderate the number of representatives in the short

---

[29] "News Releases, Regional GDP by State", bea.gov, accessed on July 1st, 2017. https://bea.gov/newsreleases/regional/gdp_state/qgsp_ newsrelease.htm

[30] "Mexico Population Totals", worldbank.org, accessed on July 1st, 2017. http://data.worldbank.org/indicator/SP.POP.TOTL?locations=MX

[31]"California Population Totals", worldbank.org, accessed on July 1st, 2017. http://data.worldbank.org/ indicator/SP.POP.TOTL?locations=CA

[32] "California Community Facts", Census.gov, accessed on July 1st, 2017. https://factfinder.census.gov/faces/nav/jsf/pages/index.xhtml

[33] "Texas Community Facts", Census.gov, accessed on July 1st 2017. https://factfinder.census.gov/faces/nav/jsf/pages/index.xhtml

[34] "Florida Community Facts", Census.gov, accessed on July 1st, 2017. https://factfinder.census.gov/faces/nav/jsf/pages/index.xhtml

[35] "New York Community Facts", Census.gov, accessed on July 1st, 2017. https://factfinder.census.gov/faces/nav/jsf/pages/index.xhtml

[36] Derivative of Mexico's population of 125.9m / California's population of 38.42m

[37] Derivative of Mexico's population of 125.9m / Texas' population of 26.54m

term but permit enough flexibility for proportional representation in the long term. Representational coefficients based on Gross Domestic Product generally distribute one vote to each resident satisfying the higher standards of Universal Suffrage. Thus, GDP based representation provides a reform that can negotiate the changing expectations of a population, over periods of instability and tumult. The promise of improved representation will bring parties to the negotiation table and impart patience and discipline in any successful reform movement.

GDP representation must provide opportunities for newly incorporated states to slowly acquire more proportional representation over time, but mature economies must also be able to protect themselves from extreme changes in the electorate during the incorporation process. Mature economies will often have a GDP growth rate large enough to moderate the GDP gains by developing economies even when they have twice the rate of increase. However, the developing nation will be the recipient of federal tax dollars which should hasten the growth rate even more. The distribution of federal tax subsidies along with the institutional power of GDP representation for the more mature economy should bend the developing economy to the institutional standards found in the older more established states.

A major theme of this book is the rural and metropolitan divide. Coastal regions typically have much larger populations than central regions resulting in more economic development. Larger populations tend to be more diverse, better educated, and populations have better economic outcomes. These geo-spatial properties are often far more important than political affiliations. These properties are held constant across different states, nations, and continents. The more densely populated regions on the coasts are the centers of trade allowing them to develop more universities, more industries, and attract a more diverse population. This urban and rural divide permeates most aspects of nation's culture and political process and is most evident in its fiscal policy. We can look at the United States as an example.

Within the United States, the coastal states pay nearly 57% of the federal taxes and the central and southern states only 43%, for a 14% difference.[38] [39] [40]. Despite the large incongruent contributions to

---

[38] "2015 Data Book", IRS.gov, accessed on July 2nd, 2017.
https://www.irs.gov/pub/irs-soi/15databk.pdf
[39] "State Summaries", USAspending.gov, accessed on July 2nd, 2017.
https://www.usaspending.gov/transparency/Pages/StateSummaries.aspx

the federal government, the funds are distributed almost equally between two groups of states. In 2015, $1.376T were paid to the coastal states and $1.38T paid to the central and southern states [41]. The two sets of states have an equal number of residents, with nearly 160 million living on the coasts and 161m living in in the central and southern regions. Cost of living is more expensive in the large metropolitan and coastal states and one would expect their federal subsidies to reflect the increased cost of business in the states[42]. If federal spending was proportional to contributions, those states would receive nearly 1.56T in subsidies while the more rural states would fall to $1.11T in subsides[43].

The coastal states pay 57% of taxes and only receive 50% of subsidies while the central and southern states pay only 43% of taxes and still receive 50% of subsidies[44] [45]. This 14% differential found in both sets equates to a loss of about 2.2% annual GDP economic activity in coastal states and a gain of 2.8% annual GDP in central and southern states[46]. The increased drag on the coastal states has reduced their GDP growth and bolstered GDP growth in the central and southern states. If federal taxes average about 20% of GDP[47], this represents more than $222B[48] GDP difference in economic activity that would be conserved within the coastal states if they received a proportional number of subsidies to taxes paid.

This differential in federal tax contributions and federal tax subsidies, has hastened the growth of the central and southern states by a non-trivial amount. According to GDP estimates for 1963

---

[41] Derivative of state expenditures from US Census for year 2015 accessed on July 2nd 2017 at https://www.usaspending.gov/transparency/Pages/StateSummaries.aspx

[42] Richard Florida "Is life better in Americas red states", Nytimes.com, last modified 01/3/2015. https://www.nytimes.com/2015/01/04/opinion/sunday/is-life-better-in-americas-red-states.html

[43] Multiplied 2015 US Census data on government spending by 57% for blue states and 43% for red states.

[44] "State Summaries", USAspending.gov, accessed on July 7th, 2017. https://www.usaspending.gov/transparency/Pages/StateSummaries.aspx

[45] "2015 Data Book", IRS.gov, accessed on July 2nd, 2017. https://www.irs.gov/pub/irs-soi/15databk.pdf

[46] "News Releases, regional GDP by state", bea.gov, access on July 1st, 2017. https://bea.gov/newsreleases/regional/gdp_state/qgsp_ newsrelease.htm

[47] John Gruber, Public finance and public policy (New York, NY: Worth Publishers, 2015), p. 14.

[48] "News Releases, regional GDP by state", bea.gov, access on July 1st, 2017. https://bea.gov/newsreleases/regional/gdp_state/qgsp_ newsrelease.htm

through 1997, the coastal states share of GDP shrank by nearly 0.99% and the central and southern state GDP grew by 0.99%[49]. This produced a total shift in GDP of close to 1.9%[50]. From 1997 to 2015, coastal states shrank nearly 1.15% and the central and southern states grew by 1.15% for a total shift of nearly 2.3%[51]. The rate of GDP growth is accelerating, with the period from 1963-1997 being nearly 3x as long as the period from 1997-2015 despite the gains in GDP being nearly equivalent. The coastal states' share of GDP shrank from nearly 58% to just over 55% and the central and southern states' share grew from 42% to nearly 45%, cutting the difference from nearly 16% to just over 10%.[52] This would translate to significant representational gains for the central and southern states if they were participating in a GDP based political union. Most nations last hundreds of years and in just 52 years, the central and southern states would have gained nearly 6% more proportional representation[53].

This is a selling point for the GDP based political union. Nations can't simply look at their historic GDP growth independent of the expectation of gaining access to more federal tax subsidy and more favorable trade and investment positions. The union itself should promote faster GDP growth in the less developed parts of the nation, helping accommodate or mitigate the superior representational position of the more developed and wealthier nation. This is the promise; a less developed nation will join a political union with an obviously inferior representational position with the expectation of acquiring perfectly proportional representation when an equivalent per capita GDP is acquired. Political unions and nations are expected to last hundreds of years and small differences in federal tax subsidies should contribute to the evening out of per capita GDP between the states of a single market economy (shared currency and regulatory environment). The expectation of more fluid representation should

---

[49] "News Releases, regional GDP by state", bea.gov, access on July 1st, 2017.
https://bea.gov/newsreleases/regional/gdp_state/qgsp_ newsrelease.htm

[50] "News Releases, regional GDP by state", bea.gov, access on July 1st, 2017.
https://bea.gov/newsreleases/regional/gdp_state/qgsp_ newsrelease.htm

[51] "News Releases, regional GDP by state", bea.gov, access on July 1st, 2017.
https://bea.gov/newsreleases/regional/gdp_state/qgsp_ newsrelease.htm

[52] Derivative of the difference in total proportion of NIAC GDP estimates for 1997-2015 and SIC GDP estimates for 1963-1997, by state party preference.

[53] Derivative of the net difference between of NIAC GDP estimates for 1997-2015 and SIC GDP estimates for 1963-1997, by state party preference.

increase the rate of union formation and improve the democratization movement.

No political union is perfect. Representational deficiencies always exist. The difference in federal tax subsidy for the Northern and West Coast States is likely caused by representational deficiencies found in the Senate. With 56% of the Senate seats from the central and southern states, typically more rural and poorer states, that favor one political party over the other, they have been able to monopolize the appropriations process and diverting huge sums of tax subsidies back to their states[54]. Only 44% of the Senate seats are located within the Coastal states, producing a natural 12% advantage for parties with higher affiliation in the central and southern states[55]. Seats do switch parties but there should be a tendency for one party to win a majority of the elected offices in the state, if that state does demonstrate a preference for political affiliation.

Despite the blue states maintaining nearly equal population with the central and southern states[56], they have a 12% deficit in representation. A 12% seat advantage is a serious benefit for one party and an almost insurmountable obstacle for the other. A 12-seat advantage will result in far more Senate majorities for the party with the seat advantage. This is even more true in environments where a filibuster is abused requiring 60 affirmative votes to pass budgetary measures or debt ceilings. Allowing the party to easily obstruct the legislative process in the bicameral legislature. Worse, the political party representing the more rural, poorer, and less educated states can preserve the austerity conditions that produce populist movements, wealth inequality, and political corruption.

The states that prefer austerity measures and weak labor laws will demonstrate a faster GDP growth and can advertise their economic policies as more successful than those that favor higher taxes and higher wages. The politicians will have superficial data that supports their claims that austerity promotes faster GDP growth. However, the data collected from these states is invalid unless it is corrected for the significant amount of economic stimulus provided by the differential in contributions and expenditures. Wealth inequality and austerity produces more poverty, and the worse the

---

[54] Derived from state party preferences demonstrated on page 42

[55] Derived from state party preferences demonstrated on page 42

[56] "2015 Population Tables", Census.gov, accessed on July 3rd, 2017. https://www.census.gov/data/tables/2016/demo/popest/nation-total.html

poverty in a region, the more federal tax subsidies they receive. This is a counterproductive feedback loop, resulting in more wealth inequality and defunded governments susceptible to government shutdowns and debt defaults.

GDP based representation can break this feedback loop. The wealthier and better educated states will have more political power and impose their economic policies on the lower GDP states. They can ensure the public has living wages and the government isn't susceptible to debt default threats of government shutdowns. They will support progressive taxes and collective bargaining. The public will make better electoral decisions, once they are elevated above poverty and subsistence living. The improved economic outcomes will provide more support for the political parties advocating for economic reform. A new positive feedback loop towards prosperity and political stability will be formed and the nation can embark on a mission for territorial expansion. The citizens of other nations will seek to adopt the culture and prosperity of the successful democracy and may enter into union with it.

Obviously, political unions that incorporate senates will attract different participants than those that support demographic chambers or econometric chambers. New states will take into account the representational deficiencies involved with the current political system and seek to exploit them or mitigate them. Nations will make concessions when entering into political unions with other nation. This is understandable from the perspective of the more established and developed nation as they benefit from the new labor and consumption markets and should be able to leverage their current representational advantages for the foreseeable future. It is also understandable for the developing nation's perspective, which gains access to larger margins of federal tax subsidy and investment capital. All of the nations will benefit from improved security with military benefiting from a larger population base for enlisted, access to the coasts, resources, and better base locations.

Don't forget, econometric representation only offers the promise of improvement. These outcomes may fail to be achieved and all parties bear risk in the unionization process. Wealth inequality is a dominant theme in politics. Even if historic GDP growth rates don't demonstrate a faster rate in the developing states, the fact that growth was distributed evenly among all states is testament to the effectiveness of extra economic stimulation through federal tax subsidies. Economic growth is usually a tautology, wealthier states grow much more wealthy than poorer states. Wealth tends to accumulate unless it is acted directly upon by public policy intended to curb the growing inequality. This is true on the macro-political or state level as much as it is true on the individual or family level. A huge imbalance in federal tax policy, might be precisely what enables a poorer state to continue growing at the same rate as the wealthier states. Without the massive imbalance is subsidy, the two political markets would continue to move apart

A nation might agree to unionization expecting a much more rapid growth in GDP but only experience static growth compared to the larger market. This is more acceptable if the union includes a Senate that might provide a huge representational advantage to a less populated state. In the United States, the smallest state has nearly 66x as much representation in the institution and the largest state[57]. Under these terms, a less developed nation with a smaller population and lower GDP might still consider unionization with the larger and more developed states. Likewise, a nation with a far larger population but lower GDP would see a benefit in unionization if it gains significant representational advantages in the demographic chamber even if it might not ever acquire a superior position in the econometric chamber. These are tradeoffs in the political markets politicians will weigh during unionization negotiations (post conflict or peaceful).

This difference in situational preference creates a more competitive market for unionization. If two nations are aggressively pursuing peaceful expansion and one offers an econometric chamber paired with a demographic chamber and the other offers an economic chamber paired with a Senate, each nation will attract different consumers. When two competing nations offer the same client different options, that client can examine growth rates in population and GDP and determine which is a more equitable relationship for them to pursue. They won't compete over the same cliental because the cliental will have their own agenda and seek to maximize their own political power within the union.

These calculations shouldn't be underweighted in terms of likelihood of occurring, when one examines the relatively short period during which both the U.S. and E.U. were formed and those conditions that enabled the two unions to thrive. Environmental and economic conditions in the near future might promote more expansion

---

[57] Comparing California to Wyoming by population constrained by terms of Senate representation.

in democratic nations. These are optimal outcomes. More mixed outcomes should be expected. The history of the world includes periods of colonialism and imperialism where democratic nations have participated. It is a reasonable expectation that the world enters another period of aggressive expansion and integration but where innovations in political representation ensure that democratic culture and rights are protected against more authoritarian regimes.

There is implicit degree of trust when forming imperial democracies. The newly incorporated states must believe the intent of the host states to achieve equilibrium in per capita GDP and distribute representation more uniformly in the union. If the States with the higher GDP abuse their institutional power by withholding federal tax subsidies while exporting austerity measures, regressive tax policies, and deregulate labor conditions they can preserve the low representational conditions for new states. This breaks the covenant, resulting in economic instability and political instability, and It could destroy the Union. The new state will rely on support from opposition parties within the more nature economies and relentlessly protest the conditions. If peaceful   resistance fails, the developing state could shrug off the imperial ties, like so many other states have in the past by taking up arms against their oppressors. The promise of proportional representation must be honored, or ruin will follow the negligent leadership.

To acquire a more representative government member states will pursue economic reforms that distribute incomes more evenly, federalist subsidies more equally, and obligations more equitably. This tendency will promote a movement to higher legislative production rates and higher quality laws. When economic conditions are corrected, the improved conditions will make future reforms more likely. Success breeds more success. When reforms are denied, it immediately elicits calls of corruption, oppression, and exploitation directly related to under representation. This can result in cultures that support rebellion or secession, undermining the productivity of the union. These conditions may make economic reform less likely as the electorate splits into partisan divides and can't reach compromises as easily.

Democratic governments need to be validated by popular support otherwise the public can start to distrust it and resist its taxes and laws. This is a dangerous situation, especially during demographic shifts and periods of wealth inequality. Economic data must be reported accurately. Reporting integrity must be ensured with an agency auditing tax data, firm accounting, and state level aggregation to ensure that all GDP figures are accurate. Newly incorporated states must have complete faith in the reporting of financial data before they agree to the political union. Firms and corporations must report their accounting data promptly and accurately. Strong institutions are a necessary component of democracy. This includes reporting laws with universal application, integrity in form, and fully enforced. The accuracy of the audits will be a strong inducement for unionization.

If the reporting isn't standardized, states will not trust each other and disrupting economy and due process. The suspicion will invite fear and anger into the union. This isn't easily cured. In the worst-case scenarios, the states fearing exploitation will organize with other states and there will be a secession or war. In the best-worst case scenario, the imperial democracy is viewed as corrupt. It won't be able to advertise its culture or political process as a benefit. It won't be able to effectively incorporate new states into the union and in more competitive environments, it will be eclipsed by larger states with larger economies. Trust is the most important component of a relationship between new states and older states. It is the cornerstone of GDP based representation.

3 GDP ELECTORATES

Wars are inevitable. It would be a productive innovation to develop a system for the integration of electorates rather than simply the occupation of other nations. The inhibitions on rapidity expanding an electorate that includes different ethnicities, religions, and cultures will still be in place. If put to a popular vote, many of the citizens might reject the incorporation of a state into the union. This doesn't mean the country won't defend itself with war, but it will moderate the number of conflicts by reducing the likelihood of coercion into a union. Wars are usually counter-productive and wasteful. The misery that accompanies them is unrivaled and rarely justified. However, war is a common response to adverse conditions and no matter how terrible the consequences, it will be rationalized as an acceptable strategy.

The destructive consequences of war should be severe enough to discourage most aggressive imperial tendencies. It is doubtful nations will embark on risk expansionist policies, if it destroys the economy of the regions and destabilizes all of the participants. Populations usually resist long wars with high casualties and forced conscription. This is dangerous for any democracy. Government may acquire substantial debts related to the war expenditures, making them susceptible to debt defaults or government shutdowns. They could see their labor forces decimated and their natural resources spoiled. Democratic expansion may not justify these risks. There are financial and political incentives to unionization, even after occupation and conflict, but the equation isn't balanced. Used defensively, democratic imperialism is productive, but nations will have to account for the full range of possibilities and consequences of conflict prior to the adventure.

JORDAN DAVID WEISINGER, M.S., M.A., M.B.A.

Democratic imperialism is much more likely to occur within a region with a similar culture and equivalent economic development. Not only do they have more religious sympathies but inclusion within a political system with GDP based representation will implicitly be more equitable. It's far less likely that a mature economy in Europe incorporates a state in Africa than it is for a democratic state in Africa to consider expanding their electorate through incorporating neighbors. The same is true in Asia and South America. The net consequences of this tendency could be an acceleration of the democratization process with a scaling of nations into larger free trade zones more able to defend themselves against authoritarian threats.

This doesn't constrain a democratic empire to its own region or continent. Modern transport and communication make it possible for a nation to incorporate a state that is not contiguous or on another continent. Democratic imperialism is still dependent on voluntary participation. No people or state can be easily coerced into union even during an occupation. The newly incorporated state must see equity and value in the statehood. This is far more likely within regions that share religion and culture, but proximity is not always necessary. Don't forget that the primary driver of expansion will be voluntary and peaceful negotiations between neighbors for free trade zones and political unions. The number of opportunities is unbound compared to those of war. War is a far less effective means to expand an electorate. The populations will be less willing, and the economy will require far more rehabilitation after the conflict. Most of the benefits from imperial expansion are gained through peaceful integration. Neighboring states have many more opportunities to form productive relationships with a strong tendency towards cooperation and voluntary union.

Conservative populations will be more susceptible to the rhetoric of econometric representation based on GDP. Culturally, Conservatives tend to trust free market ideologies and institutions found in the private sector. They will offer less resistance to the premise of econometric representation. They are often business owners or professionals who are fluent in the economic concepts like Gross Domestic Product, Free Trade, and Market Economy. This familiarity is an incentive. It also helps that the representation is variable and where expertise and patience can increase their political power outside of any immigration or demographic movements. This coincides with many beliefs in fiercely individuality and the idea that effort can overcome any obstacle or deficiency.

Conservatives will be more comfortable with both sides of the representational equation. They will accept less representation up front for the promise of proportional representation later. Business owners have a different perspective than employees or other professionals. They stand to gain more from uninhibited trade and have more material wealth making them less susceptible to economic disruptions. Business owners have more innate political power by virtue of their extra capitalization. All governments seem to recognize firms more readily than individuals. Wealthier firms have significant institutional advantages over poorer firms or individuals. The political caste sees an advantage to cultivate relationships with industrials and wealthy persons. This all contributes to surplus political power and an incentive for business owners to accept the unequal conditions of GDP based representation.

This is especially true when the business owners are in developing economies that will benefit from a political union with a more mature economy. The developing economy will receive far more in federal subsidies than it contributes to in taxes and it will be business owners who primarily benefit. The business owners will be the vendors earning such contracts for services provided to the new government. Higher paid employees contribute to more consumption for businesses. The lower labor costs could improve exports to the more mature economy. Business owners will have the most incentives to support a political union with more mature economies. This could be motivation for regime change in authoritarian nations and could accelerate the conversion rate of despotic or communist countries.

GDP based representation offers conservatives the opportunity to support a representation that closely identifies with their culture of business acumen while not trespassing on any long-standing thresholds for accurate and honest representation. GDP based representation comports to the contemporary standards in democracy for universal suffrage. Econometric representation has more appeal when it delivers high quality democratic entitlements that don't deviate from this ideal. Conservatives can finally declare support for a high-quality system of political representation based on Economy.

Recruiting conservatives into a democratization movement focused on wealth-based representation will benefit the entire community by inviting a highly motivated and energetic population into the cause for universal suffrage and high quality democratic entitlements. This will implicitly reduce the support received by non-democratic governments. Despots and tyrants are dependent on loyalist populations and wealth-based systems of representation might interrupt this relationship. Econometric representation is in a language that business leaders understand and if confidence in the establishment can be shaken or diverted, it could cause larger populations to defect to towards democratization.

GDP based representation may be critical for nation building in less developed nations. The owners class and investors class are typically involved in the more successful revolutions or regime changes. They will be attracted to the theory and the rhetoric used. The more developed regions may acquire more political power, resulting in more predictable and stable outcomes. There is an implicit legitimacy in GDP when economic activity is weakly correlated to education and population density. These characteristics often make for more sustainable and durable democracies. They also enjoy more capital support for the new government. The regions with the highest GDP will provide more proportional tax revenues. They will have more labor to draw on for public works and enlistment in the armed forces. GDP based representation confers several advantages to the fledgling democracy that may improve its chances for survival.

Even small improvements in support result in significant improvements in the odds for regime change when the affected populations are in the millions and billions. It is the law of large numbers. If a regime oppresses or upsets just a small number of its citizenry with abuses in civil liberties or due process, a segment of the disaffected public will quickly radicalize organize to protect the civil liberties like free press or the right to peacefully organize. As the number of abuses grows, so will the support for the democratization movement, representing a larger number of activists and more financial support. More importantly, it constricts the current regimes access to labor and capital. There are two sides to the single frame, one results in a gain for activists and rebels, and the other a loss of support for the loyalist, with the improvement in the odds of success squared.

Choices are always made from available options, not the ideal. The decision is evaluated through a comparison to the ideal, but that ideal is rarely satisfied during a crisis. A people may accept lower quality democratic entitlements with the expectation of acquiring a more ideal state at a future point. This was true in the early democracies which often resembled aristocracy with restricted electorates. Most improvements are earned by incremental reforms through the political process. The property that makes incremental reform most likely, is universal suffrage and a diverse electorate. With honest and accurate representation, a people will slowly acclimate to the diversity in economic outcomes, religion, and ethnicity found in most nations. Debate and peaceful protest will frame the civil rights and economic issues while the democratic process produces an opportunity to pass laws protecting their interests. GDP representation provides the basis for incremental reform. It is an immediate concession in quality of representation with the expectation of future entitlement.

Demographic representation provides an ideal form of government in most circumstances. It has the full authority and legitimacy of majority control. Proportional distribution allocates votes on an individual basis through universal suffrage, overcoming natural boundaries like region and statehood. It is easily understood and counted. It is also predictable. It is implicit that the candidates with the most supporters win most of the elections. It is imperative that the most popular policies are debated in the legislature, evaluated by the bureaucracy, and studied in academia. However, there are always those minority groups and classes that will strive to check the unbridled populism of a majority. Politicians fear populism and populism can be checked by introducing a legislative chamber decoupled from demographic representation.

This demand has historically been satisfied by senates, but the GDP chamber is more adept in this role. GDP is only weakly correlated to population (within states in a single market economy) but it still carries the potential for proportional representation when per capita GDP is equally distributed across all states. GDP can be both separate from popular representation and equivalent. This introduces a controlled measure of inefficiency into a durable political process. It actively checks populism by empowering the states with the most GDP (wealth) and therefore the least susceptibility to the animal spirits. Legislative chambers based on GDP are a more effective complement to demographic chambers than Senates. GDP imparts more value than an arbitrary assignment of representation like that found in the senate.

GDP based representation is more dynamic than senatorial representation. When GDP is positively correlated to population through more equal per capita GDP, it provides the more educated and more expert population with more proportional representation in both the demographic chamber and the GDP based chamber.

However, this relationship is inverted when it comes to political unions with less developed countries. Less developed nations will have few lower per capita GDP and representation will be less correlated to population. This is an important concept when striking the agreement for an economic zone or Union. The GDP chamber acts as a foil to the demographic chamber without completely negating the benefit of proportional representation.

GDP based representation offers better outcomes than senates for most political unions. In larger nations, senates often create the conditions for populism. It will be the more numerous and smaller states that acquire a disproportionate amount of political power in the chamber. Smaller states are generally poorer (with lower per capita GDP) and less educated making them more resistant to change and reform. Once the economic conditions deteriorate, the shorter term of a demographic chamber will make it more susceptible to the populist spirits. A senate's use of a filibuster can then preserves the poor economic conditions that moved the public to the violent throws of populism and nativism.

The senate's inverse relationship to population is counter-productive. It is often unnecessary in that a bicameral legislature is the best bulwark against populism. Setting two institutions on opposed election schedules is the most effective means to temper popular sentiment in the moment. Increasing the terms of the candidates will insulate them from populism, while an increased number of elections will improve the institutions responsiveness to contemporary conditions. It is counter-productive to diminish the legitimacy of majority rule by inserting a Senate. A bicameral process can be easily obstructed, especially when senates so often benefit the poorer states who invariably support populist candidates The GDP chamber accomplishes the same anti-populist goal while providing a pathway to proportional representation after per capita GDP equilibrates throughout the union. In both respects, the GDP based system of representation is a higher order form of organization in nations and for states.

In an environment of political instability resulting from climate change and wealth inequality, democracies can protect themselves from more frequent conflicts and conquests by democratic imperialism. There will be resources shortages, economic disasters, immigration ¡and demographic shifts all contributing to poverty, strife, and war. Democracies can put themselves in a position to better defend themselves by incorporating other states and nations into the political union. They can transmit the successes of democracy through their constitutions, their institutions, and their culture to protect those new entitlements for the fledgling states.

Wealth based representation provides an exceptional opportunity for a resurgence in the democratization movement when conservative with populations around the world can identify with a political process that more accurately reflects their preferences and ambitions while satisfying their requirements for universal suffrage and high quality Democratic standards. Wealth based representation will attract more support from business owners and conservatives who might otherwise support the current non-democratic establishment as loyalists. This will result in more frequent regime change, and a gradient towards democracy. Not all movements will be successful, but even failed efforts will impart a culture and preference for democracy in the despotic state.

Any innovation in political rhetoric or process that increases the odds of successfully converting a non-democratic nation into a Democratic nation is a permanent and significant improvement in the democratization movement. This is how we establish civil society and build a durable and equitable civilization. It is homesteading. It is establishing that outpost in the wilderness. GDP based representation is one of these innovations. Economy and finance are our immediately environments. They are an all-powerful force in our lives whether a culture or individual is compliant, or whether they rally against the general inequities and the waste created. Economy is unavoidable. GDP based representation harnesses the raw power of economy for the body politic. It makes the nation more efficient in terms of representing its own people, and it makes the state more compatible with other states. It is a variable form of representation that accommodates multiple outcomes over many periods.

GDP based representation is an implicit improvement in political science due to its ability to adjust to changing circumstances. This isn't true of senatorial representation. The senate is fixed. Its representational coefficients can change over time with population shifts coercing an inverse movement in leverage but otherwise the number of representatives is fixed and unmoving. This looks prolapsed compared to the use of GDP as a representational coefficient. GDP will generally scale up with population, but it will also increase when more appropriate economic policies are passed. This makes the promise to smaller and less developed nations of a more equitable future with GDP based representation. With hard work, patience, and expertise, a state can slowly and incrementally increase its representation of the union. This is for the benefit of the union too. If the state has more successful economic policies, it should have more representation with the opportunity to export them.

Majority rule is still the ideal. It doesn't have to mean a perfectly representational government that has a 100% legislative production rate. Too much efficiency can be counterproductive. A party could pass laws that advantage them during elections permitting them to easily preserve their majority political power. This wouldn't result in honest and accurate political representation. This is the primary driver for introducing a bicameral process. Nations may also impose conditions like a Presidential Veto or a filibuster. However, the framers must make it possible for a people to regulate themselves and govern themselves. If a political process is obstructed too easily it will result in oppression, exploitation, and political instability.

The raw probability (potential) of passing laws in a bicameral legislature is 50% with all things being equal (*perfectly competitive and binary electoral process*). Using the United States as a model, the probability falls to just 25% after a Presidential Veto is applied. However, the probability of passing laws drops to less than 9.5% in environments where the filibuster is abused and a 60-seat margin in the Senate is necessary[58]. These periods can last 40 years of more[59] resulting in increased wealth inequality and stagnant wages[60][61].

Rarely can a bill pass without the implicit consent of the opposition party. The public almost invariably overestimates the effectiveness of the opposition party because it is so easy to obstruct government and prevent laws from passing. This looks like effectiveness. It looks like expertise, and it attracts those that are

---

[58] Divided by number of times 60 seat margin in Senate overcome since 1933, where the House and President were all of the same party. "Visual Guide: The Balance of Power Between Congress and the President" Accessed on 7.8.2017. http://wiredpen.com/resources/political-commentary-and-analysis/a-visual-guide-balance-of-power-congress-presidency/

[59] Tom Donnely and Jeffry Rosen, "Political polarization killed the filibuster", Theatlantic.com. Last modified 4/8/2018. https://www.theatlantic.com/politics/archive/2017/04/ political-polarization-killed-the-filibuster/522360/

[60] Angela Monaghan, "Wealth inequality top 01 worth as much as bottom 90", Theguardian.com, last modified 11/13/2014.https://www.theguardian.com /business/2014/nov/13/us-wealth-inequality-top-01-worth-as-much-as-the-bottom-90

[61] Lawrence Mishel, Elise Gould, and Jose Bivens, "Wage stagnation in nine charts", www.edpi.org, last modified 1/6/2015.http://www.epi.org/publication/charting-wage-stagnation/

susceptible to power and abuse. It also makes the party lobbying for economic reform or political reform a lot less effective. It makes them look weaker and uncoordinated. These are illusions; ninety percent of the force behind the outcome is purely mechanical work from an inefficient and unrepresentative government.

This is extremely dangerous. The political system passes significant laws so infrequently that it is prone to corrections and catastrophe. The crisis then presents an opportunity for cults of personality to form around parties used to bullying or abusing the underrepresented populations like minorities, women, children, and laborers. This tendency was documented in the Stanford Prison Experiment and applies to macro politics as well. The culture is already present. The policies are already widely accepted, and as economic conditions get worse the rhetoric becomes more strained. It is in the vacuum of remedy through the political process that nightmares are born.

The Europeans nations avoided this fate because of the Parliamentary process. Their executive is appointed by the majority party in their representative legislature, with an almost 50% chance of having alignment in the senate (*in a perfectly competitive and binary electoral system*). This permits a coalition to identify issues and immediately address them with public policy. This doesn't mean the European states are invulnerable to wealth inequality and electoral deficiencies like Gerrymandering and private campaign finance, but it does make it far less likely to aggravate. They are more likely to use public policy to address the critical issues than force.

Their second-generation democracies only reduce the risk of compromise. It doesn't complete exclude the risk of crisis. Over the centuries, they have developed long histories of abuse and demographic violence[62]. Their proximity and population density make conflicts more likely, and probably more violent. Prior to 1945, Europe had many of the bloodiest wars[63] . Since 1945, most of the genocides and conflicts were outside of Europe[64]. The greater number of European countries certainly increases the chance of an outbreak,

---

[62] "European Wars and Battles", Thoughtco.com, accessed on 7/10/2017.
https://www.thoughtco.com/european-wars-and-battles-4133312

[63] Jennifer Rosenberg, "The Major wars and conflicts of the 20th century",
Thoughtco.com, last modified on 8/13/2018. https://www.thoughtco.com/major-wars-and-conflicts-20th-century-1779967

[64] "Genocides, Politicides, and Other Mass Murder since 1945", Genocidewatch.net,
accessed on 7/12/2017. http://genocidewatch.net/genocide-2/genocide-and-politicide/

but the more representative government and more efficient government provides as much an inoculation as possible.

Low legislative production rates aren't the only threat. Climate change has already occurred. With it will come political instability from rapid environmental changes. Populations will be on the move and this will disrupt economy and alter electorates. Automation and the computer era may produce more unemployment and more disparate wealth accumulation[65] These are the conditions where discontent breeds conflict and violence[66]. It is where the spores of dangerous rhetoric spread. The poor economic outcomes and worse political outcomes will make reform necessary but less likely as populations lose confidence in due process. Their judgment will be compromised making them more susceptible to worse decisions.

A people could retreat into empires based on value voting and the ancient instinct to rely on an aristocracy. It may not be just a few years of bad outcomes that can be corrected with term limits and off cycle elections. This could be 400 years or more of decline and instability while humans acclimate to the new conditions. No doubt, there should be a flight to more representative and efficient government, but people generally don't think well during prolonged crises. Instead, they succumb to the same fear and loathing of generations before them and organize into authoritarian systems that promise security and stability but only produce misery.

Nations with higher quality democratic entitlements will be able to protect themselves better. Democratic governance makes a people less likely to conquer other nations for sport, power, prestige, or treasures. This should decrease the frequency and intensity of conflicts just as European conflicts have decreased since 1945[67]. However, when attacked they could defend themselves from invaders and despoilers, and possibly expand their electorate to include the conquered peoples. There is safety in larger numbers. Imperial democracies should have higher GDP and larger populations to

---

[65]   Aaron Frank, "Could automation lead to chronic unemployment? Andrew Mcafee sounds the alarm", forbes.com, last modified 7/19/2012 https://www.forbes.com/sites/singularity/2012/07/19/could-automation-lead-to-chronic-unemployment-andrew-mcafee-sounds-the-alarm/#60603fda1a31

[66] "The economics of violence", economist.com, last modified 4/14/2011 http://www.economist.com/node/18558041

[67] Jennifer Rosenberg, "The Major wars and conflicts of the 20th century", Thoughtco.com, last modified on 8/13/2018. https://www.thoughtco.com/major-wars-and-conflicts-20th-century-1779967

marshal during periods of war. There is also safety in representative government. The allure of democratic votes could effectively coerce enemy combatants to surrender more easily. It could improve the conditions for people living under hostile and non-democratic regimes. It certainly provides more stability after a conflict with the hostile population now successfully placated.

4 GDP SIMULATIONS

There is some evidence that imposing independence and democracy on a formerly despotic nation does not work with a high enough success rate to justify the process. It could be argued that nation building would be far more effective if formerly despotic nations were incorporated within larger democracy rather than be made independent. These nations could slowly adopt the culture of democracy while still under the stewardship of the conquering nation. It is a better guarantee of due process and strong civil liberties. It is also an incentive for democracies to aggressive pursue nation building in regions or areas where democracy is still under-represented.

If a democratic nation can export its culture and its political process it makes its environment far less dangerous. It is a form of homesteading. Neighbors will be more trustworthy and less hostile. The democratic process makes conflict less likely, but when it is inevitable, they can convert the offender to democracy. This promotes a geometric growth in positive outcomes. As the imperial democracy expands, it will discourage possible invaders, and make wars of conquest less likely. The more it defends itself, the less likely future conflict occurs. This creates a strong tendency towards peace and prosperity. Imperial democracy makes it more likely the culture and expertise involved in the democratic process survives the dangerous and inhospitable conditions created by climate change and wealth inequality.

The democratization movement would be accelerated and improved if mature democracies started incorporating electorates from formerly despotic or communist nations. Democracies tend to be more peaceful and more stable. Despotic nations tend to suffer from internal instability and engage in warlike behavior more often. This will establish a trend in the democratization movement towards expanding the size of democracies, thus the proportion of populations protected by them in the world. Democracies rarely go to war with other democracies but when they do, they can be guaranteed to preserve their democratic entitlements with an emphasis on universal suffrage.

Democratization through expanding electorates, may be sounder than installing democracies in individual states that have not developed the institutions or culture to support them. Democracy isn't always secure or stable, and younger less experienced states are at greater risk of failing. The efforts of the United States in Iraq and Afghanistan are in question. Both states have suffered insults to their system, including civil wars, secessions, and abject corruption. It could be argued that if they were incorporated into a larger more secure and stable democracy, the fledgling nations would thrive instead of floundering.

The population data and economic data on Iraq and Afghanistan can be used to peer into what the result of this processes will look like. It is understandable that most people will initially object this exercise   based on ethical concerns but the notion of growth is critical when comparing different representational coefficients. Iraq and Afghanistan were simply the last two examples of large scale war efforts made by the United States. It should also be understood, that societies change over time, economies change over time, and environments change over time. It is expected that smaller populations incorporated into larger more moderate position have then tendency to moderate over time. The future is unknown, and this represents an opportunity for both nations involved in the conflict.

In the 1980's Iraq had a population of 13 million[68] and a GDP of 53.4[69] billion. By 2015 Iraq had a population of 36[70] million and a GDP of 168[71] billion. This represents nearly a 276% increase in population and a 314% increase in GDP. These figures can be used to estimate the total change in representation if it were included in a political union with the United States after the last war.

The other conflict involved Afghanistan. In the 1980's Afghanistan had 13 million citizens [72] and 3.6 billion dollars in GDP[73]. By 2015 Afghanistan had 32 million citizens[74] and 19.19 billion dollars in GDP[75]. This represents a 246% growth in population and a 533% growth in GDP. These figures appear as though they would have significantly more growth and would jeopardize the political power of the United States if they were included with in the electorate, but this simply isn't true.

---

[68] "Iraq GDP", Worldbank.org, accessed on July 14, 2017.
http://data.worldbank.org/indicator/NY.GDP. MKTP.CD?locations=IQ

[69] "Iraq Population", Worldbank.org, accessed on July 14, 2017.
http://data.worldbank.org/indicator/ SP.POP.TOTL ?locations=IQ

[70] "Iraq Population", Worldbank.org, accessed on July 14, 2017.
http://data.worldbank.org/indicator/ SP.POP.TOTL ?locations=IQ

[71] "Iraq GDP", Worldbank.org, accessed on July 14, 2017.
http://data.worldbank.org/indicator/NY.GDP. MKTP.CD?locations=IQ

[72] "Afghanistan Population", Worldbank.org, accessed on July 14, 2017.
http://data.worldbank.org/indicator/ SP.POP.TOTL?locations=AF

[73] "Afghanistan GDP", Worldbank.org, accessed on July 14, 2017.
http://data.worldbank.org/indicator/NY. GDP.MKTP.CD?locations=AF

[74] "Afghanistan Population", Worldbank.org, accessed on July 14, 2017.
http://data.worldbank.org/indicator/ SP.POP.TOTL?locations=AF

[75] "Afghanistan GDP", Worldbank.org, accessed on July 14, 2017.
http://data.worldbank.org/indicator/NY. GDP.MKTP.CD?locations=AF

The United States had a population of 227.25 million citizens[76] in the 1980's and a GDP of $2863B[77]. By 2015 the population had grown to 321.4 million persons with a 141% increase in total citizenship[78]. By 2015 the United States GDP had grown to $17.947T with a 626% increase in value[79].

Although, the United States had slower population growth than both Iraq and Afghanistan, it had a much faster economic expansion. This would help preserve the majority political power of the United States. One must consider the fact that both Iraq and Afghanistan had disproportionately smaller economies than the United States. The ratio of representation would be nearly 53:1 in favor of the United States over Iraq in the 1980's and then grow to nearly 107:1 in 2015. The ratio is even larger for Afghanistan with the ratio being 795:1 in 1980 and 935:1 in 2015.

These outweigh even the largest representational deficiencies in the United States Senate when comparing the states of Vermont or Wyoming to Texas or California. Iraq and Afghanistan would be protected under a "Method of Equal Proportion" leveraging their minimal economic output to one seat in a chamber of just a few hundred legislators[80]. In this respect, they would be elevated to the same standing as Vermont or Wyoming are in the House of Representatives within the United States. Each of these states receive just one representative due to their lack of residents. They receive nearly 0.25% of total representation which should nearly equivalent to the same 0.25% of total representation Iraq or Afghanistan would receive in a GDP based system, if based on a 435-seat chamber[81] [82]

The total proportion of demographic representation for Afghanistan, Iraq, and the United States can be extrapolated from the available figures. Referencing the World Bank 2015 figures, Afghanistan would command only 8.2% of the popular vote, Iraq would gain only 9.2%, and the US would maintain the majority with nearly 83% of the popular vote[83]. Even, when taken together, the two Middle Eastern states will represent only 17% of the

---

[76] "United States Population", Worldbank.org, accessed on July 14, 2017. http://data.worldbank.org/indicator/ SP.POP.TOTL?locations=US

[77] "United States GDP", Worldbank.org, accessed on July 14, 2017. http://data.worldbank.org/indicator/NY. GDP.MKTP.CD?locations=US

[78] "United States Population", Worldbank.org, accessed on July 14, 2017. http://data.worldbank.org/indicator/ SP.POP.TOTL?locations=US

[79] "United States GDP", Worldbank.org, accessed on July 14, 2017. http://data.worldbank.org/indicator/NY. GDP.MKTP.CD?locations=US

[80] "Population apportionment", Census.gov, accessed on July 14, 2017. https://www.census.gov/population/apportionment/about /computing.html

[81] "The house explained", house.gov, accessed on July 14, 2017. https://www.house.gov/the-house-explained

[82] Derivative of the demographic data on U.S., Afghanistan, and Iraq from http://data.worldbank.org/

[83] Derivative of the demographic data on U.S., Afghanistan, and Iraq from http://data.worldbank.org/

total demographic representation in the nation[84]. The United States could effectively protect its majority position for decades and generations to come.

The total proportion of econometric representation for Afghanistan, Iraq and the United States can be projected from current figures. Afghanistan has only 0.01% of total economic output while Iraq had 0.09% of GDP[85]. The United States would almost completely monopolize the political power of the econometric chamber despite losing 17% of representation in the demographic chamber[86].

Iraq had a 4% net gain in demographic representation compared to a net loss of 0.9% in GDP based representation[87]. Afghanistan had a 3% gain in demographic representation and a 0.01% loss in GDP based representation[88]. The United States had a loss of 7% in demographic representation and a gain of 0.09% in GDP based representation[89]. These are stable trajectories for representation within a political union. The fears one population might have from losing sovereignty to another population aren't founded when constrained to a 35-year period. The ratios of total representational proportions also look promising for the new and improved Union.

After 70 years of current demographic representational trends, the United States would only lose another 14% of total proportional representation, leaving it 69% of overall demographic representation[90]. Any fears of loss of majority political power are unfounded, especially when offset by a dominant position in the econometric chamber with no trends suggesting long term changes in proportion. In 70 years, civil society and equitable economy could reform the more evangelical or extremist components of the new electorate. The democratic institutions of media and freedoms of speech and organization would allow the newly incorporated electorate to develop a culture of integration within the new political union.

The simulations found in this section are based on histories that don't include the extra stimulus provided by federal subsidies. It is expected that many of the states involved have smaller populations and developing economies and would benefit from a surplus of federal investment. This could alter the expected growth in representation within the econometric chamber.

---

[84] Derivative of the demographic data on U.S., Afghanistan, and Iraq from
http://data.worldbank.org/

[85] Derivative of the GDP data on U.S., Afghanistan, and Iraq from http://data.worldbank.org/

[86] Derivative of the GDP data on U.S., Afghanistan, and Iraq from http://data.worldbank.org/

[87] Comparison of demographic data and GDP data for U.S., Afghanistan, and Iraq from
http://data.worldbank.org/

[88] Comparison of demographic data and GDP data for U.S., Afghanistan, and Iraq from
http://data.worldbank.org/

[89] Comparison of demographic data and GDP data for U.S., Afghanistan, and Iraq from
http://data.worldbank.org/

[90] Comparison of demographic data and GDP data for U.S., Afghanistan, and Iraq from
http://data.worldbank.org/

More federal subsidies will hasten the speed of economic development with the expectation of more equitable distribution of representation in the GDP chamber. The federal tax subsidy will allow the occupying nation to financially engineer the newly incorporated state, remaking it in the image of itself. The business networks, improved employment and profitability, and improved civil liberties will help inculcate the new culture into the culture of the larger electorate.

Make no mistake. Seeking to expand the electorate by war is a worse strategy than peaceful negotiation and economic integration. Not only is it more likely to be exposed to poorer partners if war is used for expansion, but using violence on persons with similar policy preferences, ethnicities, and religions will only sharpen those sectarian divides that do persist. Trade should be the basis of most political integration. Regulatory systems can be integrated through treaties. Economic unions can become free travel zones and currency zones. International law enforcement agencies can overcome the conventional boundaries of borders. There are few differences outside of regulation, law enforcement, free movement of labor and commerce, and unified currency. It is only a matter of regressing political markets and making elections compatible.

The choice for imposing a demographic form of representation on Iraq was a poor one. For decades, a minority of Sunni had preserved authoritarian control over the Shia majority population. To make matters worse, a highly independent Kurd minority was also present. The United States had decided to impose a Parliamentarian government with demographic representational coefficients. The United States thought it was organizing Iraq for optimal success, but it did not recognize the long history of sectarian tensions. The result was a civil war followed by sectarian violence[91]. This was not the fault of government architects. Parliamentarian governments were far more efficient than Presidential governments (with vetoes and filibusters) and their decision was constrained by the options available to them.

There are better options. Nations with extreme sectarian tensions or predictable demographic shifts may be served better by no-demographic systems of representation. GDP based representation satisfies this condition. It decouples political power from population, minimizing the aggregate political power awarded to populations with numerical superiority. Demographic majorities still have tremendous political power in GDP based representational systems, but non-majority demographic groups have more minority political power. Demographic representation also permits class-based representation by splitting nations in "haves" and "have nots".

---

[91] Zana Khasraw, "Who is responsible for Iraq's sectarian violence", last modified June 7, 2013. https://www.opendemocracy.net/zana-khasraw-gul/who-is-responsible-for-iraq%e2%80%99s-sectarian-violence

Class based representation may be superior to demographic representation in that the sectarian interest groups are all dissected along above GDP and below GDP lines. Regardless of ethnicity or religion, the nation will be split into Urban populations and Rural populations. This should diffuse some of the anger, angst, or mistrust that divides the sectarian groups. Class division based on incomes and tax liabilities will be successful as well as long as they can be adequately justified by the elite and academic interest groups designing the political system. The occupying power should be fluent in the representational technologies to enhance the nation building phase of the war. Econometric representation will contribute to far better outcomes for fledgling democracies than those that have been achieved with demographic representation.

By far the best option is to integrate the nation into an established democracy that is stable and sound enough in economy to sustain the fledgling democracy. The sectarian interest groups will be absorbed into the larger and more diverse nation. However, if that nation also supports a class-based system of representation it will provide a much more secure environment for the incorporated state. The sectarian aspects of the society will be divided along class-based line and then integrated into a larger community with similar divisions. Economy is all important. It encompasses most aspects of life and the sectarian properties of regional affiliation, ethnicity, and religion will be secondary to class based decisions.

Often sectarian tensions contribute to economic disparities and wealth inequality. Class based representation will improve the likelihood of addressing these core problems without invoking tribalism. The economic reforms should cut across multiple demographic groups making it more likely to pass a median partition. Otherwise, majority demographic groups will vote along tribal or sectarian lines and contribute to austerity measures and exploitative labor policies. If the nation can address these inequities, it is far more likely to succeed as a democracy. If the high unemployment and wage inequality is persistent, minority demographic groups may take adversarial positions and be more susceptible to secessionist or rebellious rhetoric. Class based representation improved the odds of success regardless of whether the nation is incorporated into another electorate or it is a standalone.

It is obvious that demographic representation has some major vulnerabilities that can be exploited by sectarian interest groups. However, they are still highly effective when stable and most of the optimal outcomes from the democratization movement included demographic based systems. Demographic systems of representation impart a high-quality voter entitlement with universal suffrage and aspects of majority rule. However, occupied nations should be able to choose from a number of options and those options should include econometric representation and class-based representation. Let the nation choose for itself the dominant virtues and characteristics of their democratic form of government. It is a form of empowerment for the fledgling democracy. It results in their identity and is major determinant of culture. Often, it's not a binary choice between either demographic or econometric systems of representation. Compromised can be made with bicameral legislatures or more complex systems. They can have both.

Class based representation has one profound advantage over demographic representation. Demographic tensions are typically resolved with restricted entitlements, mass incarceration, mass murder, or a peaceful transfer of political power between different ethnicities. There has never been a case of a peaceful transfer of political power during a demographic shift and demographic shifts occur all the time. Class based systems of representation can avoid poor outcomes by diverting attention away from demographic trends. Class based representation contributes to the deliberation process with role specialization, so the electorate identifies the issues, and then the bicameral process allows the nation to solve their most pressing issues. Economics tensions can be solved with due process. Demographic issues cannot be if the expectations are impossible.

Demographic shifts result when demographic groups previously in the majority try to resist the transition to minority demographic status with minority political power. Class based representation will raise wages, improvement employment outcomes, and fully fund their governments to resolve political instability. If there are better economic outcomes, demographic groups wont over-value the political power associated with majority demographic status. With better outcomes, they will have more trust, and exhibit more patience reducing the probability of conflict. This is why nation building must incorporate econometric and class-based systems of representation into it portfolio of solutions.

The second political union treated in this chapter will be the realignment of Canada, Mexico, and the United States along the two axes of demographics and econometrics. In this respect, the demographic changes will be more accepted among a greater proportion of the population, with Hispanics already a growing group in the electorate, and Canada contributing to the plurality of an integrated and well-educated population. In terms of economic capability, Mexico represents an opportunity to integrate a large workforce from a developing economy with an emerging market for export to. This might contribute to more integration and cooperation with Central and South America in terms of trade and political maneuvering. Canada is a resource rich country with a strong currency from a more mature economy. They also have significant cultural and political connections with other allies like Australia and the United Kingdom.

Many people think the U.S. made the first effort in forming a more comprehensive union with Mexico and Canada to hedge the growing economic and political power of the European Union. These processes can take decades and generations as is evidence by the pace in economic and political reform in Europe. The premise was set up immediately after the World War II, and although it has progressed to a free travel zone, a

Eurozone, and limited political control over Central Banking and regulation, it is still in a formative phase fully dependent on the support of the individual members. NAFTA could be the first attempt at forming a North American Union between the United States, Mexico, and Canada. This is an important process as it can be repeated over and over again in South America, Africa, and Asia.

In the 1980's, Mexico had a population of 69.3 million[92] and a GDP of 194.4 billion[93]. By 2015 Mexico had a population of 127 million[94] and a GDP of 1.144 trillion[95]. This represents nearly a 183% increase in population and a 588% increase in GDP. These figures can be used to estimate the total change in representation if it were included in a political union with the United States and Canada.

Canada is possibly our most important trading partner. In the 1980's Canada had 24.6 million citizens[96]and $273.85 billion in GDP[97]. By 2015 Canada had 35.9[98] million citizens and $1.551 trillion in GDP[99]. This represents a 146% growth in population and a 566% growth in GDP. The population growth in Canada is nearly equal to that of the United States with a slightly lower GDP growth rate.

To reiterate the statistics from the last simulation, the United States had a population of 227.25 million citizens[100] in the 1980's and a GDP of $2863 billion[101]. By 2015 the population had grown to 321.4 million persons[102] with a 141% increase in total citizenship while the United States GDP had grown to $17.947T[103] with a 626% increase in value.

---

92 "Mexico Population", Worldbank.org, accessed on July 14, 2017.
http://data.worldbank.org/indicator/ SP.POP.TOTL?locations=MX

93 "Mexico GDP", Worldbank.org, accessed on July 14, 2017.
http://data.worldbank.org/indicator/NY. GDP.MKTP.CD?locations=MX

94 "Mexico Population", Worldbank.org, accessed on July 14, 2017.
http://data.worldbank.org/indicator/ SP.POP.TOTL?locations=M

95 "Mexico GDP", Worldbank.org, accessed on July 14, 2017.
http://data.worldbank.org/indicator/NY. GDP.MKTP.CD?locations=MX

96 "Canadian Population", Worldbank.org, accessed on July 15, 2017. http://data.worldbank.org/
indicator/SP.POP.TOTL?locations=CA

97 "Canadian GDP", Worldbank.org, accessed on July 15, 2017.
http://data.worldbank.org/indicator/NY.GDP.MKTP.CD?locations=CA

98 "Canadian Population", Worldbank.org, accessed on July 15, 2017. http://data.worldbank.org/
indicator/SP.POP.TOTL?locations=CA

99 Canadian GDP", Worldbank.org, accessed on July 15, 2017.
http://data.worldbank.org/indicator/NY.GDP.MKTP.CD?locations=CA

100 "United States Population", Worldbank.org, accessed on July 14, 2017.
http://data.worldbank.org/indicator/ SP.POP.TOTL?locations=US

101 "United States GDP", Worldbank.org, accessed on July 14, 2017.
http://data.worldbank.org/indicator/NY. GDP.MKTP.CD?locations=US

102 "United States Population", Worldbank.org, accessed on July 14, 2017.
http://data.worldbank.org/indicator/ SP.POP.TOTL?locations=US

103 "United States GDP", Worldbank.org, accessed on July 14, 2017.

The combined total population of the United States would grow to 484.3 million which is nearly the entire population of the EU at 509 million[104]. The new GDP of the North American Union would be $20.642T compared to the European Unions $16.23T[105]. There are shared benefits for all parties. The US population may retain majority power, but Canada will gain political influence over its biggest trading partner for exports. Mexico will gain access to federalist tax dollars to battle the mafia and make infrastructure improvements. Mexico will also gain access to more investment dollars from US market while US employers gain access to lower cost labor with equivalent regulatory structure. The United States gains a much smaller border to the rest of the Continent and a larger population to draw on for enlistment during times of emergency.

If the political union was formed in the 1980's, Mexico would command almost 22% of the demographic based representation, with Canada managing just 8%, and the US maintaining majority political power with 70% of the electorate[106]. Compare this to 2015, where Mexico would climb to nearly 26% of the electorate, Canada would shrink to just 7%, and the United States would continue to hold majority party status with 66% of the demographic based representation[107]. Most of the population growth occurred in Mexico but populations tend to stabilize once they acquire mature market status[108], like the US and Canada, so the projections could change after labor standards are improved and Mexican law enforcement receiving substantial increases in funding.

The econometric representation within the NAU presents a different trajectory. In the 1980's, Mexico would capture nearly 6% of the total econometric representation. Canada would claim 8% while the United States would monopolize the chamber with close to 86% of the total GDP based vote. In 2015, Mexico's total proportion would remain at just 5%, while Canada's share would shrink to 7.5%[109]. The United States would retain almost 87% of the total econometric representation in the NAU.

The representational ratios earned by Canada are much lower than most of the states within the Union. In 1980, the Canadians would suffer under a 10:1 ratio in representation. This would grow to 12:1 ratio in

---

http://data.worldbank.org/indicator/NY. GDP.MKTP.CD?locations=US

[104] "EU Population", Worldbank.org, accessed on July 15, 2017.
http://data.worldbank.org/indicator/ SP.POP.TOTL?locations=EU

[105] "EU GDP", Worldbank.org, accessed on July 15, 2017. http://data.worldbank.org/indicator/ NY.GDP.MKTP.CD?locations=EU

[106] Comparison of demographic data and GDP data for U.S., Canada, and Mexico from http://data.worldbank.org/

[107] Comparison of demographic data and GDP data for U.S., Canada, and Mexico from http://data.worldbank.org/

[108] "Mature Economy", Thefreedictionary.com, Accessed on July 15,2017. http://financial-dictionary.thefreedictionary.com/Mature+economy

[109] Comparison of GDP data for U.S., Canada, and Mexico from http://data.worldbank.org/

representation by 2015. These are in line with the moderate population states in the United States Senate. For instance, Washington has a 7.17 million resident population with a representational ratio of 12 in the U.S. Senate[110]. Missouri also has a representational ratio of 10 with 6 million residents[111].

The representational ratios for Mexico slightly higher but far from the most extreme ratios in the Union. In 1980, the Mexicans would suffer under a 15:1 ratio in representation[112]. This would grow to 16:1 ratio in representation by 2015[113]. These are in line with the moderate population states in the United States Senate. For instance, New Jersey has an 8.96 million resident population with a representational ratio of 15 in the U.S. Senate[114]. Michigan also has a representational ratio of 16.9 with 9.92 million residents[115]. This is a compromise that most states make. Mexico should assent to GDP based representation referencing the precedents set by Missouri and Maryland, and accept a moderate deficiency in representation like a huge majority of contemporary states.

Representational ratios of 12:1 and 16:1 is far better than the ratios bore by the biggest and largest states in the United States. California has a ratio of approximately 67:1, Texas has a ratio of nearly 47:1, Florida has a ratio of almost 35:1, with New York suffering under a ratio just slightly under 34:1[116]. The median representational ratio is between Louisiana at 7.969 and Kentucky at 7.54[117]. Both Canada and Mexico would be in the above median group indicating a slight deficiency but when they are broken into smaller states, there will be some high higher per capita ratio of GDP than others, although the aggregate representation afforded to the group will remain constant.

Canada would own an 8% margin in both chambers. This was stable over the entire 35-year period. Mexico experienced a 4% gain in the demographic chamber but see no improvement in the econometric chamber. The United States will continue to maintain a majority in both the

---

[110] "Factfinder", census.gov, accessed on July 15th, 2017.
https://factfinder.census.gov/faces/tableservices/jsf/pages/productview.xhtml?src=bkmk
[111] "Factfinder", census.gov, accessed on July 15th, 2017.
https://factfinder.census.gov/faces/tableservices/jsf/pages/productview.xhtml?src=bkmk
[112] Comparison of demographic data for U.S., Canada, and Mexico from
http://data.worldbank.org/
[113] Comparison of demographic data for U.S., Canada, and Mexico from
http://data.worldbank.org/
[114] "Factfinder", census.gov, accessed on July 15th, 2017.
https://factfinder.census.gov/faces/tableservices/jsf/pages/productview.xhtml?src=bkmk
[115] "Factfinder", census.gov, accessed on July 15th, 2017.
https://factfinder.census.gov/faces/tableservices/jsf/pages/productview.xhtml?src=bkmk
[116] "Factfinder", census.gov, accessed on July 15th, 2017.
https://factfinder.census.gov/faces/tableservices/jsf/pages/productview.xhtml?src=bkmk
[117] "Factfinder", census.gov, accessed on July 15th, 2017.
https://factfinder.census.gov/faces/tableservices/jsf/pages/productview.xhtml?src=bkmk

demographic and econometric chambers of representation. The fears of loss of sovereignty through a political union with Mexico and Canada is not founded on reason or evidence. This is especially true when GDP is used as the representational coefficient for the second chamber.

Over another 70-year period, the United States might be challenged by an 8% increase in Mexican performance and an 8% loss in their own performance, but the spoiler will then be Canada which without coincidence represents a nearly 8% share of the demographic representation[118]. If the trajectory of Mexican population growth starts to conform to other mature economies, the demographic majority enjoyed by the United States and Canada will hold over several more generations. More stability in the demographic representation will result in more support for the N.A.U. in the United States and Canada.

The next most likely change in Union participation will be the United Kingdom with a movement away from the E.U. and towards its historic partners Canada and Australia. The Union can be modeled through the twin axes of demographics and econometrics. There are few sectarian rifts in the populations and it could easily be expected to be one of the premier political unions in the world.

Australia had 14.7m citizens in 1980 and 23.8m citizens in in 2015[119]. Canada had 24.6m citizens in 1980 and almost 35.9m citizens in 2015[120]. The United Kingdom had 56.3 million persons in 1980 and 65.1m in 2015[121]. The total proportion of population for Australia in 1980 was 15.4%, for Canada it was 25.7%, and for the United Kingdom it was 58.9%[122]. The proportions changed to 19.1% for Australia in 2015, 28.8% for Canada, and 52.2% for the United Kingdom[123].

In the 1980's Australia had 149.66B in GDP and $1.340T in 2015[124]. Canada had $273.85B in GDP in the 1980's and that grew to $1.551T GDP in 2015[125]. The United Kingdom had $564.9B GDP in 1980 and $2.849T GDP in 2015[126]. The proportion of GDP representation in 1980 set Australia at

---

[118] Comparison of GDP data for U.S., Canada, and Mexico from http://data.worldbank.org/

[119] "Australian Population", Worldbank.org, accessed on July 15, 2017.
http://data.worldbank.org/ indicator/SP.POP.TOTL?locations=AU

[120] "Canadian Population", Worldbank.org, accessed on July 15, 2017.
http://data.worldbank.org/ indicator/SP.POP.TOTL?locations=CA

[121] "UK Population", Worldbank.org, accessed on July 15, 2017. http://data.worldbank.org/ indicator/SP.POP.TOTL?locations=EU

[122] Comparison of population data for Australia, Canada, United Kingdom from http://data.worldbank.org/

[123] Comparison of population data for Australia, Canada, United Kingdom from http://data.worldbank.org/

[124] "Australian GDP", Worldbank.org, accessed on July 15, 2017. http://data.worldbank.org /indicator/NY.GDP.MKTP.CD?locations=AU

[125] "Canadian GDP", Worldbank.org, accessed on July 15, 2017.
http://data.worldbank.org/indicator/NY.GDP.MKTP.CD?locations=CA

15.1%, Canada at 27.7%, and the U.K. at 57%[127]. This changed in 2015 when Australia was allocated 23.3% of GDP, Canada maintained 27%, and the U.K.'s share shrank to just 49.6% of GDP[128].

The largest representational gains were made by Australia with an 8.2% improvement in proportional GDP and a 3.7% gain in proportional Population[129]. Canada also increased their proportion of population by 3%. The biggest representational losses were 7.5% in proportional GDP by the U.K. and a 6.7% loss in proportional population[130]. Canada had a near nominal loss in GDP.

The representational ratios for the GDP representation are minimal with the ratio between 1980's Australia and U.K. being just 3.77 and then shrinking to 2.12 in 2015[131]. The ratio for Canada in the 1980's was 2.06 with it decreasing to just 1.83 in 2015[132]. These are much more moderate than the extremes found in the United States. Australia managed a ratio closer to New Mexico at 3.55 with and Maine at 2.26 when compared to California at 66.8[133]. Canada is best compared to Maine and Rhode Island at 1.80[134]. This demonstrates the GDP ratio between the smaller and larger states are much closer with more parity in representation. This power sharing between similar cultures should result in stronger bonds between the nations.

This would be the most natural movement for the three Crown countries seeing that the European Union is moving towards political union and that the United States has a static state of political union. There is safety in numbers and a 120m person economic bloc is far more capable than a 60m person bloc. The new United Kingdom would have access to all three of the biggest markets in the world. It would have Australia in Asia, Canada in North America, and the U.K. in Europe. A perfect situation for industry that can remove most barrios to transport between the allied countries.

The United States would likely forgo a union with Mexico if it could instead forma new economic and political block with the U.K., Canada, and Australia. The total GDP would be equal to $23.687T[135]. This is far larger

---

[126] "UK GDP", Worldbank.org, accessed on July 15, 2017. http://data.worldbank.org/indicator/NY.GDP.MKTP.CD?locations=GB

[127] Comparison of GDP data for Australia, Canada, United Kingdom from http://data.worldbank.org/

[128] Comparison of GDP data for Australia, Canada, United Kingdom from http://data.worldbank.org/

[129] Comparison of GDP data for U.K., Canada, and Australia from http://data.worldbank.org/

[130] Comparison of GDP data for U.K., Canada, and Australia from http://data.worldbank.org/

[131] Comparison of GDP data for U.K., Canada, and Australia from http://data.worldbank.org/

[132] Comparison of GDP data for U.K., Canada, and Australia from http://data.worldbank.org/

[133] "Factfinder", census.gov, accessed on July 15th, 2017. https://factfinder.census.gov/faces/tableservices/jsf/pages/productview.xhtml?src=bkmk

[134] "Factfinder", census.gov, accessed on July 15th, 2017. https://factfinder.census.gov/faces/tableservices/jsf/pages/productview.xhtml?src=bkmk

than the E.U. and might gain parity with the GDP growth expected in China over the next 20 years. The total population would be 446.2m[136] which will be just shy of the European Union's population of 509m[137]. It will also expand the U.K. and U.S. reach into the Pacific with trading possible through both Australia. It would also provide access the Artic region near the North Pole which could be an important source for natural resources and trade route when the ice melts.

The total proportion of population in the 1980's was Australia with just 4.6%, Canada with 7.6%, the U.K. with 17.4%, and the U.S. with 70.3%[138]. The proportions changed slightly by 2015 with Australia gaining 5.3% of total demographic representation, Canada acquiring 8.0%, the U.K. shrinking to 14.5%, and the U.S. growing to 72.0%[139]. Demographic shifts shouldn't disrupt politics too any great degree with most positions holding steady and where cultural integration and shared identity is already present. If anything, the growth in Hispanic populations will be checked by the expansion of the Anglo populations in the U.K., Australia and Canada, but their inclusion will open relations with the developing countries in Central and South America. Diversity is a huge advantage when demographic concerns are mitigated with the use of an econometric chamber based on GDP.

The total proportion of GDP in the 1980's was 3.9% for Australia, 7.1% for Canada, 14.7% for the U.K., and 74.3% for the U.S.[140]. By 2015, Australia grew to 5.65%, Canada shrank to 6.5%, the UK decreased to 12.0%, and the United states increased to 75.8%[141]. The changes in GDP reflected similar changes in population. This arc might be altered by the flow of federal tax subsidies and investment dollars after the union is formed. The unrestricted trade zones will also benefit those partners losing ground in the GDP based chamber. The promise of econometric representation is one that accommodates these short-term trends by allowing the participants to adjust and change the expected outcome. Despite interim losses, the act of unionization may substantially change the current trajectory and this uncertainty should be enough incentive to strike agreement. The biggest

---

[135] Summation of GDP data for U.S., Canada, Australia, and U.K. from
http://data.worldbank.org/

[136] Summation of population data for U.S., Canada, Australia, and U.K. from
http://data.worldbank.org/

[137] "EU Population", Worldbank.org, accessed on July 15, 2017.
http://data.worldbank.org/indicator/ SP.POP.TOTL?locations=EU

[138] Comparison of population data for U.S., U.K., Canada, and Australia from
http://data.worldbank.org/

[139] Comparison of population data for U.S., U.K., Canada, and Australia from
http://data.worldbank.org/

[140] Comparison of GDP data for U.S., U.K., Canada, and Australia from
http://data.worldbank.org/

[141] Comparison of GDP data for U.S., U.K., Canada, and Australia from
http://data.worldbank.org/

representational gains were found in Australia with a 1.8% gain in proportional GDP and the United States with a 1.43% gain in proportional GDP[142]. The United States also earned a 1.6% gain in demographic representation over the 35-year period[143].

The biggest representational losses were in the U.K. with a 2.6% loss in GDP and a 2.9% loss in population[144]. All other values remain stable over the 35-year period. Despite the gains and losses in representation, the partners would be far better off with the political union than if they remained independent of the E.U. and U.S. Military cooperation is a huge component of any political union, and access to new territories will benefit all. If the partners accept the higher ratio of defense spending found in the United States, with greater parity in technological capacity, the inclusion of another 120m persons[145] will improve the West's ability to counteract an activist China attempting to export its despotism to the world. It is the implied threat that will discourage misbehavior and facilitate stronger trade between the spheres.

Looking at the unthinkable is also justified. For the next simulation, the United States will separate into two independents and competing blocs. This section doesn't advocate for a split, but it certainly entertains its possibility citing the debt default threats and numerous government shutdowns during a period of demographic shifts and unprecedented wealth inequality. Hints of secession have precedent. Not only was one war over secession already fought in the U.S. with the culture still frequently referenced but the U.K. recently voted to leave the E.U.[146]. Scotland has reciprocated threatening an exit from the U.K. There are parts of Spain currently entertaining secession and years ago Quebec threatened to leave Canada. It isn't farfetched to suggest a split between urban states and rural states in context of the growing political divide and economic disparity between regions.

A dissolution could be peaceful after a debt default or violent after a compromised Presidential election. Any permanent split in the union would be a less than optimal outcome. There is a strength in numbers and if the United States can preserve its territorial boundaries while improving the quality of its democratic entitlement, it will be far better off than any other outcome. Any outcome other than preserving the union would result in a

---

142 Comparison of GDP data for U.S., U.K., Canada, and Australia from
http://data.worldbank.org/

143 Comparison of Population data for U.S., U.K., Canada, and Australia from
http://data.worldbank.org/

144 Comparison of GDP data for U.S., U.K., Canada, and Australia from
http://data.worldbank.org/

145 Summation of GDP data for U.K., Canada, and Australia from http://data.worldbank.org/

146 "EU Referendum results", bbc.com, accessed on KJuly 16, 2017.
http://www.bbc.com/news/politics/eu_referendum/results

catastrophic loss in GDP and violent change in the electorate. These simulations are Gedanken experiments, motivated only by the access of demographic and economic data in the U.S. with the convenience of declared political sympathies.

Dividing the nation between urban states and rural states is a theoretical exercise. This book uses heuristics and assumes that the more urban states are on the coasts and the more rural states are in the southern and central regions. To be clear, there are some sparsely states included within the urban group and some densely populated states included within the rural group. These boundaries are hardly fixed and static with political affiliation changing over time and subject to electoral outcomes that won't be considered in this treatment of the subject. Often, the affiliation is due to proximity to other states that share these geo-spatial properties.

These simulations fix the coastal states (urban) to California, Colorado, Connecticut, Delaware, Hawaii, Illinois, Maine, Maryland, Massachusetts, Michigan, Minnesota, Nevada, New Hampshire, New Jersey, New Mexico, New York, Oregon, Pennsylvania, Rhode Island, Vermont, Wisconsin, and Washington. Washington D.C. is added to the GDP and population for the urban states although it is not a state. The central and southern states (rural) are fixed to Alabama, Alaska, Arizona, Arkansas, Florida, Georgia, Idaho, Indiana, Iowa, Kansas, Kentucky, Louisiana, Mississippi, Montana, Missouri, Nebraska, North Carolina, North Dakota, Ohio, Oklahoma, South Carolina, South Dakota, Tennessee, Texas, Utah, Virginia, West Virginia, and Wyoming. This isn't an arbitrary assignment, although it is not substantiated by any specific history.

For convenience, the coastal states are considered one independent bloc of nations with the central and southern states relegated to a competing bloc. If the rural states seceded from the union, they would have 161m persons in 2015[147] with a little more than 8.00T in GDP in 2015[148]. This is contrasted to the urban states having 160m persons[149] in 2015 with 9.83T GDP in 2015[150]. They would have nearly equal populations, but the urban states would have almost 122% advantage in GDP[151]. This has profound effects on demographics and econometrics of the new nation. This is more evident when examining the prospects of an economic union with the other allied nations or proximate nations.

---

[147] "Factfinder", census.gov, accessed on July 16th, 2017.
https://factfinder.census.gov/faces/tableservices/jsf/pages/productview.xhtml?src=bkmk
[148] "Tools (interactive data, regional data, GDP in current dollars, by year)", bea.gov, accessed on July 16, 2017. Reports run for each year, only "Red States" from page 42.
[149] "Factfinder", census.gov, accessed on July 16th, 2017.
https://factfinder.census.gov/faces/tableservices/jsf/pages/productview.xhtml?src=bkmk
[150] "Tools (interactive data, regional data, GDP in current dollars, by year)", bea.gov, accessed on July 16, 2017. Reports run for each year, only "Red States" from page 42.
[151] Comparison of 2015 GDP for Red Stats and Blue States

The first union examined will be the central and southern states and Mexico. This looks like an unorthodox or unlikely combination but if war can provoke future union formation, then this simulation is warranted. It should be noted that Hispanic populations are growing within the border states, including Texas and Florida, and they will have a dominant role in any democratic society and political system in the newly incorporated states. Although the current proportions aren't accurate for an immediate incorporation, the trends may hold true for the incorporation of the union after a period of occupation. By occupying Mexico, a 1933-mile border[152] can be transformed into an approximate 400-mile border[153] which has obvious implications for a population that sets border control as a high priority.

In 2000, the central and southern states had a population of 136 million[154] and a GDP of 4.44T[155] while Mexico had only 98.9m persons[156] and a 683.6B economy[157]. This shifted to nearly 161m persons[158] in the US by 2015 with 7.99T GDP[159]. Mexico acquired 127m persons[160] in 2015 with 1.144T GDP[161]. The total population of this new nation would be 288m persons[162] which is nearly 89% that of the current 321m[163] person population of the United States[164]. The total economic output is 9.143T[165] falling short of the standalone GDP of the coastal states as well as the current GDP of China.

---

[152] Janice Beaver, "U.S. International Borders: Brief facts", CRS Report for Congress, accessed on September 19.2017. https://fas.org/sgp/crs/misc/RS21729.pdf

[153] Randal Archibald, "In Trek North, First Lure is Mexico's Other Line", New York Times, last modified April 26, 2013. http://www.nytimes.com/ 2013/04/27 /world/americas/central-americans-pour-into-mexico-bound-for-us.html

[154] "Factfinder", census.gov, accessed on July 18th, 2017. https://factfinder.census.gov/faces/tableservices/jsf/pages/productview.xhtml?src=bkmk

[155] "Tools (interactive data, regional data, GDP in current dollars, by year)", bea.gov, accessed on July 16, 2017. Reports run for each year, only "Red States" from page 42.

[156] "Mexico Population", Worldbank.org, accessed on July 18, 2017. http://data.worldbank.org/indicator/ SP.POP.TOTL?locations=MX

[157] "Mexico GDP", Worldbank.org, accessed on July 18, 2017. http://data.worldbank.org/indicator/NY. GDP.MKTP.CD?locations=MX

[158] "Factfinder", census.gov, accessed on July 18th, 2017. https://factfinder.census.gov/faces/tableservices/jsf/pages/productview.xhtml?src=bkmk

[159] "Tools (interactive data, regional data, GDP in current dollars, by year)", bea.gov, accessed on July 16, 2017. Reports run for each year, only "Red States" from page 42.

[160] "Mexico Population", Worldbank.org, accessed on July 18, 2017. http://data.worldbank.org/indicator/ SP.POP.TOTL?locations=MX

[161] "Mexico GDP", Worldbank.org, accessed on July 18, 2017. http://data.worldbank.org/indicator/NY. GDP.MKTP.CD?locations=MX

[162] Summation of Mexico and Red States' population 2015 estimates.

[163] "Factfinder", census.gov, accessed on July 18th, 2017. https://factfinder.census.gov/faces/tableservices/jsf/pages/productview.xhtml?src=bkmk

[164] Summation of Mexico and Red States' GDP 2015 estimates

[165] "Mexico GDP", Worldbank.org, accessed on July 18, 2017. http://data.worldbank.org/indicator/NY. GDP.MKTP.CD?locations=MX

Mexico does help them make up ground in terms of population and GDP, but they must consider other options to achieve parity with their competitors.

Mexico lost nearly 13% of its total proportion of GDP[166] compared to the U.S.[167] based representation over the period of 2000-2015 while gaining nearly 10% in demographic representation[168]. This is still a net loss of nearly 3% over the 15-year period. This may be enough incentive for the central and southern states to seek out the union. If the trends continue, the central and southern states will capture more of the electorate and have a developing economy to resource for labor efficiencies and maximize exports to other markets. The Mexicans will capture federal tax subsidies and investment dollars at a high ratio due to the disparity in currency values. Mexico will gain nearly 44% of the entire demographic based chamber by 2015 which will be incentive to agree to the terms[169].

The central and southern states might only have a 55% majority in the demographic chamber[170] but the ratio grows to nearly 87% in the GDP based chamber[171]. They can effectively dictate the terms of reform and economic management through a bicameral process with emphasis on free market tendencies or outcomes. This current trend demonstrates an increase in the disparity in GDP favoring the central and southern states despite the faster economic growth in Mexico. The Mexicans may only have 13% proportion of representation in the econometric chamber[172] but they will contribute nearly 44% to Presidential elections[173]. Through the dichotomy between demographic representation and econometric representation, power can be effectively shared between developing economies and mature economies.

In 30 years, Hispanic populations may have significant majorities in Texas, Florida, Nevada, New Mexico, Arizona, and other states. Incorporating Mexico into a union may make more sense to a larger proportion of the population of that period. This simulation is predicated on the central and southern states maintaining high quality democratic entitlements after secession, which is not necessarily guaranteed. However, simulations of non-democratic nations are out of bounds of this book. If the

---

[166] "Mexico Population", Worldbank.org, accessed on July 18, 2017.
http://data.worldbank.org/indicator/ SP.POP.TOTL?locations=MX

[167] "Tools (interactive data, regional data, GDP in current dollars, by year)", bea.gov, accessed on July 16, 2017. Reports run for each year, only "Red States" from page 42.

[168] Comparison of 2015 populations in Mexico and the Central and Southern States.

[169] Comparison of previously cited 2015 populations in Mexico and the Red States found on page 42

[170] Comparison of previously cited 2015 populations in Mexico and the Red States found on page 42

[171] Comparison of previously cited 2015 GDP for Mexico and the Red States on page 42

[172] Comparison of previously cited 2015 GDP between Mexico and the Red states on page 42

[173] Comparison of previously cited 2015 population between Mexico and the Red States found on page 42

central and southern states form an imperial democracy and incorporate Mexico, they may seek to expand their border to Cuba as well.

Cuba represents a mistake made by the American established decades ago. New administrations might want to correct those passed errors. Support for this agenda will be found in Florida and the larger voting Cuban population. Cuba has a nominal economy and won't disrupt the proportion of representation apportioned through GDP, but it does have a viable population of nearly 12 million making it one of the larger states in the hypothetical Union[174].

Cuba would capture nearly 4% of the total popular vote in the new nation according to 2015[175] populations. Mexico would drop to just 42%[176] and the central and southern would drop to nearly 54%[177]. GDP representation would be almost unchanged by the inclusion of Cuba's paltry 77B economy[178]. However, due to the proportional method of representation, Cuba would gain exactly 1 representative. This would be an over-representation of the state, but most contemporary democracies have equivalent examples to justify the relationship. With 87% of the GDP based representation still in central and southern states' possession[179] they won't feel threatened by the expansion of the electorate to include Mexico and Cuba. The central and southern state will seek to acquire an equivalent level of power and prestige to the station they previously held while part of the United States. This will require them to incorporate states they wouldn't otherwise pursue.

The coastal states are slightly more formidable than the southern and central States. The coastal States have approximately the same population at 160m[180] but they capture slightly more than 60% of GDP with $9.85T GDP in 2015[181]. If the coastal states joined in union with Mexico and Canada, it would regain almost 100% of the lost population from the former United States[182]. The new nation would have 323m persons[183] with approximately 70% of the former Economy at $12.5T GDP[184]. It is far from the $18T[185]

---

174 "Cuban Population", worldbank.org, accessed on July 18, 2017.
http://data.worldbank.org/indicator /SP.POP.TOTL?locations=CU

175 Comparison of Mexico, Cuba, and U.S. 2015 populations

176 Comparison of Mexico, Cuba, and U.S. 2015 populations

177 Comparison of Mexico, Cuba, and U.S. 2015 populations

178 "Cuban GDP", worldbank.org, accessed on July 18, 2017. http://data.worldbank.org/indicator/NY.GDP.MKTP.CD?locations=CU

179 Comparison of Mexico, Cuba, and U.S. by GDP

180 "Factfinder", census.gov, accessed on August 9th, 2017.
https://factfinder.census.gov/faces/tableservices/jsf/pages/productview.xhtml?src=bkmk

181 "Tools (interactive data, regional data, GDP in current dollars, by year)", bea.gov, accessed on August 9th, 2017.

182 "Factfinder", census.gov, accessed on August 9th, 2017.
https://factfinder.census.gov/faces/tableservices/jsf/pages/productview.xhtml?src=bkmk

183 Accessed on 8.9.2017 and retrieved from US Census data and World Bank data

economy they used to manage, but the United American States (UAS) would still be able to accomplish many of the goals and tasks it previously favored. There is strength in numbers and the coastal will seek out permanent alliance with its neighbors to mitigate the counter-productive relationship it has with the Red States.

The coastal states will seek to incorporate the Canadians for two major reasons. First, they represent a mature economy with a diverse and educated electorate. Secondly, the represent a free movement zone and will connect the states on one coast with the states on the other coast. Mexico represents a developing economy for the investment dollars of the coastal states. In this respect, the central and southern states occupied a similar position being the recipient of the majority of federal tax subsidies. Mexico may also bring with it improved relations to Central and South America. A multi-cultural and multi-lingual UAS should improve trade between the three regions.

From 2000-2015, Mexico's proportion of demographic representation would grow from 36% to 39% of the total union[186], Canada would remain stable at just 11%[187], and the coastal states will fall from 53%[188] to just 50%[189]. A 4% improvement for Mexico is their incentive to join the Union[190]. However, during the same period, Mexico will stabilize at only 9% of the econometric representation[191], while the Canadians grow from 10% to 12%[192], and the coastal states fall from 80% to 78%[193]. The coastal states will continue to maintain a huge majority in the GDP based chamber providing incentive to form the Union.

The coastal states have more homogenous populations than the central and southern states and aren't in crisis over recent demographic shifts. This will keep them open to political union with its neighbors. Mexico offers a bridge into Central America and South America. It also represents a growing market for exports and investment. The coastal states have other options available to them. The UK recently voted to exit the EU and may be an opportunity for Union with the coastal states, Canada, and Australia.

---

[184] "U.S. GDP", Worldbank.org, accessed on 8.9.2017.
http://data.worldbank.org/indicator/NY.GDP.MKTP.CD?locations=US&view=chart
[185] $12.5T/$18T "U.S. GDP", Worldbank.org, accessed on 8.9.2017.
http://data.worldbank.org/indicator/NY.GDP.MKTP.CD?locations=US&view=chart
[186] "U.S. GDP", Worldbank.org, accessed on 8.9.2017.
http://data.worldbank.org/indicator/NY.GDP.MKTP.CD?locations=US&view=chart
[187] Derivative of demographic data from US Census and World Bank
[188] Derivative of demographic data from US Census and World Bank
[189] Derivative of demographic data from US Census and World Bank
[190] Derivative of demographic data from US Census and World Bank
[191] Derivative of BEA data and World Bank data
[192] Derivative of BEA data and World Bank data
[193] Derivative of BEA data and World Bank data

A union between Canada, Australia, England (UK), and the former United States would have 284m citizens[194] with nearly $15.6T GDP[195]. It might have lost 50m persons[196] but it would limit its GDP loss to just 14% of GDP[197]. The United States (dropping America from the title) would have to adopt a 2nd generation government to increase efficiency, and this can be accomplished by either eliminating the Filibuster and Presidential Veto or by adopting a Parliamentarian structure. The nations already have extremely tight military relationships and their citizens have similar ideas about healthcare, education, and civil liberties. They could integrate fairly quickly and easily. It would be a formidable association that would be nearly equivalent to the EU in GDP[198] post Britain exit, with territory in both Europe and Asia.

From 2000-2015, Australia would gain nearly 1% in demographic representation[199], the United Kingdom would see a loss of just 1%[200], Canada would lose only 0.5%[201]. and the coastal states would lose almost 1%[202]. These are stable trajectories over 15 years. It is assumed they can be sustained indefinitely. The former United States retains most of political power, but the Crown Countries capture almost 44% giving them plenty of opportunities to negotiate with the individual parties in the coastal states[203]. Most political markets are very competitive with alternating administrations and each region would be effectively split between multiple political parties. It is doubtful nationalist attitudes would divide the nation by region rather than party.

The econometric chamber demonstrates other trends. Over the period of 2000-2015, Australia increased from 5% to nearly 9%[204], the UK saw zero growth maintaining 18%[205], while Canada's representation grew from 9% to nearly 10%[206]. The coastal states saw their majority shrink from 68% to just 63%[207]. However, the coastal states would still have clear majorities in both

---

[194] Derivative of World Bank data and US Census data

[195] Derivative of World Bank data and BEA Data

[196] Derivative of World Bank data and US Census data

[197] Derivative of World Bank data and BEA Data

[198] "EU GDP", Worldbank.org, accessed on August 9, 2017.
http://data.worldbank.org/indicator/NY.GDP.MKTP.CD?locations=EU&view=chart

[199] Derivative of World Bank data and US Census Data

[200] Derivative of World Bank data and US Census data

[201] Derivative of World Bank data and US Census data

[202] Derivative of World Bank data and US Census data

[203] Derivative of World Bank data and US Census data

[204] Derivative of World Bank data and BEA data

[205] Derivative of World Bank data and BEA data

[206] Derivative of World Bank data and BEA data

[207] Stephen Castle, "Scotland Votes to Demand a Post "Brexit" Independence Referendum", Nytimes.com, last modified March 28, 2017.
https://www.nytimes.com/2017/03/28/world/europe/scotland-britain-brexit-european-union.html?_r=0

chambers. Their citizens will be open to trade up on representation formerly apportioned to the central and southern being allocated to Canada, Australia, and the UK. Despite the loss in GDP and population, the new United States might be a more viable and capable nation. '

Great Britain might be able to retain the support and cooperation of Scotland[208] and Northern Ireland[209], both of which are concerned over the split with the EU, if it considered a political union with the US. Otherwise, it could fracture amidst the calls for secession circulating in the world. The UK would be the hub for all European exports from its allies helping to replace its former status as EU financial capital. The UK has a long history of alliance with the United States and this might influence Canada and Australia to make similar decision.

The last simulations will be central and southern states with Mexico and Canada. It is assumed that many of the citizens in the central and southern states will actively seek to offset the demographic changes caused by integrating Mexico with the populations found in Canada. Mexico, Canada, and the central and southern states combined to form nearly 324m persons[210] and $10.69T GDP[211]. This is almost equivalent to the current GDP of China[212] and with a large portion of the economy remaining developing with a faster GDP growth rate, the Central States of America (CSA) could make some gains on the emergent economic superpower.

One concern, is the precipitous drop in federal revenues after the loss of the coastal. Despite the coastal states paying 57% of taxes[213] they only receive 50% of the federal tax subsidies[214]. One of the reasons for this discrepancy is base location in the country and the huge disparity in enlistment. Most of the military bases are in the central and southern states with a huge nearly 2:1 advantage in enlistment for those states[215]. The central

---

[208] , "What does brexit mean for northern ireland", Newstatesman.com, last modified June 24, 2016. https://www.newstatesman.com/politics/uk/2016/06/what-does-brexit-mean-northern-ireland

[209] , "What does brexit mean for northern ireland", Newstatesman.com, last modified June 24, 2016. https://www.newstatesman.com/politics/uk/2016/06/what-does-brexit-mean-northern-ireland

[210] Derivative of World Bank and US Census data

[211] Derivative of World Bank and US Census

[212] "Chinese GDP", Worldbank.org, accessed on August 9, 2017. http://data.worldbank.org/indicator/NY.GDP.MKTP.CD?locations=CN&view=chart

[213] "Tools (interactive data, regional data, GDP in current dollars, by year)", bea.gov, accessed on July 16, 2017. Reports run for each year, "Red state GDP" compared to "Blue State GDP" in proportion, found on page 42.

[214] "2015 Data Book, state revenue data", irs.gov, accessed July 2nd 2017. https://www.irs.gov/pub/irs-soi/15databk.pdf

[215] "Military Active-Duty Personnel, Civilians by State", governing.com, accessed on August 9, 2017. http://www.governing.com/gov-data/military-civilian-active-duty-employee-workforce-numbers-by-state.html

and southern states won't be able to support the military they control and the loss of federalist tax support.

The 20% difference in federalist tax subsidies will contribute to massive public finance deficits for the central and southern states after secession or dissolution of the union[216]. In some cases, the loss of Blue state subsidies could represent a loss of economic stimulus by a margin of nearly 2-3% of GDP. In the same respect, New Jersey and Connecticut would almost double the amount of money they receive back from the economic union once the dependency of the central and southern states is ended. On average, New Jersey and Connecticut only receive back 60% of the contributions they make to the federal government[217]. The repatriation of $60B in federal spending represents nearly 10% of annual GDP to New Jersey[218].

The central and southern states' tentative grasp on democracy in the region could suffer an immediate insult to their economies and public finance systems. However, if the central and southern states did pursue union formation it could produce a more equitable and stable outcome. A union with a population of 324m[219] with a GDP close to 11T[220] would continue to be a potent force in the world, especially if it remains democratic. The United States is one of the largest oil producing nations in the world and these resources are concentrated in the central and southern states. This is a double-edged knife. It could be a hugely lucrative outcome for residents helping offset the initial loss of federal tax subsidy, but it could also invite instability. The newly incorporated states might succumb to the allure and curse of oil production and metamorphosis into a state resembling the OPEC nations or those like Russia, Venezuela, or Nigeria.

If these deficiencies can be overcome, the combined benefits of increased military prowess and massive oil production could make the republic an incredibly successful ally and trading partner. Mexico, Canada, and the central and southern states combined to form nearly 324m persons[221] and 10.69T GDP[222]. This is almost equivalent to the current GDP of China and with a large portion of the economy remaining developing with a faster GDP growth rate, the Confederated States of America (CSA) could make some gains on the emergent economic superpower.

---

[216] Derivative of BEA data and IRS data – comparing differences in state revenues with contributions made.

[217] "2015 Data Book, State Revenue Data", irs.gov, accessed August 9th 2017. https://www.irs.gov/pub/irs-soi/15databk.pdf

[218] "2015 Data Book, State Revenue Data", irs.gov, accessed August 9th 2017. https://www.irs.gov/pub/irs-soi/15databk.pdf

[219] Derivative of World Bank data and US Census data

[220] Derivative of World Bank data and BEA data

[221] Derivative of World Bank data and US Census data

[222] Derivative of World Bank data and BEA data

For instance, Mexico would fall to just 37% of the entire electorate in 2000, with the central and southern states retaining 51% of representation, and Canada capturing almost 12%[223], Canada represents another mature economy with ideologies that reflect strong democratic institutions. Mexico is also strongly rooted in democracy, but it is suffering under terrible corruption and crime at the moment. By 2015, Mexico will represent only 39%, with the central and southern states falling to 49%, and Canada declining to 11%[224]. The central and southern states will need to form coalitions to lead the union, which will be complicated by internal demographics, and external relationships with both Mexico and Canada.

GDP based representation provides an opportunity for the central and southern states to maintain a clear representational advantage despite the majority in the cumulative electorate diminishing. In 2000, Mexico will have nearly 12% of the GDP representation, while Canada has 13%, and the central and southern states maintain 75%[225]. The former United States will have a clear majority to lead from. This is reinforced over the 15-year period, with Mexico falling to 11%, Canada growing to 15%, and the central and southern states declining slightly to 74% in 2015[226]. This large majority in representation should be incentive enough for the central and southern states to entertain the union, especially if they are attempting to recover after a split with the coastal who controlled nearly 60% of the GDP of the former United States[227].

The central and southern states don't have to fear from losing representation in the demographic chamber if they retain their influence in the econometric chamber. Politics is complicated, and the central and southern states will already have some of the most complicated demographics in the world. They will have a large and growing Hispanic population in the Border states and Florida, with a large and stable African American population in the South. They will need to navigate the political environment as a minority demographic group anyway, so the inclusion of Mexico and Canada don't do much to alter their current or expected future state.

The point of these simulations is not to predict likely outcomes. It is to suggest how economic representation could provide more opportunities for union formation or nation building. The peaceful integration of states is a far more effective method for expanding free trade and improving civil liberties and voting rights. However, war is a feature of our geo-political environment and the rise in wealth inequality and expected disruptions from climate

---

[223] Derivative of World Bank data and US Census data

[224] Derivative of World Bank data and US Census data

[225] Derivative of World Bank data and BEA data

[226] Derivative of World Bank data and BEA data

[227] "Tools (interactive data, regional data, GDP in current dollars, by year)", bea.gov, accessed on July 16, 2017. Reports run for each year, "Red state GDP" compared to "Blue State GDP" in proportion, found on page 42.

change will accelerate the rate of conflict. The world has benefit from an unnatural state of peace for the last 70 years. This period might be over with the contraction in the European Union, the loss of authority and power in the United States, and the rise of a despotic China as economic and military superpower. Nation building will be an important component for foreign policy in the near future and econometric representation may offer unique benefits.

5 PROPORTIONAL GDP

If majority rule is the bar to measure political systems, representative government is already a lower quality form of self-governance when compared to direct democracy. Political influence concentrated in a smaller number of people, who are detached from the public by wealth, privilege, and power. This lack of sympathy should introduce inefficiency with the legislature hesitating to respond quickly to issues related to incomes, civil liberties, and health or education. Instead, the body politic will focus on property rights, security, and budget austerity. The government will be more concerned with protecting itself from change than in addressing poverty or other concerns. This will only cause more distrust and disdain from the lower classes and shrinking middle class.

However, representative government has proved itself to an extremely effective form of government, with direct democracy associated more with populism and nativism. Direct democracy makes public policy more accessible to an uninformed and selfish public. In many Western nations, only a minority of the public has college degrees, even fewer have advanced degrees. In larger countries, urban populations diversify while rural communities homogenize. It opens the public sector to crises related to user error and partisan conflict. Direct Democracy presents an argument against majority rule. The tyranny of the masses is often less stable and less equitable than the tyranny of the elites.

Non-democratic countries may call themselves republics, but they don't have free and open elections. They render large segments of the population ineligible for suffrage. They do this be coercing and threatening the public with arrest or violence. These countries can claim their Republic status despite failing to conform to even the lowest standards of free speech, the right to organize and protest, an independent media, and legitimate elections. This sets a terrible precedent for the leaders of other nations who might see opportunity and advantage in those strategies. An Industrial agenda wins out, where the political elites run the country for their own benefit. Companies protect their profits with a leadership caste comes from their corporate boards or the law enforcement and intelligence agencies in the non-democratic country.

Older democracies will pick up deficiencies like gerrymandering, private campaign finance, noted suppression that will make its elections less accurate and less honest. Like economy and commerce, most of politics is based on tradition and trust. It hinges on peaceful transfers of power after free and fair elections. Mistrust and fear can provoke dangerous rhetoric and destructive behavior. A culture of populism can erupt from the lack of faith in democracy and the lack of trust in the media. It only takes a generation of political corruption and challenged elections before a population loses its inhibitions. In just a few short years, the lack of cooperation can produce counterproductive and self-validating histories for abuse. In this respect, stoic and traditionally strong democracies can sink into decline and start resembling the non-democratic countries that only call themselves Republics.

The younger democracies are at even more risk. They don't have well established histories. They may not have developed the culture necessary to support democracy and civil liberties. More importantly, they don't have the long histories of tradition around civil liberties and democratic process. Tradition is critical. It is a social mechanism that accommodates for the deficiencies of laws by creating agreed upon assumptions. All actors will comport to the behavior or expectation because it is predictable and productive. A younger democracy has none of these things. An interruption in the peaceful transition of power could destroy the tradition and culture supporting democracy while its institutions are too understaffed and underfunded to protect themselves.

During demographic shifts, certain political parties will attempt to pass counterproductive policies like gerrymandering, private campaign finance, and voter suppression to empower the majority during their transition to minority. This will distort representation making it inaccurate and dishonest. Populations will react with mistrust in the government and disdain for the agencies that no longer protect their interests or civil liberties. Once faith is lost in the democratic process, a public will stop peacefully resisting with nonviolent protest. This will aggravate the situation inviting more egregious abuses by the minority party trying to maintain power. The enfranchised minority party might even attempt to permanently alter the demographics of the country to reassert itself with majority status. If one looks at history demographic based violence is one of the most common occurrences.

One of the most important attributes of universal suffrage and one person one vote system is their ability to overcome deficiencies like gerrymandering and private campaign finance. There is no more critical aspect of democracy when reforming the economy and electorate. Universal suffrage will correct for wealth inequality and political corruption. It also makes it easier to expand the electorate with women's suffrage and minority suffrage. Without universal suffrage, a nation might otherwise succumb to political instability and rebellion from underrepresented groups and the aristocracy.

Universal suffrage sets a pathway through the deleterious effects of low quality Democratic entitlements like gerrymandering and private campaign finance. Despite its use to oppress minority groups, gerrymandering and private campaign finance will only give the new ascending minority tremendous advantages when finally acquire majority status. The body politic will be more energetic and more erratic, swinging towards the poles, with universal suffrage eventually the majority with more seats and a greater probability of protecting them.

Universal Suffrage will continue to be the foundation for democracy but if majority rule can be challenged as a pre-requisite for democracy, it opens the door for econometric systems of representation. Representational Coefficients based on GDP will provide universal suffrage without demographic representation. A political system can be engineered exclusively on GDP by simply replacing a demographic parliament with a GDP based parliament. Gross Domestic Product is often derivative of population, so the chamber is reminiscent of majority rule without being wholly dependent on it. The **Imperial Union** is an example of this possibility.

Imperial Union

Primary Traits:

- Unitary Legislature

- GDP representational coefficient

- Parliament

Advantages:

- Representation is decoupled from demographic information reducing the likelihood of violence during demographic shifts.

- GDP Representation incentivizes unions between mature democracies and less developed states with larger populations. The less developed nation should be the recipient of significant federalist tax support and business investment, offsetting the lower net representation.

- The variable representation rewards sound economic policy by providing more representation to states with faster economic growth.

- GDP based representation promotes a more aggressive expansion of political boundaries for more developed nations who can be more certain of prolonged political majorities.

- The Unicameral Parliament ensures the majority party can enact laws with little resistance from the minority party.

- Universal Suffrage is preserved with GDP based Representation. Econometric representation qualifies as high quality democratic entitlements on par Senates and demographic chambers

Disadvantages:

- Majority Rule isn't achieved with the Imperial Union, but most contemporary democracies already offer only a diminished quality by including Senates and other inhibitions.

- More populous states with low GDP will resent the greater representation of wealthier states. This might promote political instability if the political power is used to preserve current economic conditions.

- The Unicameral Parliament has few checks and balances installed to ensure minority rights. It may be more susceptible to populism or nationalism than bicameral systems with external executives. It is suggested that the nation maintain a strong Constitution with Independent Judiciary to protect civil liberties and voting rights.

Executive:

- 2.iii (Abolished Executive), 5.a. (National)

Legislative:

- **1.i.x (Unicameral legislature)**, ii.x (Representative), iii.1.2.a.3.4.a.5.7.10.13.a.i.b.ii.c.i (Laws, Oversight, Ratification, Unitary Executive Powers, Appropriations, Appointments, Taxing, Unilateral Amendments with supermajority), **iv.1.b.2.a (Independent, 3/5ths rule, majority party)**, 5.a (National), 6.a.iii (6 year terms), b.iv (Unlimited), c.iii (Unlimited), d.iv (no restraints), **7.a.i (Publicly Funded)**, b.i.xx (parliamentary), **ii.xxxx (Universal Suffrage)**, c.x (direct elections), 8.a.v.b (Citizen), b.i.ii (to vote and to hold office), c.ii (non -exclusive), 10.b (voluntary), 12.b (Districts), **13.b.i (Representative of GDP Straight)**

Judicial:

- 3.A.i (Judicial, Hierarchical), b.i. (Judicial powers only), c.ii.x.1 **(appointed by the Prime Minister),** 5.a.(National), 6.a.iv (Unlimited), b.iv (unlimited), c.iii (Unlimited), d.ii (sum of elected), 8.a.v.b, b.ii (citizen to hold office)

The Imperial Union decouples it republican form of representation from population. States acquire representation based on raw economic power. This allows it to assemble a larger number of satellite states under its immediate control. Wealth is the determinant of political power not demographics. However, universal suffrage still applies and populations with numerical superiority in their states will continue to exert tremendous political power. Each state will earn a number of representatives equal to its proportional GDP allowing wealthier nations to aggressive incorporate smaller or less developed nations into a democracy without disrupting the balance of power.

The larger and less developed states will view the GDP based representation as a limitation, but this only extends on the federal level. The newly incorporated state will have complete control over state level politics with local elections and local laws. The Imperial Union should have a strong constitution for civil liberties and state sovereignty through federalism. These two conditions will limit the frustration a less developed state has with the higher rate of representation a more developed state has in the federal tier. After a number of years, there will likely be free travel and work for citizens of the recently incorporated state diminishing the negative externalities of less representation for the state.

The Imperial Union is one of the darkest and least equitable configurations, but it will certainly have advantages in scale compared to other democracies. This may be more successful in an environment dominated by climate change and wealth inequality. Although imperfect, the imperial democracy is till superior to despotism or communism and the rate at which it can accumulate satellite states should allow it to thrive in more dangerous environments. The world has passed through other dark periods of colonialism and imperialism. It would not be out of bounds to suggest we fall into decline again. The imperial Union is an excellent vector for preserving voting rights, constitutions, and state sovereignty even in the dark ages.

Unlike most other forms of econometric representation, the Imperial Union doesn't use any other representational coefficients. It relies on a single unicameral parliament based on GDP. This gives the demographic majority from the wealthiest states a durable platform to lead the empire. Despite, the econometric representation satisfying the conditions of universal suffrage it doesn't comply with majority rule on a macro-political level. There are strategies for mitigating these representational deficiencies. The unicameral legislative chamber will be able to identify issues and more easily address them.

One of the most counterproductive aspects of conventional government is the Senate. Contemporary democracies can be oppressed and exploited by a Senate just like an economic power controls its colonies. This is apparent when a Senate and low legislative production rate produces a deregulated economy with low wages and low taxes. A landed aristocracy of business owners and investors can obstruct all efforts to improve the economy from the labor classes perspective. This is especially true in bicameral legislature systems with filibusters and Presidential Vetoes. The rate of laws passed can drop to almost nominal levels with the quality quickly declining during periods of great stress, like war, like economic depression, or wealth inequality and corruption.

A Senate is an inverse of most demographic based representation, allowing it to effectively negate or cancel any reform movements from the other chamber. It will imbue the least economically developed states, with the most homogenous and least education population, the most political power. This is a form of populism which is very similar to direct democracy. In fact, the low legislative production rates found in bicameral chambers can produce the conditions where populism gains support and momentum. If the Senate obstructs economic reforms like unions, progressive taxes, and minimum wage, the nation will become much less stable and more susceptible to violent rhetoric and extremism. The obstruction of the legislative process will result in the continued exploitation and oppression of a people.

In this respect, the Senate will preserve a colonial relationship much better than a representative chamber based on Gross Domestic Product. GDP generally increases at a faster rate than GDP in mature economies during these conditions. This naturally disrupts or inhibits the ability of a mature economy to extract rents from a developing state without the state improving its reciprocal representation. This is the promise of GDP based representation. It invites investment dollars with low wages, which will quickly inflate GDP, and while the state is making a transition from developing to mature economy, it can better impose those reforms that would benefit the lower and middle classes like progressive taxes, unions, and higher wages. By that time, the developing nation will acquire the institutions and culture to fully integrate with a nature economy with a durable democracy.

Unicameral legislatures eliminate this condition. Improving the legislative production rate makes it far more likely that the nation is able to regulate itself and tax itself in a manner that promotes more equitable economy and stronger civil liberties. However, unicameral parliaments lack one a major component of democratic governance. They don't have strong checks and balances in place. The Senate would normally bear the burden of moderating the rate of laws passed. It is a check against authoritarian governments sweeping the elections and passing anti-democratic laws. In its absence, the unicameral parliament will have to rely on state sovereignty (federalism) and a strong constitution to protect civil liberties and the democratic process. Unicameral parliaments might consider more oversight by state level governors or living constitutions that set thresholds for changing laws based on the number of votes acquired to pass the law. Without state sovereignty (federalism) and a strong constitution to dictate powers, the high efficiency of the Imperial Union could result in frequent bouts of Populism.

Higher GDP growth in developing nations rarely offsets the slow growth in developing nations. A 3% growth rate applied to 18T in GDP is much larger than a 7% growth rate in 2T economy. Most nations won't experience the GDP growth that China and India have over the last 30 years. When unions rely on GDP based representation, this could preserve a superior position for wealthier nations. The Senate then becomes the best option for newly incorporated states to protect themselves against economic monopolization. In federalist systems, the states have a high degree of sovereignty. Introducing a Senate means the states will be able to regulate themselves. The inefficiency becomes a benefit. This may be especially true, when larger more mature states are assuming new less developed states into their political union. The new state would receive federal tax subsidy and investment dollars, without the fear of over regulation. If the arc of GDP growth is not known, then a political union moderating its GDP based representation with a Senate may be more successful in attracting satellites.

The Economy Union (EU) substitutes a GDP based chamber for the Demographic chamber while preserving access to a Senate and separate elections for the President. States incorporated into the Union can be more certain of equal representation in the Presidential system at the onset, with expectations of improved representation with a proportional increase in the GDP based system. If the equilibration of GDP between states is slower than expected, the less represented states can rely on the fixed representation in the Senate. The net representation afford to it through a Senate might even be larger than the proportional representation in GDP. If the Senate is modeled like the US Senate, individual Senators have tremendous powers including the filibuster. They can effectively moderate the laws coming from the Union promoting self-rule on the state level. The Economy Union is intended to provide incentives for the expansion of a democratic electorate in a safe and more controlled manner.

The Economy Union

Primary Traits:

- President with Veto

- Bicameral Legislature

- Straight GDP representational coefficient

- Senate

Advantages:

- This configuration maintains a presidential veto and bicameral process to moderate the speed and quality of legislation passed. Normally this is a deficiency but if provides the more developed nations some security when taking on new client states.

- The union promotes econometric representation by GDP for wealthier nations who have higher per capita GDP. This chamber provides some security for wealthier states that they will preserve their superior representational position in at least one chamber of the legislature.

- The Senate should attract a larger number of smaller clients which will make it more likely to expand at a faster rate. Smaller nations will seek the security of a larger and more developed nation for protection, while ensuring it can protect itself from aggressive regulation or legislation.

- National Presidential elections still comply with majority rule. Demographics dominate the outcomes of elections as the popular vote determines the winner.

- The lack of a demographic chamber may limit the electorates exposure to violence resulting from demographic shifts. Changes in population don't equate with changes in representation, although they do result in internal representational outcomes.

Disadvantages:

- A nation with a presidential veto, bicameral process, and filibuster really underperforms in legislative production. Not only are there a low number of laws but they can be of lower quality. This might increase the odds of a future event ending the union.

- Low legislative production often results in populism and populism can hurt trade and provoke demographic or class based violence.

- This configuration lacks a demographic chamber decoupling all due process from the theoretical legitimacy of majority rule. Most contemporary democracies temper demographic representational power with senates but continue to defer to limited majority rule. This is not true of the Economy Union.

Executive;

- 2.i (Unitary Presidential), 5.a (National), 6.a.ii (6 year terms), b.i (1 term maximum), c.i (lifetime maximum), d.ii (sum of elected), **7.a.i (publicly funded, citizens),** b.i.x (Presidential), **ii.xxxx (Universal Suffrage),** c.x (direct elections), 8.a.v.b (Citizen), b.i.ii (eligibility for voting and holding office), c.i (exclusive), 10.b (voluntary voting), 14.1.a.2.a (Executive, Veto)

Legislative:

- 1.i.xx.z (Bicameral legislature, House), ii.x (Representative), **iii.1.2.a.5.10.13.a.ii.b.ii.c.i (Laws, Oversight over Unitary, Appropriations, Taxes, Amendments),** iv.1.b.2.a (Independent, 3/5th rule, majority party), 5.a (National), 6.a.iii (6 year terms), b.iv (unlimited terms), c.iii (unlimited); d.iv (no restraints), **7.a.i (publicly funded, citizens),** b.i.x (Presidential), **ii.xxxx (Universal Suffrage),** c.x (direct elections), 8.a.v.b (Citizen), b.i.ii (to vote and hold office), c.i (exclusive), 10.b (voluntary), 12.b (Districts), **13.b.i (Representative of GDP Straight)**

- 1.i.xx.zz (Bicameral legislature, Senate), ii.x (Representative), **iii.1.2.3.7.13.a.ii.b.ii.c.i (Laws, Oversight, Ratification, Appointments),** iv.1.b.2.a (Independent, 3/5th rule, majority party), 5.a (National), 6.a.iii (6 year **terms**), b.iv (unlimited terms), c.iii (unlimited); d.iv (no restraints), **7.a.i (publicly funded, citizens),** b.i.x (Presidential), **ii.xxxx (Universal Suffrage),** c.x (direct elections), 8.a.v.b (Citizen), b.i.ii (to vote and hold office), c.i (exclusive), 10.b (voluntary), 12.a (Jurisdictions), **13.j.ii (Senatorial, two)**

Judicial:

- 3.a.i (Judicial, Hierarchical), b.i.a (Judicial powers only, general), c.ii.x.2 **(appointed by the President),** 5.a.(National), 6.a.iv (Unlimited), b.iv (unlimited), c.iii (Unlimited), d.ii (sum of elected), 8.a.v.b, b.ii (citizen to hold office)

The Economy Union relies on an external executive so that the election is predicated on a demographic variable. This will provide an advantage to less developed states that have larger populations and small per capita GDP. A state may still consider incorporation in the union, despite the low likelihood of capturing a superior position with GDP, if it knows it will have an advantage in the Presidential election. Nations will always have tradeoffs when forming Unions. Presidential elections are a direct form of representation. The President maintains a Veto will be an important check against economic exploitation coming from the more mature economy in a GDP based system. The President will seek re-election by favoring this high population but low per capita GDP region by leveraging the Veto to ensure more equitable budgets and subsidies. It is expected that access to Presidential election and Senate Filibusters will induce a high rate of participation or less resistance after inclusion.

Another option is pairing the GDP chamber with a democratic chamber. The Democratic chamber compensates for the lack of majority rule in econometric systems of representation. This provides some security to larger less developed nations that are under-represented in the GDP based chamber. The democratic chamber provides a source of legitimacy on top of the popular elections for the President. The **Econometric Democracy** satisfies both universal suffrage and majority rule, unlike many of the other econometric systems of representation. If anything, it is right shifted towards populism rather than more moderate forms of governance. Demographic changes will have a greater impact on legislation production and executive elections.

Econometric Democracy

Primary Traits:

- President

- Bicameral Legislature

- Straight GDP representational coefficient

- Democratic chamber – executive filter

Advantages:

- The legislature remains bicameral and without the Senate filibuster it should preserve a high enough legislative production rate.

- The legislators have 6 year terms. This allows them to have midterm elections and full-term elections, paced to the term of the president.

- The union will attract larger nations which will have more confidence in their ability to impact national elections and national democratic votes.

- The President has more legislative power in this organization but the GDP chamber retains all rights to author bills and provide oversight over executive agencies.

- The democratic chamber offers the legislature an opportunity for higher order organization between the state tiers and municipal tiers. Laws voted on by the democratic chamber can be used to pass laws on the lower levels of government, even if they don't pass on the federal level.

- The democratic chamber can only vote on bills authored by the legislature restraining the issues the public has access to. This constraint protects the nation from Presidents pursing populist or nationalist policies.

- The democratic chamber loses the ability to excise legislators, but it gains the ability to repeal legislation. If a majority of 65% is achieved, the laws based by the econometric chamber can be repealed. This is the only mechanism in the democratic chamber that operates independently of the legislature, but it is still constrained to previously passed laws.

- The representative legislature has a more competitive committee selection process. The number of committee seats apportioned to the parties is in proportional representation to the number of seats they manage. The parties take turns appointing members to the committees of their preference. This allows both parties to acquire majority control over a number of committees.

Disadvantages:

- Smaller less developed states will be under-represented in this system. They won't have significant representation in the GDP chamber and they won't have a major impact in national elections or the democratic chamber.

- The democratic chamber makes the nation more susceptible to populism while the econometric system insulates it from demographic instability. The frequency may be reduced but the severity may get worse due to the ability of state and municipal governments to pass bills that fail in the democratic chamber. Although a national democratic vote may fail, certain states or cities will achieve majority support in their specific jurisdictions providing the opportunity to ratify the measure.

Executive;

- 2.i (Unitary Presidential), 5.a (National), 6.a.ii (6 year terms), b.i (1 term maximum), c.i (lifetime maximum), d.ii (sum of elected), **7.a.i (publicly funded, citizens),** b.i.x (Presidential), **ii.xxxx (Universal Suffrage),** c.x (direct elections), 8.a.v.b (Citizen) b.i. (eligibility for voting), c.i (exclusive), 10.b (voluntary voting),

Legislative:

- 1.i.xx.z (Bicameral legislature, House), ii.x (Representative), **iii.1.2.3.5.7.a.b.10.13.a.i.b.ii.c.ii (Laws, Oversight, Treaties, Appropriations, Confirmations for judicial and executive, Taxes, Unilateral Amendments with supermajority),** iv.1.b.2.d (Independent, proportional, one for one, rotating), 5.a (National), 6.a.iii (6 year terms), b.iv (unlimited terms), c.iii (unlimited); d.iv (no restraints), **7.a.i (publicly funded, citizens),** b.i.x (Presidential), **ii.xxxx (Universal Suffrage),** c.x (direct elections), 8.a.v.b (Citizen), b.i.ii (to vote and hold office), c.i (exclusive), 10.b (voluntary), 12.b (Districts), **13.b.i (Representative of GDP Straight)**

- 1.i.xx.zz (Democratic chamber, 2nd house) ii.ixxxx (Direct Democracy), 1.a.i (Mono-chamber, straight), **2.b.ii.x (Executive Filter),** iii.xxx (federal), 2.a.iii (Referendum monthly), 3 b.ii (confirm laws bicameral), c (Repeal legislation), 4.a (municipal jurisdictions), 8.a.v.b (Citizen), b.i (to vote), 10.b (voluntary)

Judicial:

- 3.a.i (Judicial, Hierarchical), b.i. Judicial powers only), c.ii.x.2 **(appointed by the President),** 5.a.(National), 6.a.iv (Unlimited), b.iv (unlimited), c.iii (Unlimited), d.ii (sum of elected), 8.a.v.b, b.ii (citizen to hold office)

Democratic chambers are notorious for their susceptibility to populism. The Econometric Democracy limits its exposure by maintaining 6-year terms for their legislators. The extended term will make them far less susceptible to strategies for pursing short-term goals. They will be able to patiently wait out the animal spirits that grip the public and other institutions with shorter terms. The econometric chamber already distances itself from pure demographic representation dampening the risk of mob psychology or impaired inhibitions that may result from certain demographic conditions. Hopefully, this moderates the frequency of populist uprisings in the electoral system but it may make them more severe. If economic conditions deteriorate considerably, and populism roots itself in the legislature, then the democratic chamber will provide a pathway for their reforms.

Political architects should not under-value the coordination a democratic chamber provides. The laws considered by the chamber for passage may have profound effects on state laws or city laws regardless of whether they pass the national vote. Even if the vote fails to pass on the national level, it may acquire a majority in the municipal or state jurisdiction providing a pathway for the state legislature or city council to ratify the measure with the support of only a single chamber. This extra coordination will help root public policy in the culture. Outcomes matter. Success matters. Political parties are evaluated on the measures they pass rather than the measures they support. The democratic chamber allows for a party to acquire more political successes on the state and municipal levels, resulting in more data points and more evidence in the success of those policy platforms.

Most of political science is an applied science. This naturally moderates the number of reforms offered and the number of theoretical systems considered. It requires tremendous labor and capital to reform a nation. This is true in cases of despotism and democracy. Even if an idea appears viable it can fail to be executed correctly removing it from subsequent considerations. Real structural reforms require constitutional conventions and amendments with overwhelming support on the state and federal level. Even with popular movements behind them, it can take decades of peaceful protest and public debt before they are accepted and passed. As a result, innovation in the political sciences is almost nonexistent. Theoretical reforms are far too risky to pass without historical data supporting their conclusions, but no reform can acquire the evidence to substantiate their claims until it is passed. It is a catch 22. Political rhetoric will prove more useful than complex formulas and algorithms in gaining the support of the public for reform and this is a dangerous prospect. Reforms are passed under duress, during extreme conditions, with a lack of debate or consensus.

Popular movements often over react to stimulus and over emphasize less critical issues. They tend to ignore core causes of dysfunction. The reforms demanded are often due to some culture misconception of justice or due process. However, reform movements are much sounder than revolutions. They will produce more productive results many more times as often as violent revolts. Regime change invites disaster as elections can be suspended reversed, invalidated. Term limits can be removed. Due process can be temporarily revoked all in the name of emergency powers. Reforms build on institutions that already have long distinct histories. Reforms account for known deficiencies with higher expectations for improved efficiency. Unless conditions are so poor and there is absolutely no recourse for reform, revolution is often the worst choice a people can make. They will trade democracy for despotism, and civil society for extremism.

The democratic chamber fosters an environment of reform, where a larger number of lower level governments can pass similar laws and collect data on their effectiveness. This data will provide the support the reform needs for national implementation. Without the historical evidence, reforms are generally perceived as too risky or dangerous to pass. The democratic chamber will provide the political parties and government bureaucracies the evidence they need to make data driven decision. Without the coordinated legislative efforts, reforms might occur too infrequently for effective data collection and analysis. Unfortunately, this also means that ineffective laws will be passed at a higher rate with the data or evidence provided after the consequences have been expressed in the economy or electoral system.

Replacing the Senate with a GDP based chamber while preserving the bicameral process is an option that may contribute to sounder legislative production. This configuration combines the legitimacy of a demographic chamber with the effectiveness of a GDP chamber. Within the **Unity Parliament** each chamber is a parliament with its own executive branch. The demographic chamber is the seat of government with its representatives electing a Prime Minister with all the traditional executive powers. Majority rule isn't a requirement for democracy, but it certainly adds a significant amount of credibility. GDP based representation will invoke mistrust in the people at first impression. This will be true for the citizenry in both mature nations and developing nations. If the GDP chamber managed the seat of the government, it might be criticized as elitism or colonialism. Other Unions will see an advantage in this outcome, but for most nations that are more similar in demographic or GDP attributes, the clear choice will be to couple demographic representation to the executive functions.

Unity Parliament

Primary Traits:

- Bipartite Parliament split into President and AG/Treasurer

- Upper House is Representative of population : President

- Upper House allows legislative brokers

- Lower House is Representative of straight GDP : AG/Treasurer

Advantages:

- The nation maintains a bicameral parliament with the chief executive rooted in the demographic chamber. This provides more legitimacy to the office in support of majority rule.

- A reliance on a demographic chamber will induce more conservative attitudes for expansion of the electorate. There will be a real risk of electorate change if it accepts cliental with larger populations.

- States with smaller populations will have far fewer incentives to join the union, especially when per capita GDP are equivalent. This won't exclude such possibilities, but it may discourage them.

- The Demographic chamber maintains legislative broker powers allowing the primary chamber to consolidate seats from the GDP chamber.

- The Demographic chamber has a competitive committee selection process which permits the minority party to capture majority control if it sacrifices representation on other committees.

- The GDP Chamber has a secondary role, but it preserves appointment confirmation powers and has a much more variable committee selection process. Legislators are appointed to committees on a rotating and incrementing schedule almost guaranteeing the minority party has control over one or more committees.

- The bicameral process produces a 50% probability for passing laws regardless of which party is in power. This slows the pace of legislative production allow more debate to occur and more recourse for minority parties.

- When minority parties have majority control over certain committees they have access to investigative and subpoena powers vastly improving their ability to protect themselves during periods of political instability.

- Most contemporary democracies suffer risks of populism but the substitution of a GDP chamber for a Senate does mitigate some concern. This is truer of unions where a larger number of more rural and poorer states have a majority of political power in the Senate. A GDP chamber will favor the more developed states and these populations should be more resistant from the xenophobia and class warfare rural populations are more susceptible too,

Disadvantages:

- Although minority parties having majority control over some committees sounds like an exception power sharing plan, it may result in some inefficiencies in the Parliamentary government. This will invite the judicial branch into the process by compelling performance or issuing injunctions.

- The legislative broker powers weaken the check provided by a second chamber. The legislators from the parliament will sit on committees providing oversight or using confirmation powers. In severe situations, the parliament could effectively coopt the GDP chamber and reduce diversity in the chambers. The total number of representatives can be cut in half during outlier environments with high convergence.

- The Demographic chamber is primary, and this might induce more risk of violence during demographic shifts. States with faster growth rates and of different ethnicity of the current majority demographic will be viewed as adversarial or dangerous. This will provoke more austerity measures from those states, creating more wealth inequality and greater risk of populism.

Executive:

- 2.iii (Abolished Executive), 5.a. (National)

Legislative:

- **1.i.xx.z (Bicameral legislature,** 1ˢᵗ House) , ii.x (Representative), iii.1.2.d.e.4.a.5.7.b.iii.iv.13.a.ii.b.ii.c.i (Laws, Oversight over A.G./Treasurer, Foreign Executive Powers, Appropriations, Appointment over A.G./Treasurer, Amendments bicameral and supermajority), **iv.1.b.2.b (Independent, 3/5ths rule, one by one, rotating),** 5.a (National), 6.a.ii (4 year terms), b.iv (Unlimited), c.iii (Unlimited), d.iv (no restraints), **7.a.i (Publicly Funded)** b.i.xx (parliamentary), c.x (direct elections), 8.a.v.b (Citizen), b.i.ii (to vote and to hold office), c.ii (non -exclusive), 10.b (voluntary), 12.a (jurisdictions), **13.a.i (Representative of Population), 13.h (Legislative Broker)**

- **1.i.xx.zz (Bicameral legislature,** 2nd House), ii.x (Representative), iii.1.2.c.3.7.a.ii.10.13.a.ii.b.ii.c.i (Laws, Oversight over foreign executive, Ratification, Appointment over judicial and foreign executive, Taxes, Amendments bicameral and supermajority), **iv.1.b.2.c (Independent, 3/5ths rule, incremental, rotating),** 5.a (National), 6.a.ii (4 year terms), b.iv (Unlimited), c.iii (Unlimited), d.iv (no restraints), **7.a.i (Publicly Funded),** b.i.xx (non-parliamentary), c.x (direct elections), 8.a.v.b (Citizen), b.i.ii (to vote and to hold office), c.ii (non -exclusive), 10.b (voluntary), 12.a (jurisdictions), **13.b.i (Representative of GDP Straight)**

Judicial:

- 3.a.i (Judicial, Hierarchical), b.i. (Judicial powers only), c.ii.x.2 **(appointed by the President),** 5.a.(National), 6.a.iv (Unlimited), b.iv (unlimited), c.iii (Unlimited), d.ii (sum of elected), 8.a.v.b, b.ii (citizen to hold office)

There are few political solutions that will satisfy all parties when the difference in population or GDP is so great that one party will be at a tremendous and permanent disadvantage. One would have to see it as a predatory behavior if this discrepancy existed. This is not to say that a nation wouldn't see benefit to unionization with a larger and wealthier nation, for tax subsidies and investment, but the terms will be spelled out in negotiations. If nations are seeking partnerships, they will negotiate with equals. If they are seeking to exploit natural resources or labor, then they will entertain lower quality relationships. When the nations or states are more similar, there is less of a need to make structural inhibitions on representation to compensate for some vast inequality in population or wealth.

This doesn't rule out a larger and wealthier nation incorporating a smaller and poorer nation, but the new citizens must see the benefits in a voluntary relationship. In a true union, the newly incorporated citizens will be able to travel throughout the entire country and reside in any state they want. This diffuses the inequities of GDP based representation. Not only would it receive more federal tax support and more investment, but the free movement of residents will allow them to seek out entrepreneurial, academic, or social opportunities throughout the rest of the union. The low GDP of the newly incorporated state wont unfairly and unjustly segregate the population and exploit them. The representational deficiencies are still obstacles to adequate public administration, but the severity of the problem diminishes when travel restrictions are lifted.

The representatives in the demographic chamber will have legislative broker powers. This way the two legislative chambers will be positively correlated in intent and capacity. To maximize the impact of the broker power, both chambers are elected in jurisdictions rather than districts. The number of seats remain proportional to the representational coefficient used but all citizens vote for all of the political officers coming from their state. The number of correlated seats is not limited so that exceptional politicians in the demographic chamber can acquire a large number of seats in the GDP chamber. Wealthier jurisdictions with larger populations will have significantly more coordinated offices. This concentration of political power and expertise should lend itself to more productive parliamentarian governments. The more successful representatives will be authorized to have staff sit on committees, negotiate legislation, or provide labor to agencies.

Instead of legislative broker powers, a nation could organize its representatives around executive representation. This would reduce the number of representatives to the number of states in the union and make political outcomes far more predictable. An **Executive Union** utilizes a bicameral process with one demographic chamber and one GDP chamber. Each chamber operates with executive representation concentrating the political power within a single officer. Each chamber functions as a parliament electing their own executive officer. The demographic executive maintains the military and judicial appointments while the GDP executive controls domestic law enforcement, treasurer, and economic regulation.

Executive Union

Primary Traits:

- Bipartite Parliament split into President and AG/treasurer

- Upper House is representative of population with executive rep

- Lower House is representative of straight GDP with executive rep

Advantages:

- Executive powers are divided among two parliaments. This reduces the chances of authoritarianism rooting in any single chamber.

- Military powers are preserved by demographic chamber to couple the responsibility to majority rule.

- Taxing powers are preserved by the demographic chamber to couple the responsibility to majority rule.

- The judicial appointment powers are preserved by the demographic chamber to couple the responsibility to majority rule and to check the GDP chamber's authority to regulate commerce and pursue law enforcement.

- The two parliaments may appeal to nations of different populations or wealth if the union is seeking to expand membership. A nation will typically have an advantage in one aspect and will be more satisfied by the specialization in powers.

Disadvantages:

- The use of executive representation cuts the number of legislators down to the number of participating states. This diminishes diversity and consolidates power to a degree not seen within conventional democracies. This could invite anti-democratic interventions and a risk of authoritarian culture dominating the public.

- Executive Representation introduces representational deficiencies as the ratio of the public represented to the number of representatives scales up to the size of the state. If political parties are competitive and the population is split in half, the single executive representative will only have the support of half the population. Larger numbers of representatives will be more heterogenous with more representation split between the competing parties.

Executive:

- 2.iii (Abolished Executive), 5.a. (National)

Legislative:

- **1.i.xx.z (Bicameral legislature**, 1st House) , ii.x (Representative), iii.1.2.d.e.4.b.f.5.7.iii.iv.10.13.a.i.b.ii.c.i (Laws, Oversight over A.G/Treasurer, Foreign Executive Powers, Appropriations, Appointments over A.G./Treasurer, Taxes, and unilateral amendments with supermajority), **iv.1.b.2.d (proportional, one by one, rotating),** 5.a (National), 6.a.iii (6 year terms), b.ii (2 terms), c.iii (Unlimited), d.iv (no restraints), **7.a.i (Publicly Funded)** b.i.xx (parliamentary), c.x (direct elections), 8.a.v.b (Citizen), b.i.ii (to vote and to hold office), c.ii (non -exclusive), 10.b (voluntary), 12.a (jurisdictions), **13.a.i (Representative of Population), 13.f (Executive Representation)**

- **1.i.xx.zz (Bicameral legislature,** 2nd House), ii.x (Representative), iii.1.2.c.3.4.c.d.5.7.a.b.ii (Laws, Oversight over Foreign Executive, Ratification, Domestic Executive Powers, Central Banking/Treasury Executive, Appropriations, Appointment confirmation over judicial and foreign executive), **iv.1.b.2.d (proportional, one by one, rotating),** 5.a (National), 6.a.iii (6 year terms), b.iii (3 terms), c.iii (Unlimited), d.iv (no restraints), **7.a.i (Publicly Funded),** b.i.xx (non-parliamentary), c.x (direct elections), 8.a.v.b (Citizen), b.i.ii (to vote and to hold office), c.ii (non -exclusive), 10.b (voluntary), 12.a (jurisdictions), **13.b.i (Representative of GDP Straight), 13.f (Executive Representation)**

Judicial:

- 3.a.i (Judicial, Hierarchical), b.i. (Judicial powers only), c.ii.x.2 **(appointed by the President),** 5.a.(National), 6.a.iv (Unlimited), b.iv (unlimited), c.iii (Unlimited), d.ii (sum of elected), 8.a.v.b, b.ii (citizen to hold office)

The two legislative chambers will make their own rules for committee formation. Due to the executive representation, they might consider sitting on all of the committees. The legislators can simply dedicate staff to the committee to accommodate the large amount of required labor hours. The party with the simple majority in the chamber will have majority control over the committees and the members can elect their own chairs. This is a parliament and the majority party will form the government while the opposition party provides oversight. Power will be concentrated within a small number of people. In competitive political markets, each state would produce one officer with the government comprised of half the seats. An incoming executive will have to delegate authority to each of the representatives in their party, although the number of committees and the scope of authority will differ between administrations.

The participation of representatives in an administration does expose them to challenges in the next election. The administration is under much more scrutiny than the opposition party and this will increase the rate of party rotations in the office. This should mitigate claims that executive representation concentrates power too much in too few persons. Term lengths are slightly longer than most contemporary democracies, but the total number of terms is truncated due to their exposure to executive level repressibilities.

The chamber with military powers is more limited than the regulatory and banking chamber but both have firm maximum terms. It should be fairly rare that a single representation last until their maximum term if elections remain free and open with a strong independent media. Otherwise, the distribution of powers among a bicameral legislature should inhibit coercive or exploitative public policies.

The offices of the executive representatives will resemble regional or state level agencies. They will acquire staff to attend committees and to manage executive functions. Otherwise, the job responsibilities couldn't be discharged by the single political officer. Most nations have hundreds of representatives in addition to hundreds of political appointments. Replacing these people would overwhelm the small number of elected representatives and the quality of work would suffer tremendously. We are already comfortable with executives establishing deputies and agents who work towards the principles goals within the parameters of their appointment. The executive representatives will have similar agents and authority to replace them at will. Executive representatives should be thought as legislative governors in the respect of concentrated political power and executive responsibilities.

Despite the Executive Union maintaining only a small number of elected officials, the representation is still proportional in representation. Proportional representation is a critical element for union formation. Nations will measure whether they benefit from proportional demographic representation or proportional econometric representation (GDP) when deciding to join a political union or economic union. The variance between the two, with their respective growth rates will create the dual conditions of uncertainty and promise necessary to attract participation. There will be no doubt, that unions are far more versatile and viable than individual nations. They are able to improve their economic influence and their military power. They are better able to defend themselves and organize their environment to an order that benefits them.

6 MEDIAN PARTITION OF GDP

Nations face tradeoffs; all systems are inherently deficient or risky, with the most efficient systems carrying as much risk as the least efficient systems, but where moderately efficient systems have the least risk. Optimal configurations of political systems include some inhibitions on majority rule with no restrictions on universal suffrage. They also want to slow down the rate of legislative production without enabling compete obstruction. There is a habitable zone for political representation that reduces the risk of regime change and economic catastrophe. It has to allow the people to regulate themselves and tax themselves while protecting itself from populism or other threats to sovereignty and civility. This Goldilocks zone is achievable through the use of median partitions. This book describes median partitions based on GDP, but other values can be used.

Nations can form a bicameral legislature by separating states into districts of equal population and determining the number of representatives each state receives by an LCD. The lowest common denominator is usually population, but other representational coefficients can be used. The districts are then arranged in descending order from highest GDP to lowest GDP with the middle value becoming the median (*or the average between two middle vales in even number of districts*). The median value is then used to separate districts into either the above median GDP chamber or below median GDP chamber while preserving proportional representation with majority rule and universal suffrage.

Splitting states and districts into above median "haves" and below median "have nots" is far safer than dividing natural persons into classes. Each district will contain a normally distributed population of incomes that should be near the median values for the state and nation. This will reign in some of the more divisive rhetoric around class and wealth inequality but still encourage the topics to be discussed openly in the legislative chambers. Natural persons have a much more intimate or visceral relationship with wealth inequality and a class based representation based on personal incomes will invite entirely different electoral outcomes than a class based representational system based on GDP (macro-political income). GDP provides a few degrees of separation between the person and their participation in a below median or above median legislative chamber.

GDP can vary wildly from one district to the next resulting in different economic experiences for residents. Arranging the below median districts in one chamber and the above median districts in another will allow districts with economic sympathies to organize themselves more effectively. A median partition based on GDP will cut across state lines with poorer regions in one state able to coordinate with the poorer regions of other states. States often have different histories and cultures promoting diversity among both the above median and below median districts.

Each district will have an equivalent amount of political power despite certain states having more representative than another. Each citizen receives one vote and each representative has one vote within their respective chamber. This is a tenant in contemporary democracy. Participants will have more confidence in a system that preserves both universal suffrage and majority rule. GDP based representation has one major advantage over a demographic chamber. A median partition will split the residents of a state between the two chambers, effectively decentering the locus of control a larger state may otherwise have. This should inhibit region disputes and contribute to more cooperation along representational lines.

For example, New Jersey may have 12 representatives, but if 70% are in the above median chamber and 40% are in the below median chamber, it will limit the total proportion of representation the state receives in any single chamber. Seven Representatives are sent to the above median chamber while five are sent to the below median chamber. The Representatives within each chamber should have mixed party affiliations, despite strong tendencies in the population to support one party over the other. If elections remain competitive, seats will often switch between parties. This is an effective check on the accumulation of political power in larger states and it breaks up the monopoly a party may have in the state. It has all of the components of high quality democratic representation with the added benefit of class based incentives and arguments.

This division into rural and urban classes might improve minority rights if certain demographic groups prefer cities. They could effectively double their net representation by concentrating their population in one of the two chambers. If a minority group favors urban areas over rural areas, they can increase their proportional representation in the chamber. A demographic group of 12% the total population might have 20% of the electoral power in the above median GDP chamber. A larger population with mixed habitation preferences would split their representation between the two chambers, reducing the effectiveness of their majority status. Although they would preserve most of their representational advantage in the above median GDP chamber, they would perform only slightly better in the below median chamber. When a habitation preference concentrates a minority group in one chamber, it effectively doubles their representation in that chamber. This is a bicameral legislative process, so bills must be confirmed by both chambers to become law. This magnifies the representation of populations concentrated in one chamber and not the other.

There are other benefits. The median partition could be a huge advantage when trying to overcome or avoid regional conflicts like civil wars. Rebel states would be split between two chambers of the legislature with a depreciated capacity to organize protests or revolts in the legislature. By dividing the urban population from the rural population, a state may not be able to effectively organize a resistance within a democratically elected government. Wars are devastating to GDP and can permanently alter the trajectory of an electorate. They should be avoided at all costs, unless the democratic process itself is jeopardized by anti-democratic measures, authoritarian challenges to civil liberties and the free press, or voter suppression and fraud. The dislocation of representation across two adversarial chambers and the urban/rural divide should delay or disrupt organized resistance for long enough to acquire the economic reforms or electoral changes necessary to avoid the conflict.

This could have tremendous value in nation building. Nations with sectarian divides within the population could be pacified by splitting states into above median and below median parts. This is especially true in cases where a nation is divided by demographics into specific regions. Each region will be split into two parts by median GDP. Each half will be absorbed into a larger more comprehensive electorate made up of different demographic groups. This is precisely what is necessary to dislocate and disrupt sectarian tensions. This won't cure incurable rifts in demographic groups, but it may cause enough hesitation to promote reconciliation during conversion to democracy or some other nation building exercise. Any diversion or interruption could prove the difference between success and failure.

Urban districts should have far higher GDP making it far more likely that for districts in cities to be included in the above median GDP chamber. This will produce a stark divide with rural communities which will tend to be poorer and located in the below median GDP chamber. Class division doesn't occur only within personal incomes. Cities by themselves are a form of equity. They are wealth generators where proximity equals access, and population density produces economic opportunity. There is a huge difference between being poor in a city and being poor in the country.

Cities have huge advantages over rural communities despite the districts having the same number of voters within them. Cities are concentrated populations that aggregate health and education services more effectively. Information can be disseminated far more quickly with higher accuracy to residents. Job creation is more frequent, and they usually pay much higher salaries. Cities rebound more quickly after large economic corrections and they are far more resistant to smaller crises. More importantly, cities are more proficient at mobilizing for war and defending their real estate and superior economic position.

The largest cities are often global cities with large components of Employees falling under the classification of NIDL (New international division of labor)[228]. Global cities will typically fall into the above median GDP chamber and contribute to the stereotype that urban environments favor elites and globalization. Cities tend to attract the most educated persons due to their higher incomes and more satisfying living conditions towards the core of the city[229]. The high frequency of digital transactions and the large volumes of financial capital give global cities more influence in the global economy[230].They establish more business contacts and they have a greater impact on other regions in the world. This attracts dissent from rural communities with worse economic outcomes and fewer connections with the other cities or nations in the world.

Conflict in identity and class should contribute to sounder public policy. If the issues are more easily identified by the group after their role specialization or class differentiation, the group can seek to negotiate compromises and seek concessions from the other chamber. Rural communities can examine their specific circumstances and design policies that will remedy their deficiencies in job creation, wages education, and access to healthcare. Urban communities will do the same. The two will then reconcile their bills to accommodate both agendas, or negotiate concessions on one aspect to win concessions on another. Class identity will improve the representative's ability to identify their constituents needs and lobby for them. This is true of all class based representation.

Demographic representation lacks the differentiation in class and therefore produces more cohesive but less effective coalitions. Parties often form around sectarian or tribal criteria reducing the effectiveness of a political platform. If the party is not organized around discrete economic interests, it will fail to acquire reforms that will satisfy their demands. For example, if the party aligns around the tribal property of ethnicity, it may be comprised of low wage earners and small business owners. The group, can't effectively pursue policies that satisfy the demands of both economic groups because raising the minimum wage for workers will raise labor costs for business owners. Thus, the political platform and rhetoric used by candidates will be weaker and less cohesive. It will make the party appear untrustworthy or ineffective.

This is an oversimplification of a complex argument. Economic interests are often mixed between demographic or special interest groups. For example, cities have higher costs of living so the poorer citizens will have much more in common with the voters on the poorer rural districts. Even if city dwellers have median wages more than 30% that of rural residents, the

---

[228] Brenner, N. and Keil, R. (2006). *The Global Cities Reader.* New York, NY. Routledge.

[229] Brenner, N. and Keil, R. (2006). *The Global Cities Reader.* New York, NY. Routledge.

[230] Sassen, S., (2012). *Cities in a World Economy.* Thousand Oaks, California: Pine Forge Press

costs of living could be 50% higher, making the disposal income rates between the two groups much more similar. Workers and families will still be concerned with retirement savings, healthcare, and taxes. However, cities are organized differently than rural communities and therefore produce different classes. There is the urban class and the rural class, and each will develop the facility to pursue their economic interests better than if they remained undifferentiated.

Hopefully the intersection of interests provides for more fluid class based debate and reform. City dwellers will seek economic reforms that benefit the rural workers and vice versa. Economic sympathies and incentives will remain the primary driver of voters with many of the regional or cultural boundaries overcome by the allocation of districts by GDP rather than state lines. Cities are distributed across a large cross section of disparate states, cutting across current political divides that segregate the nation into regions. The class division is intended to be constructive rather than destructive.

Don't forget, each district has an equal number of citizens in it and the nation is split precisely in half by GDP. Despite the country being divided into an above median chamber and a below median chamber, the two interest groups will have equal political power. This makes the class division into Urban and Rural communities productive and equitable. Rural classes can expect to have as much power as the Urban class, with permanent access to a bully pulpit. The class specialization wouldn't be an effective or productive property if one group had more innate political power than the other. However, the bicameral legislature remains representative of population, preserving universal suffrage with one person and one vote and allowing majoritarian control.

Urban districts will have another important advantage. They are the primary economic drivers of the nation. City populations generally have access to more government services and there is less urgency to pass new laws. This will allow their legislative representatives to utilize the political power of obstruction. Urban populations are typically far wealthier than rural population, even in relative terms of wealth. They can patiently wait out calls for more extreme reforms and pursue more moderate remedies. Urban populations have more education and are often exposed to more diverse environments making it more appropriate that they play the role of cooling the animal spirits of the electorate. Modest delays in passage produces more debate and more debate improves the quality of the laws. Deliberation optimizes outcomes as long as a filibusters or presidential veto dont drop the rate of legislative production down to an unsafe level.

The opportunity is reciprocal with both chambers able to slow down the pace of legislation. Both chambers can force negotiations on issues more important to them by refusing to address issues more important to the other chamber. The rural communities may be hurt more by obstruction, but it is a political weapon they will become apt as using. There is another innate check to this possible obstruction. Civil Service and military enlistment are more attractive to rural populations. Government services are poorer, and wages are far smaller. Jobs are also scarcer. Rural populations will seek enlistment to maximize their employment outcomes. This should mitigate the natural organizational advantages cities have during crises and accommodate the urban chambers ability to cause conflict with obstruction. It is the threat of the military supporting the below median GDP chamber that keeps the above median GDOP chamber more moderate.

Elections have consequences and parties should be competitive in both chambers. When economic conditions change, the public will favor one party over another and this support will result in the majorities needed to pass economic reform. With mixed economic sympathies, majority parties in both chambers will continue to seek compromise and concession to achieve their constituencies goals. The shifting majorities in the two chambers will mitigate the tendency for obstruction. The frequency should be nearly equivalent to conventional bicameral legislative chambers. The nation must be wary of anti-democratic measures like private campaign finance or gerrymandering due to the fact it is more susceptible to obstruction. Class based representation is dependent on honest and accurate representation predicted on unencumbered elections.

The most conventional median partition is the presidential system. It allocates its districts between above median GDP and below median GDP chambers and preserves am external executive branch. **The Presidential Median Partition** is intended to resemble the United States. It retains proportional representation but eliminates the Senate and along with its filibuster. It gains the innate advantages of class divisions between urban and rural communities without the threat of prolonged periods of legislative obstruction.

The bicameral legislature is moderated by a Presidential Veto producing a below average number of laws but far more than the filibuster permits. When a filibuster is abused, it can slow legislation to a standstill for decades or generations. A Presidential Veto only halves the prospective number of laws in more competitive electoral systems. This prolongs the legislative cycle, but it gives plenty of opportunity to parties to pass laws when they are in the majority. Nations should be able to pass enough economic reforms to overcome the obstacles that may threaten other nations without the organizational advantages found in class based representation and efficient due process.

Presidential Median Partition

Primary Trait:

- Unitary President with Veto

- Median Partition split by GDP, national median

- Population used for representational coefficient

Advantages:

- The class based representation intersects states by dividing them into above median GDP districts (urban) and below median districts (rural). This is a natural limitation on regional affiliation trumping national allegiance or class identity.

- The two chambers will independently prioritize economic issues and then promote negotiations toward compromises and concessions between the bicameral chambers.

- Both chambers are representative of population, having an equal number of legislators. This preserves universal suffrage and majority rule while limiting the systems susceptibility to populism.

- The President retains a veto and this might extend the length of debate before a party gains majority control of both the executive and legislative branches to pass the reform. Longer debate may improve the quality of laws despite reducing the frequency of attempts.

- Despite the two chambers being divided into above median and below median groups, the political parties should remain competitive, thus increasing the odds of a single party gaining majority power in the bicameral process. A chamber might favor one party over another, but it is unlikely this will result in permanently fixed outcomes within the institution. Conditions will dictate outcomes, with different environments making one party more likely to win more seats than the other.

- Due to the lack of a Senate, a filibuster is not present. This will double the legislative production of the Presidential system, despite the system remaining only half as effective as many Parliamentary systems.

Disadvantages:

- There is no filibuster, but the political process still relies on a bicameral process. If the two chambers can't agree on legislation, then it will remain incomplete. It's a bicameral process requiring the consent of both chambers and those chambers are divided into below median and above median components. In hyper-partisan environments, it could pose problematic.

Executive;

- **2.i (Unitary Presidential),** 5.a (National), 6.a.ii (4 year terms), b.ii (2 terms maximum), c.i (lifetime maximum, d.ii (sum of elected), 7.a.i (publicly funded), b.ii.xxxx (One citizen = One vote), c.x (direct elections), 8.a.v.b (Citizen), b.i.ii (to vote and hold office) c.i (exclusive), 10.b (voluntary voting), 14.1.a.2.a **(Macro-political vote, Veto)**

Legislative:

- 1.i.xx.z (Bicameral legislature, 1st House), ii.x (Representative), iii.1.2.3.7.13.a.ii.b.ii.c.i (Laws, Oversight over unitary, Ratification, Appointments, and Amendments), iv.1.b.2.b (Independent, 3/5ths rule, one by one, rotating), 5.a (National), **6.a.iii (4 year terms), b.i iv (unlimited terms),** c.i (lifetime maximum, d.ii (sum of elected), 7.a.i (publicly funded), b.ii.xxxx (One citizen = One vote), c.x (direct elections), **8.a.iv.b.i.f.ii.z.d.zz.a.zzz.i (GDP, below median, independent, national median),** v.b (Citizen), b.i.ii (to vote and hold office), c.i (exclusive), 10.b (voluntary), 12.b (Districts), **13.a.i (Representative of Population, by jurisdiction)**

- 1.i.xx.zz (Bicameral legislature, 2nd Chamber), ii.x (Representative), iii.1.2.a.3.5.10.13.a.ii.b.ii.c.i (Laws, Oversight over unitary, Appropriations, Taxes, and Amendments), iv.3 (majority rule, one for one rotation), 5.a (National), **6.a.iii (4 year terms), b.i iv (unlimited terms),** c.i (lifetime maximum, d.ii (sum of elected 7.a.i (publicly funded), b.ii.xxxx (One citizen = One vote), c.x (direct elections), **8.a.iv.b.i.f.ii.z.d.zz.a.zzz.i (GDP, below median, independent, national median),** v.b (Citizen), b.i.ii (to vote and hold office), 10.b (voluntary), 12.b (Districts), **13.a.i (Representative of Population , by jurisdiction)**

Judicial:

- 3.A.i (Judicial, Hierarchical), b.i.a (Judicial powers only, general), c.ii.x.2 **(appointed by the President),** 5.a.(National), 6.a.iv (Unlimited), b.iv (unlimited), c.iii (Unlimited), d.ii (sum of elected), 8.a.v.b, b.ii (citizen to hold office)

The Presidential Median Partition preserves proportional representation which is the highest standard for democratic entitlements. Although the nation is split between above median GDP and below median GDP, the representational ratio between districts remains equal. This will smooth out the difference between above median and below median districts creating a large class of middle GDP districts. The median voter will be split between both chambers moderating the policy preferences of the two adversarial perspectives. This should result in more deliberation and negotiation between the "haves" and "have nots".

Class is important, especially if it is divided along an urban and rural divide. Each class will separate into its own above median and below median components so that perspective is more diversified among the districts. The aggregate of individual interests within the districts will result in more specialized policy coming out of the chamber. With better identity of issues, concessions and compromise between the two chambers will better satisfy the demands of the constituents. To move laws and public policy out of committee and through the bicameral process, a larger number of spatial and class based perspectives must be satisfied. The laws will have a higher order than those passed through a simple demographic chamber with a senate.

Presidential systems aren't favored in nation building. The Presidential Veto presents an obstacle to legislative production that could impede the progress a nation makes towards universal suffrage, majority rule, or more egalitarian economic policies. Presidential systems typically have half the passage rate of a Parliament even when a filibuster isn't abused. The median partition can be improved by eliminating the President and replacing it with a bifurcated Parliament. The twin parliaments aren't perfect but they do provide many important checks on executive power while also providing advantages in legislation production.

Certain parties will want to limit the frequency and quality of laws passed. When the states are divided by GDP these tendencies may be more evident and it should provoke an electoral response. The worse the economic conditions get with no legislative output, the more likely a seat is to switch parties. Those parties that offer more solutions to a larger proportion of the population should win, at least temporarily. Hopefully, this more competitive electoral environment will contribute to a more equitable economy with more oversight and accountability in government. This will help mitigate the party preference within a particular chamber and contribute to an increased rate of legislation production. More competitive elections will ensure parties can't simply obstruct laws and remain in power as conditions deteriorate.

A higher rate of legislation production might be critical to maintain civil society considering the more polarized nature of the constituency. The districts will be split by spatial and class divisions, with the below median in one chamber and the above median in another. If the raw probability of passing a law is low, there is a considerably higher probability that a larger proportion of laws will be obstructed. It will become more cultural acceptable and the expectation will chill most attempts at reform. The chambers are adversarial already and if given the opportunity they may actively inhibit laws to negotiate for more aggressive compromises. This may result in a tendency for conflict or violence between the two classes. Class based violence is almost as dangerous as demographic based violence and should be discouraged at every opportunity.

In environments of higher legislative production, the value of obstruction is significantly lower given the probability of passing laws over a longer period. This will counteract the more partisan environment a class based system of representation harbors. The improved role identity and class specialization will aid debate rather than inhibit it. The higher quality laws should mitigate any tendency towards conflict and violence yielding a more equitable economy and a more stable nation. This is an optimal outcome and with a higher frequency of high quality laws, they should be able to compete more effectively in international trade and accumulate GDP more quickly.

Parliaments offer improved legislation production, but the standard median partition is not compatible with unitary parliaments. It would be disastrous to allocate all of the executive power to one chamber in the bicameral legislature when the system of representative is inherently class based. This is practically the only time a Presidential structure is a higher order than a parliamentary structure. This can be improved too. One of the more effective ways to organize a median partitioned is to complement it with a bipartite President.

The bipartite Presidents has an important advantage over the standard Presidential median partition. The two executives will have a combined confirmation power allowing them to choose which chamber and class to support. In this respect, the other chamber can be bypassed until the next election results in a change in leadership. This is practically the only way for a party to gain a consistent single party majority in the two legislatures. Otherwise, the two chambers are more likely to be split due to the class preferences of their constituents. The frequency of one party maintaining power in at least one legislature and both executive branches will be relatively small with equivalency to a single party maintaining majorities the bicameral legislature and executive.

The **Bipartite Median Partition** has another significant advantage. Separate elections determine the Presidential election outcomes, ensuring more power sharing between the parties and the Offices. Competitive elections in the executive offices introduces some variability in the appointment processes for both judges and executive cabinets. A more competitive committee selection process in the legislature will ensure that the minority party has oversight over at least a few appointments. This should be enough power sharing to offset the party preference within the median partition chamber.

Bipartite Median Partition

94

Primary Traits:

- Bipartite Presidential split between Foreign and AG/Treasurer

- Presidents have confirmation powers when aligned

- Median Partition split by GDP, national median

- Population used for representational coefficient

Advantages:

- This is one of the highest orders of median petition. It combines proportional representation with an executive office split between two persons. Not only does this limit the threat of authoritarian usurpation but the confirmation powers in the executive contribute to a faster legislative production rate.

- The classed division between above median and below median will benefit from an executive confirmation power split between two offices. The confirmation power will be used infrequently but it will still be often enough to help the nation overcome significant obstacles that are too difficult for an ordinary legislative process.

- The number of districts allocated to the two chambers is identical. If there is an odd number of seats, the district occupying the precise median value will choose whether they join the above median or below median chamber. Institutions with even numbers may have ties and an executive officer will have to be allocated as tie breaker.

- Each executive has a single 6-year term. The two legislatures each have 6-year terms, with elections held in the midterm at 3 years and the full term at 6 years. The two executive elections are spaced by three years so that one executive's midterms are another executive full term.

- Judicial confirmation powers are so powerful that the below median chamber gains sole authority to offer amendments for passage. Amendments may not be confirmed by the two executives and must be ratified by both chambers and 3.5[ths] of participating states.

Disadvantages:

- Appointment powers are arbitrarily assigned to the two median partitioned chambers. This is dangerous if an institution starts demonstrating favor or preference for those constituencies. Open elections for the nation office should mitigate this but that might invite retaliation from the chamber.

- Splitting the executive into two parts will create information asymmetries between the two executive branches. This invites some inefficiency but with a regulatory framework and communications infrastructure, the deficiency can be overcome.

Executive;

- 2.ii.x.c. (**Executive Presidential**), 5.a (National), 6.a.iii (6 year terms), b.i (1 terms maximum), c.i (lifetime maximum), d.ii (sum of elected), **7.a.i, b.i., ii.xxxx, c.x (publicly funded, presidential, one person = one vote, direct elections),** b.i.ii (eligibility for voting and holding office), 10.b (voluntary voting), 14.1.a.2.b (Executive, Confirmation)

- 2.ii.x.cc.ccc (**Executive Attorney General and Treasury**), 5.a (National), 6.a.iii (6 year terms), b.ii (2 terms maximum), c.i (lifetime maximum), d.ii (sum of elected), **7.a.i, b.i., ii.xxxx, c.x (publicly funded, presidential, one person = one vote, direct elections),** 8.a.v.b (Citizen), b.i.ii (eligibility for voting and holding office), 10.b (voluntary voting), 14.1.a.2.b (Executive, Confirmation)

Legislative:

- 1.i.xx.z (Bicameral legislature, 1st House), ii.x (Representative), **iii.1.2.3.5.7.a.b..ii.10.13.a.ii.b.ii.c.i (Laws, Oversight, Treaties, Appropriations, Appointments Judicial & Presidential, Taxing, and Amendments),** iv.1.b.2.b (Independent, 3/5ths rule, one by one, rotating), 5.a (National), 6.a.iv (6 year terms), b.i iv (unlimited terms), c.i (lifetime maximum, d.ii (sum of elected), 7.a.i (publicly funded), b.ii.xxxx (One citizen = One vote), c.x (direct elections), **8.a.iv.b.i.f.ii.z.d.zz.a.zzz.i (GDP, below median, independent, national median),** v.b (Citizen), b.i.ii (to vote and hold office), c.i (exclusive), 10.b (voluntary), 12.b (Districts), **13.a.i (Representative of Population, by jurisdiction)**

- 1.i.xx.zz (Bicameral legislature, 2nd Chamber), ii.x (Representative), **iii.1.2.5.7.b..iii.iv.13.a.ii.b.ii.c.i (Laws, Oversight, Appropriations. Appointments Executive – Attorney General & Treasurer, Amendments),** iv.1.b.2.b (Independent, 3/5ths rule, one by one, rotating), 5.a (National), **6.a.iv (6 year terms), b.i iv (unlimited terms),** c.i (lifetime maximum, d.ii (sum of elected 7.a.i (publicly funded), b.ii.xxxx (One citizen = One vote), c.x (direct elections), **8.a.iv.b.i.f.ii.z.d.zz.a.zzz.i (GDP, below median, independent, national median),** v.b (Citizen), b.i.ii (to vote and hold office), 10.b (voluntary), 12.b (Districts), **13.a.i (Representative of Population, by jurisdiction)**

Judicial:

- 3.A.i (Judicial, Hierarchical), b.i. (Judicial powers) c.ii.x.2 **(appointed by the President),** 5.a.(National), 6.a.iv (Unlimited), b.iv (unlimited), c.iii (Unlimited), d.ii (sum of elected), 8.a.v.b, b.ii (citizen to hold office)

The two executives don't have to be from the same party to effectively leverage the legislation confirmation powers. Moderates will typically seek to compromise on laws to earn concessions on one aspect while making concessions on another aspect. They will have two chambers to choose from and the chamber that produces the most reasonable or effective laws can expect them to be passed more often, even without the sympathy of the other chamber. This will produce a positive gradient towards regulation and taxation and permit the nation to overcome more of the obstacles other less productive nations suffer from. Laws aren't necessarily passed every 6-year presidential term, but the odds increase after every election that the electorate reorganizes itself to pass the laws that will satisfy their security or economic concerns.

Each President has a single 6-year term with a delay of three years between the two offices. Each of the two legislative chambers split their elections between midterm and presidential elections. The above median GDP chamber is synchronized with the domestic executive while the below median GDP chamber is synchronized with the foreign executive. The intersection of Presidential elections and midterm elections across the two chambers should help randomize the election outcomes between the two parties. All parties should be competitive despite each chamber having a party preference. Introducing strong minority party rights will reduce the risk of populism or authoritarian culture rooting in any single institution.

There is another configuration that permits higher legislation production. The A bifurcated parliament ensures that executive power isn't concentrated in one chamber by splitting military functions form commercial and law enforcement functions. Each of the two chambers preserves administrative control over one of the two functions. This is an awesome check on the power of the executive. In the **Median Partitioned Parliament,** the above median GDP group retains control over the commercial and law enforcement aspects of government while the below median maintains control over the military and judicial appointments. The assignment isn't completely arbitrary but urban areas typically are wealthier and their higher concentration of professional expertise will be more useful for managing the foreign executive office. Rural areas typically have more military enlistment validating the assignment of foreign executive powers. Both chambers contribute to the laws and oversight over the other, defraying some of the risk in the role specialization in executive function.

Parliamentary Median Partition

Primary Traits;

- Bipartite Parliament split between President and AG/Treasurer

- Lower House has Foreign and Judicial Executive Powers

- Upper House has AG/Treasurer Powers

- Median Partition split by GDP, national median

- Population used for representational coefficient

Advantages:

- The below median chamber maintains control over foreign policy, the military, and judicial appointments. All tax laws must originate from the chamber to mitigate the tendency towards wealth inequality.

- The above median chamber maintains control over domestic law enforcement and the treasury. All treaties must be ratified by this chamber to diffuse some of the risk of concentrating the foreign executive power in the below median chamber.

- The above median chamber has sole authority to offer amendments, but this must be passed by simple majority in both chambers and 50% of all states. The lower threshold is intended to accommodate the concentration of judicial power in the below median chamber.

- All judicial appointments must be confirmed in the above median chamber, protecting against one party dominating the third branch of government. Although this mitigates the advantage in the near term, more competitive electoral systems will in a fair number of opportunities for one party to control both chambers resulting in at least a few opportunities to appoint more partisan candidates.

- The bifurcated parliament has a much higher legislative production rate than presidential systems, allowing it to compensate for the more partisan political divide among the two chambers.

- The committee selection process is incremental. The political parties take turns appointing party members to the committees of their choice. The number of members appointed increased by one each time a turn is taken. This will quickly escalate the number of members appointed each turn, allowing a minority party to acquire majority control over one or more committees and achieving more effective oversight and power sharing. The Prime Minister is the party leader and will be able to appoint members to individual committees. This lets the executive office install the leaders of government agencies, unless a minority party capture administrative control through the more competitive selection process.

- The terms are limited to 4 years with the election of the prime ministers staggered by 2 years. This creates some space between the two elections and minimizes the possibility that a single populist movement captures both executive offices. The bifurcated parliament is an effective check on populism, with the two classes split by the median partition, and time separating the two executive elections.

Disadvantages:

- Culture is derivative of politics and allocating an executive function to a class could be dangerous across generations. Rifts accumulate and economic conditions are cyclical. A political party or region with almost exclusive access to a branch invite more serious insults to the integrity of the nation.

- Maintaining control over the military is a powerful advantage during man made crises. However, this will be checked by a national guard system distributed to the states. These states already employ police forces that act as militias. In this environment, control over the treasury and central bank may be able to discourage all bad behavior.

- Allowing minority parties to control agencies within the executive government would pose significant obstacles for the majority party, but even these ministers will have to abide by the laws and budgets previously passed. Ultimately, they will be constrained by the judicial system who can reign in under-performing ministers. There are enough checks within the political system to accommodate this check on executive power.

Executive;

- 2.iii (Abolished Executive), 5.a (National)

Legislative:

- 1.i.xx.z (Bicameral legislature, 1st House), ii.x (Representative), iii.1.2.c.d.4.b.f.5.7..iii.iv.10 (Laws, Oversight over Domestic and Commerce Executive, **Foreign Executive Powers, Executive Judicial Powers, Appropriations, Appointment powers over A.G./Treasurer, and Taxes**), iv.1.b.2.c (Independent, 3/5ths rule, incremental, rotating), 5.a (National), 6.a.iii (4 year terms), b.i iv (unlimited terms), c.i (lifetime maximum, d.ii (sum of elected), 7.a.i (publicly funded), b.ii.xxxx (One citizen = One vote), c.x (direct elections), **8.a.iv.b.i.f.ii.z.d.zz.a.zzz.i (GDP, below median, independent, national median),** v.b (Citizen), b.i.ii (to vote and hold office), c.i (exclusive), 10.b (voluntary), 12.b (Districts), **13.a.i (Representative of Population, by jurisdiction)**

- 1.i.xx.zz (Bicameral legislature, 2nd Chamber), ii.x (Representative), iii.1.2.b.3.4.c.d..5.7.10.13.a.i.b.i.c.i (Laws, **Ratification,** Oversight over Foreign Executive, **Domestic Executive Powers, Central Banking/Treasury Executive, Appropriations, Appointment confirmation powers over judicial and foreign, Amendments),** iv.1.b.2.c (Independent, 3/5ths rule, incremental, rotating), 5.a (National), **6.a.iii (4 year terms), b.i iv (unlimited terms),** c.i (lifetime maximum, d.ii (sum of elected 7.a.i (publicly funded), b.ii.xxxx (One citizen = One vote), c.x (direct elections), **8.a.iv.b.i.f.ii.z.d.zz.a.zzz.i (GDP, below median, independent, national median),** v.b (Citizen), b.i.ii (to vote and hold office), 10.b (voluntary), 12.b (Districts), **13.a.i (Representative of Population, by jurisdiction)**

Judicial:

- 3.A.i (Judicial, Hierarchical), b.i. (Judicial powers only), c.ii.x.2 **(appointed by the President),** 5.a.(National), 6.a.iv (Unlimited), b.iv (unlimited), c.iii (Unlimited), d.ii (sum of elected), 8.a.v.b, b.ii (citizen to hold office)

The assignment and specialization of executive function might suggest structural advantages for one class over the other if minority parties weren't empowered by more competitive committee selection processes. Parties will form coalitions and then competitively bid on the committees that constitute the executive government. This ensures that minority parties will maintain control over a select agency in the government, with oversight applied from the other chamber. Even if the Prime Minister is allowed to appoint all agency heads, the committees will act as corporate boards with significant powers to remove persons or check authoritarian powers. The specialization in executive function within the above median and below median chambers should be stable across generations due to the power sharing innate in more competitive committee selections processes.

The constituencies within the districts aren't static. People migrate from one region to another. This helps alleviate the concern over certain regions exerting too much control over one aspect of the government. Constituencies also tend to acquire higher incomes and more wealth during their lifetimes, contributing to changing perspectives on foreign policy and economy. Age is often the biggest predictor of party affiliation or policy preference, with younger generations being more liberal and older persons more conservative. These demographic and preference changes helps diversify the perspectives within the districts allocated between the two adversarial chambers.

A median partition will be an effective means to interject class based issues into the representational system. It does so safely by relying on a macro-political organization. States are aggregators of individual political preferences and within even territory will be a mix of good outcomes and poor outcomes. States that find themselves within the below median chamber with still have middle class and wealth residents voting within their electorate. This will naturally diversify the electoral outcomes, or at least introduce some uncertainty. The same is true for the above median chamber. Those states with higher GDP's will continue to have poor populations. This cross section of economic interests between the two classes of states will ensure that the political environment isn't overly polarized.

The public won't be divided into above median and below median electorate, but the states will. Poorer citizens from the above median GDP chambers might have incomes that are closer to the above median income earners in the below median GDP chamber. The shared economic interests should help moderate both electoral outcomes and legislative output. Half of all the districts will fall into the middle GDP Class, with 68% of the population with 1 standard deviation of GDP from the median. The other districts may have a larger variance between GDP, but they will be polar opposites and won't likely cooperate to pass the same quality of laws. This will contribute to a gradient of political preference that more closely resembles actual economic conditions. Representatives should be highly responsive to stimulus or argument that impacts their citizens. The class based rhetoric should improve the tendency.

Another moderating property is per capita GDP. Less wealthy districts may naturally have smaller GDP and find themselves in the below median GDP chamber despite having above median per capita GDP. The states wont simply be split between the 'Haves" and the "Have Nots" but the tendencies will certainly be present. This will allow bills that would not normally be present in a below median chamber to be introduced, and vice versa. The opportunity for compromise is present every time elections may cause the chamber to switch parties. When economic conditions cause significant electoral shifts, one of the parties will earn representational advantages and pass laws to remedy the problems its constituents are more concerned with.

The class division of states should help parties and representatives identify the issues contributing most to the economic gap and they will work more strenuously to overcome the natural or artificial obstacles to greater wealth equality among persons and districts. The electorate will view a whole host of issues through the prism of state based class. They will look at deficiencies in federalist tax policy. They will look more closely at the laws that contribute to poverty, like lax labor laws, regressive taxes, and absent wage controls. This is an important concept. A more homogenous chamber should allow it to focus more intently on issues related to its constituencies preferences. The two chambers will then reconcile those bills and compromise on others. The more intense concentration on issues should highlight the differences among the parties better, producing more accurate representation.

The median partition has several different configurations. Instead of the standard configuration, the median partition can form a bicameral senate. The participating states can be divided by GDP into a below median GDP cohort and an above median GDP cohort forming a co-equal chamber in the bicameral legislature with an identical (and even) number of representatives. Each state will report a standardized GDP value and be arranged sequentially from low GDP to high GDP. The representatives will be split by the median value into an above median GDP group and a below median GDP group. The institution will simulate a conventional Senate where the number of representatives is arbitrary and inverse of demographic representation. They may not have identical powers, but they will be equivalent in prestige and influence. This may appeal to nations with worse wealth inequality and constantly shifting demographics.

Smaller states will have equal representation as larger states in the union. Despite its lack of majoritarian rule, it continues to distribute universal suffrage. Senates are critical components of contemporary democracies with the full confidence and authority imparted to republican forms of government. The lack of proportional representation offers states an opportunity to form a union despite incongruences in population. It also comports to lower standards found in monarchies or more authoritarian systems, permitting a more incremental path towards high quality democracy. Median partitioned senates have their place within the topic of wealth based representation, but they certainly are a lower quality outcome due to its emphatically unrepresentative system for legislature.

A median partition split into two coequal chambers with the same number of representatives completely disentangles representation from demographics and majority rule. It is the equivalent of having two Senates. Larger states will have far higher representational ratios than the smaller states. However, this completely mitigates many of the fears involved in union formation. Unorthodox circumstances may provide the incentives for states and nations to agree to this arrangement. Union formation often requires participating states to make concessions and this organizational strategy doesn't fall out of bounds, especially for populations with a tendency to support more authoritarian political organizations and who fear the rapid demographic changes within their nation.

The Founding Fathers of contemporary democracy were suspicious of majority rule and discounted its legitimacy. A fully representative institution is a defect or flaw in democracy rather than a benefit. Often, a Senate is used to check a demographic chamber, but some electorates may prefer a dual Senate resulting from a median partition of GDP. This introduces a class based division of states, rather than cities or natural persons. The Founding fathers also pursued restricted electorates, excluding women, minorities, and the poor creating a stronger argument for support for the dual Senate. Larger representational ratios are a far more egalitarian property than restricted electorates, making it far more palatable to contemporary populations.

The Senate was originally conceived of as a concession to smaller states that feared unionization. They were given incentives to join. This has severely compromised the legitimacy of the government by decoupling representational power from majority rule. Majority rule is a necessary and productive component of democracy if mob rule and populism can be actively inhibited. The median partition accomplishes this by reaffirming the bicameral process. The animal spirits of the public can be cooled by the adversarial nature of the class based chambers and rotating elections. GDP based representation is intended to be a useful tool for union formation and the median partitioned senate offers another option.

The median partition senate may be a lower order than more representation systems, but some nations may offer more concessions towards unionization. If the union has a strong constitution that protects state sovereignty and individual civil liberties, a less representational federal government may be more acceptable. Many unions start as economic unions with constrained political powers. The Senatorial structure is far easier to accept with more limited powers to tax or regulate the many participating states. The primary benefit will be single currency zones and one standard regulator market.

A median portioned Senate is used with the express intent to eliminate any proportional representation based on population. This may induce smaller states to join in union with larger states. Larger states might accept the weaker form of representation if the smaller nations provide more federal tax dollars or other benefits like improved military organization. Larger and wealthier states still benefit from union with smaller or poorer nation as there is strength in numbers. States with larger populations will have more influence over nationwide elections. This will go a long way to compensate them for the higher representational ratios between the states within the two Senates. A **Bipartite Presidential Partitioned Senate** balances the less representative Senatorial elections with two nation-wide Presidential elections.

Bipartite Presidential Partitioned Senate

Primary Traits:

- Bipartite Presidential split into President and AG/Treasurer

- Median Partition split by GDP, national median

- Both chambers are Senate with arbitrary representational coefficient

Advantages:

- The two executive offices combine for a confirmation power in the legislature. They can pick and choose between the above median and below median GDP Senates and favor one class of citizens over the other. This will accelerate the rate of legislation production and contribute to higher quality laws.

- Both legislatures are non-democratic. The number of Senators is arbitrary. In fact, the representational coefficient is an inverse of population. The larger more populous states have significantly higher ratios of citizens to Senators. The nation certainly qualifies under the standard of universal suffrage, but majority rule isn't present outside of the executive elections.

- Despite all of the states having an equal number of Senators, the more populous states have distinct representational advantages in the national elections. The two executives have a combined power greater than a traditional president. The offices have access to both a veto and confirmation when in agreement.

- While the above median GDP Senate provides all appointment confirmations for the President, the below median GDP Senate provides all appointment confirmations for the Attorney General/Treasurer. Judicial appointments made by the President must be confirmed by both Senates, but neither Senate has filibuster powers.

Disadvantages:

- The empowered executives subject to national elections may not be a significant enough draw for larger states to join the union, unless there are promises of federalist tax subsidy or other concessions made.

- It is always dangerous to associate the class based chambers with a group of static states. Unlike persons, states are less likely to move between classes as their incomes improve. States might cultivate a culture of rebellion and dissent. They are already organized and will have the capacity to moderate or obstruct legislation production.

Executive;

- 2.ii.x.c. (**Executive Presidential**), 5.a (National), 6.a.ii (4 year terms), b.ii (2 terms maximum), c.i (lifetime maximum), d.ii (sum of elected), **7.a.i, b.i., ii.xxxx, c.x (publicly funded, presidential, one person = one vote, direct elections),** b.i.ii (eligibility for voting and holding office), 10.b (voluntary voting), 14.1.a.2.a.b (Macro-political vote, Veto and Confirmation)

- 2.ii.x.cc.ccc (**Executive Attorney General and Treasury**), 5.a (National), 6.a.ii (4 year terms), b.ii (2 terms maximum), c.i (lifetime maximum), d.ii (sum of elected), **7.a.i, b.i., ii.xxxx, c.x (publicly funded, presidential, one person = one vote, direct**

elections), 8.a.v.b (Citizen), b.i.ii (eligibility for voting and holding office), 10.b (voluntary voting), 14.1.a.2.a.b (Macro-political vote, Veto and Confirmation)

Legislative

- 1.i.xxx.z (Multi-cameral legislature, 1st House), ii.x (Representative), iii.1.2.b.5.7.a.b.13.a.ii.b.i.c.i (Laws, Oversight over foreign executive, Appropriations Appointment Confirmation powers over judicial and foreign executive, Amendments), iv.1.b.2.a (Independent, 3/5th rule, majority party), 5.a (National), 6.a.iii (4 year terms), b.i iv (unlimited terms), c.i (lifetime maximum, d.ii (sum of elected), 7.a.i (publicly funded), b.ii.xxxx (One citizen = One vote), c.x (direct elections), **8.a.iv.b.i.f.ii.z.d.zz.b.zzz.i (GDP, below median, aggregate, national median),** v.b (Citizen), b.i.ii (to vote and hold office), c.i (exclusive), 10.b (voluntary), 12.a (Jurisdictions), **13.a.i (Representative of Population, by jurisdiction)**

- 1.i.xxx.zz (Multi-cameral legislature, 2nd Chamber), ii.x (Representative), iii.1.2.c.d.3.5.7.a.b.10.13.a.ii.b.i.c.i (Laws, Oversight over A.G./Treasurer, Treatise, Appointment Confirmation over judicial and domestic executive, Appropriations, Taxes, and Amendments), iv.1.b.2.a (Independent, 3/5th rule, majority party), 5.a (National), **6.a.iii (4 year terms), b.i iv (unlimited terms),** c.i (lifetime maximum, d.ii (sum of elected 7.a.i (publicly funded), b.ii.xxxx (One citizen = One vote), c.x (direct elections), **8.a.iv.b.i.f.ii.z.d.zz.b.zzz.i (GDP, below median, aggregate, national median),** v.b (Citizen), b.i.ii (to vote and hold office), 10.b (voluntary), 12.a (Jurisdictions), **13.a.i (Representative of Population , by jurisdiction)**

Judicial:

- 3.A.i (Judicial, Hierarchical), b.i.a (Judicial powers only, general), c.ii.x.2 **(appointed by the President),** 5.a.(National), 6.a.iv (Unlimited), b.iv (unlimited), c.iii (Unlimited), d.ii (sum of elected), 8.a.v.b, b.ii (citizen to hold office)

The median partition senate is also intended to be improved by a triangulation chamber. This chamber ought to be more representational to offset the deficiencies of an unrepresentative bicameral legislature. However, it may make the political system too efficient with fewer inhibitions on legislation and less oversight All governance models have flaws; some err towards obstruction and other err towards efficiency. A third chamber with proportional representation would go a long way to validate the union with majority rule. Senates lack legitimacy without the temper of a demographic or democratic chamber. The **Democratic Reserve Partition** is a configuration of median partition that utilizes a Reserve chamber as a filter for a democratic chamber.

Those Senators who lose their seats in the two GDP Senates will earn seats in the Reserve chamber. The Reserve chamber elects the Prime Minister and acts as the filter for the democratic chamber. The nation is split into above median GDP chambers and below median GDP chambers with the Democratic chamber will playing king maker between the two classes for passing laws. Both legislative chambers have term limits ensuring a constant flow of high quality candidates into the Reserve chamber every midterm or full term. The PM will have strong party affiliation and class affiliation due to their prior inclusion within one of the two chambers.

When term limits expire, or candidates lose elections, legislators will move from the median partitioned senate to the Reserve chamber. If majority power changes parties, a larger number of one party's candidates will relocate into the Reserve chamber. When a party acquires a majority in the legislature, they will lose the majority in the Reserve chamber. This checks legislative power by setting it contrary to executive power. This is also a check on the Democratic chamber as the party or chamber affiliation of the PM will often be contrary to the majority party within the two senates.

Democratic Reserve Partition

Primary Traits:

- Multi-cameral legislature (3 parts)

- Median GDP Partition with national median

- Population as representational coefficient

- Democratic Triangulation chamber

- Reserve Chamber with Unitary Executive Powers

Advantages:

- The median partition is on the state level. Above median GDP states are separated from below median GDP states. Larger or wealthier states will be in one chamber. Smaller or poorer states will be in the other. This is an excellent example of class based representation.

- The democratic chamber introduces majority rule and proportional representation into a median partitioned Senate. Economic conditions will dictate where the democratic chamber allocates its votes between the above median and below median GDP chambers.

- Although larger states will have less influence in the senate, they will have considerably more influence within the democratic chamber.

- Democratic chambers are fulcrums that will improve coordinated legislation produce on the state and municipal levels. Even laws that fail to pass on the federal level might enable state legislatures an opportunity to pass the same measures.

- The Reserve chamber conserves political experience by retaining veteran legislators for use in the executive branch. Parties that lose legislative elections are more likely to win election in the Reserve, splitting power between the executive and legislative branches.

- Competitive committee selection processes in the Reserve and median partition will ensure minority parties have access to oversight and legislative influence. Minority parties can bring bills to the democratic chamber, they can assume control over agencies, and they can issue subpoenas and investigate oversight matters. These are checks that are missing from most conventional legislatures.

Disadvantages:

- Each state is reduced to just one or two Senators regardless of population or GDP. It is a leveler between the states but not all states will benefit from the lack of proportional representation.

- The democratic chamber is a disincentive for Unions between states of significantly varied sizes. The larger nation will have a superior position regarding passing laws through the triangulation chamber. Unlike executives with confirmation powers, the democratic chamber is more populist and less controllable than a single office or institution. It might be viewed as a threat to smaller states that are subject to the whims of mob psychology.

- The Reserve chamber is technically non-democratic in that there are no formal elections. Therefore, the members are limited to half the total equivalency in terms earned in the median partition Senate.

Executive:

- 2.iii (Abolished Executive), 5.a. (National)

Legislative:

- 1.i.xxx.z (Multi-cameral legislature, 1st House), ii.x (Representative), iii.1.2.a3..5.7.10.13.a.ii.b.ii.c.ii (Laws, Oversight over Unitary, Treatise, Appropriations Appointments, Taxes, and Bicameral Amendments with supermajority), iv.1.b.2.b (Independent, 3/5ths rule, one by one, rotating), 5.a (National), 6.a.iii (4 year terms), b.i iv (unlimited terms), c.i (lifetime maximum, d.ii (sum of elected), 7.a.i (publicly funded), b.ii.xxxx (One citizen = One vote), c.x (direct elections), **8.a.iv.b.i.f.ii.z.d.zz.b.zzz.i (GDP, below median, aggregate, national median),** v.b (Citizen), b.i.ii (to vote and hold office), c.i (exclusive), 10.b (voluntary), 12.a (Jurisdictions), **13.a.i (Representative of Population, by jurisdiction)**

- 1.i.xxx.zz (Multi-cameral legislature, 2nd Chamber), ii.x (Representative), iii.1.2.a.5.10.13.a.ii.b.ii.c.ii (Laws, Oversight over Unitary, Appropriations, Taxes), iv.1.b.2.b (Independent, 3/5ths rule, one by one, rotating), 5.a (National), **6.a.iii (4 year terms), b.i iv (unlimited terms),** c.i (lifetime maximum, d.ii (sum of elected 7.a.i (publicly funded), b.ii.xxxx (One citizen = One vote), c.x (direct elections), **8.a.iv.b.i.f.ii.z.d.zz.b.zzz.i (GDP, below median, aggregate, national median),** v.b (Citizen), b.i.ii (to vote and hold office), 10.b (voluntary), 12.a (Jurisdictions), **13.a.i (Representative of Population , by jurisdiction)**

- 1.i.xxx.zzz (Multicamera legislature, 3rd chamber), ii.ixxxx (Direct Democracy), 1.a.ii (Mono-chamber, Leveraged), 2.a.iii (Referendum monthly), **2b.ii.x.iii.xxx (Unitary filter, Federal tier, Reserve) 3.b.i, (confirm laws triangulation),** 4.a (municipal jurisdictions), 8.a.v.b (Citizen), b.i (to vote), 10.b (voluntary)

Reserve:

- 4.i.a (Reserves, admitting all retired members), **ii.a..2.i (Unitary Presidential sub routine), ii.d.x (repealing legislation with**

supermajority), iii.b (Unicameral), iv.1.a.2.b (Pool of retired national legislators), v.e (half total equivalent terms)

Judicial:

- 3.A.i (Judicial, Hierarchical), b.i.a (Judicial powers only, general), c.ii.x.2 **(appointed by the President),** 5.a.(National), 6.a.iv (Unlimited), b.iv (unlimited), c.iii (Unlimited), d.ii (sum of elected), 8.a.v.b, b.ii (citizen to hold office)

The Reserve chamber is completely bureaucratic. The Reserve dictates which laws are put to popular vote in the democratic chamber, but they don't vote on the laws themselves. Instead, the Reserve chamber controls the executive functions of the government. The executive functions are distributed to committees and members of the Reserve compete for control of those agencies. The Prime Minister allocates the Reserve members of their party or coalition, granting them more administrative control over the selection process. The Prime Minister does not have traditional Veto powers. However, the Office has powers to repeal laws with a supermajority. This is the equivalent of a retroactive Veto for the Reserve executive and the only mechanism for the branch to interact with laws after they are passed.

The Reserve chamber is a parliament, so the majority party elects its own leader from amidst its ranks. The party will typically only gain this majority after losing elections in the legislature. This will ensure that power will be effectively distributed among the institutions of government and the parties. Over the longer term, parties will be far more interested in winning elections as they will lose numerical viability after a few lost elections. A party could be rendered invalid or noncompetitive in just one generation if they don't win their share of elections. Term limits in legislature ensure higher turnover. This will ensure parties who win elections more often gain an advantage in the Reserve chamber, increasing the odds of maintaining both institutions.

All members of the Reserve are veteran politicians with a mix of oversight and administrative experience. If a legislator served 18 years in the Congress, the legislator will be able to serve 9 more in the Reserve chamber. If a legislator only served 4 years, then they only serve 2 more. The variable terms for Reserve members help randomize the allocation of seats among parties or states. There are two factors that impact majority control over the Reserve chamber. Not only do parties have to plan for Reserve members losing office due to term limits, but they also subject to competition in elections between the two median partitioned senates. Term limits expire every year, permitting for frequent changes in speakership, committee selection, and majority control of the chamber.

The Reserve chamber maintains more competitive committee selections to ensure minority parties contribute to the government and to optimize the allocation of experienced legislators. Each of the committees independently determines which laws are put in front on the people, allowing for minority party Reserve members to make contributions to legislative output. The Reserve chamber will have more predictable and durable output over a longer period when all parties contribute to the management of the government and the legislative agenda of the democratic chamber.

The two senates can pass laws independently of the democratic chamber eliminating some of the concern that a minority party can fully obstruct legislative production with majorities within the legislative committees of the Reserve Chamber. Parties winning majority control over both legislative chambers will have full authority to pass laws without the input of the Prime Minister or Reserve chamber. If the two senates are split between the two parties, the democratic chamber will still provide a pathway to passing laws. This results in a 100% legislative capacity, where laws can be passed regardless of the outcomes of elections, and regardless of which party has majorities in any of the chambers. However, unpopular laws will result in election losses, making the party more likely to be exhausted or permanently retired over the long term.

The Senate is not the only alternative format for median partitions. Median partitions can continue to allocate individual states to above median GDP chambers and below median GDP chamber and simultaneously comport to proportional representation. This is a weaker form of organization than the standard median partition, but it has some unique advantages. Chiefly, it concentrates state representation in one of the two chambers so that the above median chamber will have a small number of large states and the below median chamber will have a large number of smaller states. This produces representational advantages for larger states while preserving claims of high quality democratic entitlements. Universal suffrage and majority rule apply to this configuration of entitlements contributing to its legitimacy in nation building and union formation.

Each state is allocated a number of representatives determined by an LCD of population or GDP. This achieves proportional representation in a system of representation that splits states by class. State representatives are then arranged in sequential order from highest value to lowest value. The number of representatives is tallied and divided by two. The middle point determines were each state is allocated. Each representative has a value equal to its state's GDP so all of the representatives from the same state will typically be located in the same above median or below median chamber. The two chambers will have an equal number of representatives providing a pathway towards both universal suffrage and majority rule.

Unlike a standard median partition, individual districts aren't separated into below median and above median chamber. Instead, all districts in the state participate in a single above median or below median chamber.

This imparts an interesting characteristic into the legislature. The nation will be split in two equal halves with below median GDP states in one chamber and above median GDP states in the other.

More populous or wealthier states will have concentrated power in one of the chambers. If there is a high variance between the representational coefficients of participating states, then a small number states may dominate one of the two median chambers. A large state with a high GDP would gain a larger number of representatives in that chamber. This will concentrate political power around oversight committees, appropriation committees, or investigative committees in a very small group of states. This will improve productivity when the representatives of a state to continually work with other representatives from the same state.

The representational equity of a larger and more wealthy state doubles by virtue of concentrating power in a single chamber of a median partition. A state with 10% of the population may have as much as 20% of the representational power in an above median chamber. Their representatives will be more aligned with similar economic interests and civil interests and work more effectively towards those goals in the chamber. The parties will organize themselves more efficiently, negotiate more effectively, and compromise more often resulting in a high legislative production rate with higher quality laws.

For example, if the nation had 436 total representatives, with half in the above median and half in the below median chambers, then a state with a 10% of the overall population would control 20% of the representation in one of the chambers. Since larger populations generally have higher GDP, this would impact the above median GDP. There is another consequence of larger states having larger GDP. The above median chamber will have far fewer participating states. If the 5 largest states have an equal number of residents as the 45 smallest states, then the above median chamber will have 218 representatives from only 5 states and the below median chamber will have 218 representatives from the other 45 states. In a bicameral process that can be obstructed fairly easily, coordinating representatives from a small number of states might pronounce or magnify the net representation afforded to the above median GDP chamber.

The above median chamber has another advantage over the below median chamber. The more homogenous distribution of representatives increases the odds that the chamber will be able to obstruct the legislative process. The below median chamber has many more states and they won't be able to coordinate their responses to laws as effectively. This isn't only about discipline in party members. The larger number of lower GDP states will have more diversity in economic interests and sympathies. It's simply less likely the chamber will be unanimous in its judgment. Larger states will have a disproportionate impact on legislative output in the bicameral process. As a result, they will be able to exert more influence over the legislative process and assume leadership roles in domestic politics.

This doesn't mean smaller states wont present organized resistance to exploitative laws or taxes coming out of the above median chamber. It is simply less likely to occur. The smaller states also benefit from an improvement in representational equity in the bicameral process. Both chambers must consent to the laws passed, doubling the proportional representation of each state within the individual chamber. The smaller states will recognize the inherent value of laws and vote them down if they aren't in their interests. Representatives who are too permissive will likely lose office if they don't assert or protect the interests of their state. This is how political markets work. They aggregate individual self-interests with elections and promote honest and accurate representation.

Even if a state has concentrated power in a single chamber, their constituents will be normally distributed around a median income. This should randomize electoral outcomes more effectively, or at least make more elections more competitive. States aren't completely homogenous in political dispositions even if there are strong tendencies. The very act of organizing them into a single chamber may alter the politics of elections making the elections less certain. Constituents will continue to sanction poor performance and corruption while rewarding success, making the future of electoral outcomes less certain despite the concentration of states within the single chamber. Thus, political preferences won't be fixed allowing for all parties to seek majorities in the chamber

The most conventional configuration for a biaxial median partition is the Presidential system. Unlike most contemporary examples, a parliament is inadequate due to the division of states into two separate chambers. States are more highly organized, and they will exert more influence on a federal executive branch if there is a smaller number of them. The larger states already have considerable political power simply by virtue of their advantages in population and GDP. To give them unchecked power on an executive branch would imbalance the distribution of power among the states. For this reason, most biaxial median partitions retain Presidents rather than parliaments.

The **Presidential Biaxial Median Partition** maintains a simple bicameral legislature with a single unitary executive. It allocates representatives in districts and each district carries with it the aggregate state GDP. This will divide the districts into above median and below median groups by state. The largest and wealthiest states will be in the above median GDP group and the smaller and poorer states will be in the below median GDP group. Each state will retain a proportional number of representatives correlated by population. Except for the less conventional use of a median partition, this configuration satisfies all contemporary demands for universal suffrage, majority rule, and efficient due process.

Presidential Biaxial Median Partition

Primary Traits:

- Unitary President

- Median GDP Partition with national median

- Population as representational coefficient

- Districts are used in median partition, unequal concentrations

Advantages:

- The Presidential office is outside of the locus of the congress, adding a significant check on executive authority. Presidential systems introduce more uncertainty between the alignment of executive and legislative powers, and allow midterm elections to dictate those conditions.

- The above median partition will have far fewer participating states and states tend to have representatives that resemble each other. If there is less variance in electoral outcomes in the above median chamber, then it may establish a standard for the below median to measure themselves to.

- The below median chamber will be much more competitive with a larger number of seats from states with more variance in economic outcomes. Not only do the larger number of seats equal more opportunity for change, but there will be more diversity in candidates. In this respect, the legislative production rate might increase due to the interplay of fixed electoral outcomes in the above median GDP chamber and the mixed electoral outcomes in the below median GDP chamber.

- Competitive committee selection processes are used to offset the increased risk of party preference developing in the two adversarial chambers. This ensures that minority parties can provide oversight and initiate investigations to check authoritarian behaviors in the executive.

Disadvantages:

- The proportional representation may discourage smaller states from forming unions with significantly larger states due to the concentrated political power in the above median GDP chamber.

- The Presidential system has half the rate of legislation production than a typical parliament, but this may still be fast enough for it to accommodate the fiscal crises or economic crises that may regularly occur.

- Party preference may accumulate in the two chambers at a faster rate than in the districts were allocated independently by GDP. If the two chambers become predictably adversarial, then it might cause obstruction and worsening conditions. Once the economy deteriorates, the party preference might switch providing an opportunity for reform. This is suboptimal but common in Presidential systems that employ both presidential vetoes and filibusters.

Executive;

- **2.i (Unitary Presidential)**, 5.a (National), 6.a.iii (6 year terms), b.i (1 terms maximum), c.i (lifetime maximum, d.ii (sum of elected), 7.a.i (publicly funded), **b.ii.xxxx (One citizen = One** vote), c.x (direct elections), 8.a.v.b (Citizen), bi.ii (to vote and hold office) c.i (exclusive), 10.b (voluntary voting), 14.1.a.2.a (Macro-political vote, Veto)

Legislative:

- 1.i.xx.z (Bicameral legislature, 1st House), ii.x (Representative), iii.1.2.a.3.5.7. 13.a.ii.b.i.c.i (Laws, Oversight over Unitary, Ratification, Appropriations, and Appointments), iv.1.b.2.d (Independent, proportional, one for one, rotating), 5.a (National), **6.a.iii (6 year terms), b.i iv (unlimited terms),** c.i (lifetime maximum, d.ii (sum of elected), 7.a.i (publicly funded), b.ii.xxxx (One citizen = One vote), c.x (direct elections), **8.a.iv.b.i.f.ii.z.d.zz.b.zzz.i (GDP, below median, aggregate, national median),** v.b (Citizen), b.i.ii (to vote and hold office), c.i (exclusive), 10.b (voluntary), 12.b (Districts), **13.a.i (Representative of Population, by jurisdiction)**

- 1.i.xx.zz (Bicameral legislature, 2nd Chamber), ii.x (Representative), iii.1.2.5.10. 13.a.ii.b.i.c.i (Laws, Oversight over Unitary, Appropriations, Taxes, and Amendments), iv.1.b.2.d (Independent, proportional, one for one, rotating), 5.a (National), **6.a.iii (6 year terms), b.i iv (unlimited terms),** c.i (lifetime maximum, d.ii (sum of elected 7.a.i (publicly funded), b.ii.xxxx (One citizen = One vote), c.x (direct elections), **8.a.iv.b.i.f.ii.z.d.zz.b.zzz.i (GDP, below median, aggregate, national median),** v.b (Citizen), b.i.ii (to vote and hold office), 10.b (voluntary), 12.b (Districts), **13.a.i (Representative of Population, by jurisdiction)**

Judicial:

- 3.A.i (Judicial, Hierarchical), b.i. (Judicial powers), c.ii.x.2 **(appointed by the President),** 5.a.(National), 6.a.iv (Unlimited), b.iv (unlimited), c.iii (Unlimited), d.ii (sum of elected), 8.a.v.b, b.ii (citizen to hold office)

Each chamber will have their own oversight and intelligence committees. This will permit the representatives from the larger states to develop significantly more experience in those matters. The larger states will have far more discretion too. States from the below median chamber might not get appointed to a critical oversight or intelligence committee. There are simply too many states for them to all be represented and the smaller states will have to negotiate amongst themselves who gets the more important committees. This is not true for the larger states, who will have multiple appointments to each committee.

Biaxial median partition promotes union formation by creating more value for both large states and small states. Larger states get more comprehensive oversight over government while smaller states gain more security and benefit from federal tax subsidies. Smaller states will see safety in numbers and free trade with larger markets as a good reason to accept the concentration of political power in the above median GDP chamber. Both states gain representational equity by concentrating their representatives in one of the two median GDP chambers.

Although senates might incentivize smaller states to join unions, they also discourage larger states. The higher order organization in biaxial median partitions should accommodate this deficit. The smaller states can obstruct legislation if their immediate needs are not met. This reduces the representational advantages larger states have in demographic based systems. Smaller states double their effective representation by concentrating it in one chamber. A state that would have only 4 representatives out of 100 would effectively gain four more for a total of 8 representatives in the median partition. They will go from 4% of total representation to 8% in a single chamber. Since this is a bicameral legislature that requires consent from both parts, it increases their net overall representation. The division into coequal parts creates value for all participants. This value is not present in standard demographic chambers or senates. It is a significant improvement over traditional political systems that don't utilize total proportional representation in a bicameral process.

The biaxial median partition starts to resemble an imperial democracy with a few of the larger states occupying the above median GDP chamber and all of the smaller or poorer states occupying the below median GDP chamber. The number of representatives is split equally in half, but it gives the impression of a superior position. Larger states are intrinsically more organized than smaller states and the median partition attempts to accommodate this deficiency by separating them into their own chamber. Politics is not always about equality. Smaller states may accept this marginally inferior position to acquire the federal tax subsides provided by larger states and the increased security from a larger more integrated military. Ultimately, the imperial democracy is a legitimate mechanism for union formation as it provides proportional representation satisfying all conditions of universal suffrage and majority rule

The median partition offers an exceptional opportunity to form peaceful unions with neighbors and allied nations. The class based division helps eliminate rigid cultural or notational borders. Citizens from one country will quickly form economic sympathies with citizens of the other country, reducing the nationalistic tendencies of both populations. Public policy cuts through most sectarian divisions by reducing relationships to wages, taxes, or profits. If more emphasis is placed on economic self-interests and the public policy that will improve conditions, a smaller proportion of the electorate will respond to xenophobia or nationalist overtones. Politicians will appeal to more citizens than those in their immediate proximity. This will help define the new public identity of the union. Business relationships will follow and then interpersonal, and eventually the nations will merge cultures and ambitions.

The median partition is a check on the threat of populism. If a legislature is split into below median and above median parts, it is far less likely that a single populist wave will overcome both chambers of the legislature. In fact, the two chambers maintain constituents who, on average, have opposite economic experiences. The poorer states might be more susceptible to populism. They may be more likely to capture the below median chamber, but the above median chamber will move in an opposite direction. This isn't necessarily true in a conventional senate, which will have similar vulnerabilities to the rhetoric. The Senate is slightly more resistant due to its longer terms and different rotation schedule, but this is hardly as effective as the median partition. The median partition explicitly mitigates the effectiveness by establishing adversarial self-interests in the constituents of the two opposed chambers. It will be very unlikely that a populist party wins election in both chambers and the executive making the nation far more resilient.

Populism is especially dangerous in demographic based systems of representation where a single ethnic or religious group will seek to affirm and preserve their own political power at the expense of minority rights or equitable economy. Demographic based violence is extremely common and there are sectarian rifts in almost every country. Cooling the temperament by splitting the population into two classes, and providing minorities more proportional representation in a single legislative chamber might contribute to better policies prior will reduce the odds of a conflict occurring or dampen its severity. If the median partition results in better wealth equality through higher wages, union participation, and stable finance for governments, the nation will be able to avoid most sectarian tensions. Populism is less of a threat even if the electorate is split into urban areas and rural areas, or into "haves" and "have nots".

The class identity should distract from the demographic properties of the electorate and provide more opportunity to diagnose economic issues and address them with due process. The bicameral process will help mitigate the animal spirits of any specific demographic group by moderating the quality of laws and ensuring that anti-democratic reforms can't be easily passed by a majority party. If due process can be preserved over an extended period, the legislature will have the opportunity it needs to pass reforms that address the deficiencies in the economy causing the instability. Strong civil liberties and constitutional rights will create an atmosphere where peaceful protest and debate contribute to the national dialogue and problem-solving strategies of political parties. Class based representation utilizing a median portioned legislature may prove to be the most effective method for resolving demographic or class based tensions and thus increasing the odds a nation survives.

These are all aspects that should be considered during the nation building process after occupations or regime changes. The characteristics of the host nation can be assessed prior to the conflict, and a more appropriate system can be installed. Not only will this produce better outcomes with more durable peace and more equitable economy, but it also contributes to the substance and quality of rhetoric used during the war effort. Arguments can be formed that appeal to more of the sectarian groups in the host nation. This will galvanize support for the regime change and the next administration. GDP based representation is another solution in the tool box for the democratization movement.

Demographic systems of representation won't always satisfy the demands of the host nation. GDP based systems of representation won't always work. However, if the occupying nation offers more options, then the host nation is more likely to accept the outcomes. Nations suffer under different demographic or economic conditions, and political systems that emphasize one aspect over the other may be more effective. This will play out over large numbers of simulations making the actual application far more important. Mistakes are costlier after the war effort concludes with the host nation succumbing to dissent and discard only a few years later. More technology and better science will make it more likely that optimal outcomes are achieved.

There is more utility for GDP based representation in peaceful unions. GDP is a non-sectarian measure for government to use in coordinating political representation. The application of more expert public policy can improve the proportional representation of the state. It is a good indicator of economic influence and soft political power. War is an often-infrequent event. It tends to increase in frequency during adverse times like climate change and wealth inequality but for the last few decades the world has averted the wide scale destruction and misery associated with conflict. While peace reigns, nations will have an opportunity to forge durable relationships by forming unions with other nations. Although there are two large unions in the US and EU, there are many more nations that could benefit from unionization.

It is a matter of fact, economic unions and political unions create wealth with standardized currencies, regulatory zones, and uninhibited trade. Free trade creates wealth by competitive advantages in production and pricing. Unions predicated on GDP based representation will be more inclined to preserve these conditions. They will try to export their policies to other nations, and possibly expand their political boundaries. When nations aren't fixation in ethnicity, religion, or another sectarian characteristic, they are more likely to agree to reciprocal representation in a mutual beneficial economic union. More importantly, unions are a pathway to greater security and more net political power. It should be expected that more nations seek the comfort and safety of larger unions or empires. GDP based representation simply offers a strategy to combine both in a political system with universal suffrage, majority rule, and efficient due process.

7 ENGINEERING

Modern political systems are complex and dynamic institutions, but they can still be reduced to a relatively small number of fundamental attributes. These characteristics can be recombined into a large variety of more specialized or more practical systems. The refined systems can then be engineered for integration within even larger unions. This chapter lists all of the most relevant and useful of attributes in outline form and briefly describes each one. The order of the attributes is arbitrary, but the outline still serves a purpose in making a quick translation of property to code for more efficient substitution and re-organization. Although disparate and seemingly unconnected when presented within the individual system designs, they will coalesce to form the most important themes contained within the other chapters. Most of the attributes are self-explanatory but in cases of ambiguity, the term and definitions can be referenced with ease in this chapter.

The first aspect of government to be explained will be the Legislatures. Their most fundamental characteristics are the number of chambers contained within the institution. This book will focus on three broad types; unicameral, bicameral, and multi-cameral. Unicameral legislatures are the most efficient where laws can be passed with least effort and with greater frequency. It is the most basic and prototypical form of majority rule. This speed allows the nation or jurisdiction to adapt to critical environments quickly and with implied consent. The velocity at which legislation can be passed might also be viewed as a negative; changes may be made too hastily and require reversal. However, reversals are also much easier to achieve due to the fact that only a simple majority in one chamber is necessary to unwind previous legislations. This too has its dangers as a generation worth of progress can be undermined by a relatively few numbers of politicians in a very short time.

Bicameral legislatures actively inhibiting reversals but the pace at which new legislations are passed is much slower by virtue of two complementing majorities are needed within the two chambers. It is actually much more likely that a bicameral legislature is split between the parties reducing the possibility of passing significant bills while diluting their strength and integrity. Bicameral legislatures are a factor of 3x more conservative in this respect. This can have a terribly corrupting effect as the regression will produce ample opportunity for institutional powers to monopolize market share in politics and economy.

1.) Legislative
        i. Organization
                x) uni-cameral
                xx.) Bi-cameral
                    z. 1st camera
                    zz. 2nd camera
                xxx.) Multicameral
                    z. 1st camera
                    zz. 2nd Camera
                    zzz. 3rd Camera
                    zzzz 4th Camera
                xxxx.) Abolished (usurped by executive,
                      administrative laws only)

Another danger exists. Bicameral Legislatures are slow and ponderous and can be unresponsive during crises. Not only are the chances of passing a reactionary law much lower but it will take much longer. Doubling the number of politicians will triple the number of debates. This gives rise to the possibility that the Legislature not act fast enough or strong enough when a crisis presents itself.

Multi-legislatures can be as fast and nimble as unicameral chambers while as thorough and secure as bicameral chambers. The third chamber increases the chances of passing laws while still requiring two chambers to repeal. Their greatest asset is their ability to assume the responsibilities of other branches and reserve powers from each other. A multi-legislature, or complex legislature, could combine a unicameral structure for the chambers assuming executive or judicial powers with bicameral structures for those retaining legislative powers. Complexes permit multiple segments of the population to be individually enfranchised which offers opportunity for concession as well as specialization. Multi-cameral structures are more compatible with reserve system structures, triangulation powers, and legislative equivalents to tripartite executive structures all of which will be explained in more detail in subsequent chapters.

The entry of abolished legislatures is useful for manufacturing political systems where the executive branch or judicial branch usurps the legislative primary responsibilities. During emergencies, it offers significant efficiencies. Nearly half of the laws governing a nation and its economy are administrative laws derived from executive authority. With a more specialized executive department it might be able to develop the entire legal canon. This is especially true with configurations where there is no unitary order within the executive branch but rather discrete and independent parts that act as checks on the other parts for a more distributed and balanced structure.

For the contemporary history of democracy certain executives have had veto powers over the legislature. This reinforces the dictatorial aspect the original founders intended. They modeled the Presidential office on a monarchy burdened by parliament. However, this has conspired to produce some of the worst outcomes for democracies when employed with bicameral legislatures which already inhibit regulatory initiatives and reform movements. The odds of passing a significant piece of legislation are already minimal and made much less frequent when a veto adds to the number of negative solutions already produced by bicameral legislatures with opposing majorities.

It is unlikely that executive officers will abandon veto powers but there is a more appropriate substitute. Macro-political votes allow the executive branches to interact with legislatures and other branches and triangulate between multiple legislatures to confirm one version of legislation over another version. Instead of inhibiting the legislation process, the macro-political vote would increase the number of passed bills. It is simply a much more productive power than the veto, acting like a one-way valve towards more progressive regulatory and civil rights environments. The body politic still has the opportunity to repeal legislature but this requires the cooperation of the entire legislature. In cases of tripartite executive structures, the macro political vote would offer confirmation of the legislation created through agency laws in order to check each individual executive branches accumulation of power over the others.

Another important qualifier for legislative branches is whether they are representational or tyrannical. If another branch or chamber appoints legislators it qualifies as tyrannical. It is expected that terms continue to apply to the officers serving in the chamber despite its classification as autocratic. Tyrannical appointments can come from any number of executives, judicial, or legislative branches from the same tier or adjacent tier of government. Appointment powers are very common even in the most progressive of democracies. One of the more common forms of tyrannical appointment is an executive's access to the court systems. Judges are often appointed to permanent tenures on federal courts, appellate courts, or supreme courts. Another example of appointment powers comes from the original structure of the US Senate. All of the Senators were originally appointed by the various state legislatures rather than being elected directly by the population.

The term representative implies that the number of representatives elected are correlated to a proportion of the electorate. This will result in a legislative body that imparts a number of legislators to each state or region equal to its population in proportion to the other states or regions. Larger states will have proportionally more legislators. The Representational option refers to both proportional and non-proportional allocations of legislator members. Non-proportional representation includes stipulated and arbitrary representational coefficients. This means that the number of representatives can be fixed in non-proportional ratios to populations. A non-proportional legislature might assign two senators to every state regardless of its size.

Non-proportional representative criteria have their uses but is the weaker of the two forms of Representational Coefficients. It is also a clear depreciation of Universal Suffrage and typically produces a government which is which is more easily exploited by the owner's class or the politically enfranchised. Imbalanced systems of representation can still work but they require offsetting powers between demographic or economic criteria so that more segments of the populations are empowered than those disenfranchised. This is the primary source for political concession during moments of crisis.

ii. Attributes
      x. Representative
      xx. Tyrannical
            a. Appointing Tier
               1. Same Tier
               2. Lower Tier
            b. Appointing Agent
               z. Appointed by Exec
                    1. Unitary Executive
                    2. Presidential
                    3. Attorney General
                    4. Treasurer General
               zz. Appointed by legislators
               zzz. Appointed by judicial
               zzzz. Appointed by Reserve Chamber
          c. Proportion (remaining are elected)
            z. minimal 3%
            zz. Optimal 10%
            zzz. Total 100%

Tyrannical systems are qualified by the branch or tier making the appointments and produce the political levers for manufacturing extra-national tiers of government (central, federal, or economic unions).

Tyrant appointment powers occur within the same tier or lower tier. Same tier appointments are more acceptable for executive officers controlling their own branches, but control can be extended to limited degrees within the legislative branches. Often this will be a predetermined proportion of representation. The portion of legislators not appointed are then elected and representative of the population. When there are multiple executives, each appointing authority will be able to install 3% or 10% of the seats, depending upon the appointment authority.

Tyrannical appointments are also useful for emergency governments and for configurations that demand greater control over a specific tier or branch of government. One example is a President appointing the members of Congress during an occupation. This should be temporary with the seats eventually transferred to democratic control when elections are more secure. This way the government can organize the political system prior to its acceptance by the occupied people so that all of the infrastructure can be created. This should maximize the probability of success after the occupation ends.

Tyrannical systems have practical use but otherwise introduce many of the same flaws non-proportional representative appointments endure. Appointed legislatures can be representational of population in the same respects that elected legislatures can be which will impart more legitimacy to the institution as the individual senators will be accorded a proportion of power equivalent to the scale of part: whole in regard to population, GDP, or tax liabilities paid.

Atomized configurations dictate that the members of lower tier legislations appoint, by consensus, the members of the higher tier legislatures. Terms will insulate current higher tier legislatures from political turnover occurring too quickly and too often. The atomized structure operates across tiers rather than chambers. The Atomized attributes permit appointments to be made by either the executive branch or the legislative branch which will be incredible useful for constricting extra regional or extra-national governmental institutions like economic unions and satellite systems.

> xxx. Atomized (lower tier governments appoint representatives
> in higher tier, lowest tier elected by popular
> vote)
> 1. Legislators (Council members) appoint representative in federal tier
> 2. Executives (mayor or governors) appoint representatives in federal tier

Democracy is a misnomer for many nations in the West. Most contemporary democracies are actually republican forms of governments and not traditional democracies. However, modern technologies in communication and information distribution might accommodate true democratic reforms. Nations can adopt reforms that imitate the first instance of democratic government found in Ancient Greece. The term Direct Democracy typically implies an entitlement for citizens to vote directly on the issues in front the body politic. Historically, this has had disastrous consequences, but the Greek empire did persist for hundreds of years and thrive for much of it. Corruption eventually set in and an endless period of warfare followed. Only then did the empire recede. Modern economy, society, and technology is much more sophisticated than the ancient era of Greece and might contribute to a more effective deployment of True Democratic reforms.

Direct Democracies can be implemented in a popular form with no restrictions on access or without voting based on rigid economic or demographic criteria. True democracies can also be improved with an auxiliary chamber meant to filter the legislation for popular voting. These filters can be subjected to eligibility criteria and refined with procedural rules to ensure the locus of power remains with the larger voting body. More mature postal systems, telephone systems, and internet systems provide the necessary communication infrastructure permitting the true democratic structure to be distributed among a much larger population over a much larger area. Independence from a physical building allows for larger populations to participate efficiently with enough checks on voter fraud to provide a secure voting system.

The most obvious criticism of democratic reforms is the access it grants to the general public. The best way to diffuse the potentially devastating consequences is to restrain or restrict their powers and responsibilities. Many of the responsibilities maintained by the republican legislature could easily be transferred to a democratic chamber without endangering the state or nation. True democratic formats might be more acceptable within multi-legislatures where responsibilities can be delegated to the popular chamber without diluting the specialized leadership professional politicians provide.

Democratic chambers can be premised on different methods for vote calculation. Function can be engineered into the chamber by allowing the results within the individual jurisdictions to earn values not predicated exclusively on the number of affirmative votes for the measures or laws. Systems can be made more stable by reducing the standard deviation away from actual votes or by maximizing it with an averaged value from a midpoint. Predictability is an important part of engineering political systems but sometimes the measure of change itself produces more change. Producing a variable mechanism should motivate more participating from the public with incentives for public planners to actively promote more registration and active involvement. There are five primary vote calculation methods.

xxx. Direct Democracy (non-republican)
    1. Structure
           i.   Straight
                1. Representative
                2. Winner Take All
          ii. Leverage
        iii. Cumulative
        iv. Registered
         v. Senatorial
                1. Arbitrary
                2. Average

Straight voting is what one would expect. The number of votes earned by the winning argument is tallied with the other jurisdictions and the combined figure determines the outcome of the election or vote. This is also a winner take all election. Only the values for the winning argument are tallied with the other values. It is the most conventional of vote counting methods with the most familiar of voting processes. If a jurisdiction with a population of 100 residents holds a vote and only 60 people cast a ballot, with 40 affirmative and 20 contraries, 40 votes will be tallied with the affirmative votes of other jurisdictions. If the same town voted and the result was 20 in the affirmative and 40 negatives, then only the 40 No votes would be tallied. The total number of Yes votes and No votes from the various jurisdictions are compared with the result dependent on answer with the larger figure.

It is what one expects within a popular democratic election. A slight variation on this method involves counting all answers in all jurisdictions and using that figure to determine the outcome of an election or vote. For instance, if in town A 100 people vote, with 60 voting affirmative and 40 voting contraries, and in town B 80 people vote, with 40 voting affirmative and 40 voting negatives, the final result will be 100 voting affirmative and 80 voting negatives. This looks to have the same result of a winner take all system, but this method is much more accurate when polling larger populations.

If town A has 100 voters, when only 40 vote affirmatives, with 20 voting contraries, when only the 40 affirmative votes count it has a much more dramatic impact on final results than if the 40 affirmative votes were offset by the 20 negative votes. In one instance, the difference is 40 votes and with the other method the difference is only 20 votes. This could be pivotal in closer votes where the difference in votes excluded could have an impact on the final result. A Representative tally would ultimately contribute more accurate information to the analysis occurring after the vote. It would be supported better by actual demographic and ideological partitions.

Leveraged voting is only slightly more complex. Instead of tallying only those votes that carried the measure the value is comprised of total of number of residents within the jurisdictions. If a population of jurisdiction of 100 residents holds a vote and only 60 votes with 40 for the measure and 20 against the full 100 population is applied in the affirmative when tallying the result with other jurisdictions. Likewise, if 60 votes with 40 voting against and only 20 voting in the affirmative, a "No" vote captures the entire 100 votes prescribed to the jurisdiction. There are deficiencies with this method, especially when large populations have low voter turnout, but the advantages are that votes and elections can be more easily predicted with the fixed value of leveraged population used in the calculations.

A cumulative voting method is similar to the leveraged method except that it only tallies active participants. If a population of jurisdiction of 100 residents holds a vote and only 60 votes with 40 for the measure and 20 against the combined figure of 60 votes is applied in the affirmative when tallying the result with other jurisdictions. Only active voters are counted but this process provides a significant advantage to more active and larger jurisdictions. It acts as a force multiplier with advantages scaled up in accordance with population by a factor of activity.

The registered method a hybrid between the cumulative method and the leveraged method with only registered voters being applied to the result. The figure will be much smaller than total populations but larger than participating voters. It will motivate city and state planners to pursue maximum registration rates in the jurisdiction. This will improve the jurisdictions influence within the election system and will contribute to a more informed electorate.

The senatorial methods allow individual jurisdictions to come to a conclusion on a vote and translate it into a fixed figure or ratio applied to the entire system. There are varieties of senatorial democratic voting that can be applied. The first applies one fixed value to each jurisdiction regardless of the population or other attributes. The second established an average or ratio of votes per population similar in republican chambers

If a population of jurisdiction of 100 residents holds a vote in an Arbitrary Senatorial system and only 60 votes with 40 for the measure and 20 against an arbitrary value of 1 is applied in the affirmative when tallying the result with other jurisdictions. Obviously, this method overwhelmingly favors low population and more numerous municipalities. Larger jurisdictions will be under-represented if it captures an arbitrary value rather than a ratio value. Despite this failure in accuracy, Senatorial forms of representation are extremely popular in most contemporary Democracies. This demands its inclusion within True Democratic chambers.

The second option is based on ratios. If a population of jurisdiction of 100 residents holds a vote in a Ratio Senatorial system and only 60 votes with 40 for the measure and 20 against an averaged value of 10 is applied in the affirmative when tallying the result with other jurisdictions. The figure is dependent on some ratio of average population to jurisdictional population which in this scenario is 1 vote per every 10 residents. A town with 1000 residents would therefore have a value of 100 applied to the total tally of all municipalities participating in the vote. Ratio based systems are much fairer than arbitrary systems but its value is diminished when compared to the other non-senatorial methods which utilize the same strategies but are more accurate.

The frequency of votes matters when determining the scope of responsibility of the democratic chamber. A monthly voting schedule won't be able to accommodate legislation confirmation duties as the number of laws passed during a month will make the monthly vote too cumbersome when information distribution is considered. It may be appropriate for confirmation of appointments, treatise, or excising as they occur much less frequently. Weekly votes will be necessary when the democratic chamber is part of a bicameral legislative process. The schedule will accommodate more votes when needed and can be scaled down when less are needed.

> 2. Components
>> a. Echo-chamber (all functions usurped by referendum)
>>> i. Referendum weekly
>>> ii. Referendum biweekly
>>> iii. Referendum monthly

The success of a voting schedule will be dependent on the method used to distribute information regarding the votes. Democratic chambers with no auxiliary chambers or professional politicians will be exposed to information deficiencies. The state would be in crisis if the democratic chamber was a necessary part of the government structure but there was no successful method for educating and organizing the voting public. It would be disastrous for the public to vote on issues they have not read about or have not had time to contemplate. The state or nation would be set towards an immediate path of decay and decline.

Even when professional politicians are abolished, the legislature can still rely on committees. No eligibility constraints would be permitted, and terms must apply. All of the voting power remains with the public despite the allocation of committee members. These committees allow for a more precise examination of issues prior to the public referendum. This actually provides for greater specialization of candidates as each will be evaluated on the merits of their argument and not prescribed individual powers outside of debate. Committee members would only be concerned with communicating the issues and circumstances to the public which is a direct contrast to professional representatives voting on issues themselves.

The auxiliary chamber can be delegated presentation powers where they dictate which legislation is tabled for popular voting. Procedural rules will protect the franchise of the public in their responsibility for voting on the most important issues. A filter will only allow for more order with issues prioritized and emphasized according to the needs of the nation or state rather than the individual. If necessary, auxiliary chambers can be relegated to deliberation only with the tools necessary to research and argue the issues prior to a popular vote but where no filibuster controls are authorized.

> b. Auxiliary Chamber
>> i. Legislators charged with presentation/filter (veto & Schedule)
>>> x. Elected advocates (by popular vote)
>>> xx. Appointed (by Chamber leadership)

The most obvious choice for electing auxiliary officers is to resource the legislators for candidates. They are more familiar with the process and they already have a working relationship with the public. It would not be hard for an elected legislator to act in the capacity of distributing information to the public for use in a democratic chamber. The elections should remain separate but double coverage is acceptable. It would certainly be a major benefit for the legislators to be able to prioritize the voting schedule and control the filter for the democratic chamber. Those legislators working for the Democratic chamber would have more access to the media and have many more opportunities to address the public. This could translate to more successful elections.

Legislators can come from the either the state tiers or the federal tiers. Both have their advantages. Legislators from the state tiers will align the state governments with the federal democratic chamber. Legislators from the federal tier will align the democratic chamber with the republican legislature. This is a significant decision for political unions and nations. Those unions that favor stronger state rights will benefit from state legislators appointed to the auxiliary chamber. Those nations with federalist characteristics will favor federal representatives acting in the capacity of filter for the democratic chamber.

Legislators can be elected by the democratic chamber through a popular vote or they can be appointed by the leadership within a designated republican legislature. The same division between state rights and federalism exists. Appointed positions will strengthen ties between the republican and democratic chambers making it easier to coordinate and pass legislation.

ii. Executives act as filter (veto & Schedule)
and appoints advocate for presentation
x. Unitary
xx. Presidential
xxx. Attorney General
xxxx. Treasurer.

When executive officers appoint representatives, it introduces a check and balance within the legislative process. Executives normally have a veto but control over the democratic chambers schedule and filter may be more effective. It combines the bully pulpit with the veto and aligns the executive branch with a popular legislative chamber. In many respects, the executive can be viewed as the equivalent Speaker or Prime Minister. In more complicated systems the executive branch may be split into more specific parts in these occasions access to the democratic chamber must be enumerated or stipulated.

When state level executives are able to control the filters of a federal democratic chamber it allows significant influence to be transmitted from the states. State level executives will be more vested in the legislative process within the federal tier when their appointed officials set the schedule and prioritize the votes. It will certainly be easier to organize retroactive passage in the state level legislature when governors can coordinate votes across larger jurisdictions.

iii. Auxiliary Executives Tier
x. Municipal
xx. State
xxx. Federal
iv. Number of Auxiliary Representatives
x. Senatorial – one per jurisdiction
xx. Representative – ratio coupled to
population (or GDP, taxes, etc.)

Municipal officers may be useful if the democratic chamber is organized around municipal jurisdictions. It also decreases the ratio of population served by democratic advocates. However, the number of representatives can be correlated to any population metric or economic metric that can be reasoned. Increasing the number of advocates can accommodate a lower ratio and make municipal tier auxiliaries redundant. A larger number of committee officers will help diversity in the dissemination of information. It will promote diversity in opinion and be less susceptible to coercion or compromise.

All of the powers of a true democratic legislature imitate those of a Republican legislature except they are much more limited and specialized. The fact that most powers are predicated on triangulation and confirmation makes it a powerful partner for other government branches. The powers focus on legislative responsibilities including appointment powers, treaties, and laws. There are five principal domains of power within the democratic chamber. The democratic chambers can excise, appoint, pass legislation, repeal legislation, and confirm treatise.

3. Powers
a. Excising
i. Appointments
ii. Legislators
iii. Executives
iv. Judicial

Excising politicians is a potent power and should be restricted in most charters. It should demand a super majority in support from the popular chamber as simple majorities will make it too accessible and destabilize the government branches. The power can be reformed to only apply to appointed executives rather than any elected officials. This might just inhibit government rather than decimate it. The only other ways a people can exert control over appointed officials is during the legislature's appointment process and this this only proactive.

There is no real way to censure appointments after they are in office. Executive elections are too far in between to be an effective means to reform wayward appointments and the Executive is not likely to be swayed from public opinion only. The dilemma is a double-edged sword in that both the status quo and the reform are unsatisfactory. Prohibiting excising exacts too loose of a control and permitting it applies to much scrutiny with too much volatile. Still, the option for entitlement should be available to the electorate and body politic.

The power to excise elected officials is partitioned into executive, legislative, and judicial aspects to add specialization in the checks and balances between the different institutions. Excising can be an important aspect when dealing with longer term limits and unregulated terms for legislators. Excising may be critical in dealing with those appointed to Supreme Courts with no term limits. It would also be an effective tool to reign in wayward or overly ambitious Excising does not require confirmation from any bicameral process but an Executive might be given veto power in lieu of a supermajority needed.

> b. Confirms Legislation
>   i. Triangulation
>   ii. Bicameral
> c. Repeals Legislation

Confirming legislation is a major component of democratic chambers responsibilities. It is certainly the least controversial. It is important to determine whether the duty can be discharged by virtue of a bicameral process or a triangulation process. Triangulation chambers are generally much more productive than bicameral chambers by virtue of the increased likelihood of successfully passing legislation.

Repealing legislation is more akin to the excise power in that supermajorities should dictate access to this powerful tool. The loss of legislation can leave a vacuum in regulatory power or taxing power that can cripple a state or administration. It can deny citizens access to voting entitlements or welfare benefits. It can also be a powerful measure to check the animal spirits of an earlier legislative session. If reckless legislation is passed in a prior year the recourse to correct must be available. Repeal powers will be a potent power to check dangerous advances in powers from the other chambers or government institutions.

> a. Confirms Appointments (Circuits)
>   i. Exclusive
>   ii. Bicameral

The democratic chamber can be given exclusive responsibility for confirming or it can be relegated to just one part of a two-part bicameral process. Appointment powers often preside over executive agency employees as well as over judicial circuit allocations. Most appointments should proceed without much resistance and a simple majority vote will suffice. This will aid the nation by producing seamless transitions from one administration to the next. A bicameral process for appointments will slow it down tremendously if the public is less cooperative than the republican senators but otherwise the up and down vote can be scheduled immediately after the vote in the Republican chamber. Even if debate is necessary, it should be shorter and more concise having occurred subsequent to the Republican legislature which already dedicated significant resources to the debate.

Confirmation of treatise must occur within a bicameral or triangulation process. Most are simply too complex for a democratic chamber to consider in entirety without the help of a republican chamber. However, by virtue of a treatise's intent most should be reviewed by the masses with access to a popular vote to confirm the agreement. This is a check on the alignment of commercial interests with political interests at the expense of consumer or employees. It is never acceptable for a trade agreement or defense pact to be agreed to without public discourse and popular consent.

    e. Confirms Treaties
        i. Triangulation
        ii. Bicameral

Oversight is another typical legislative power that isn't readily compatible with true democratic chambers. No discrete committees are formed with the intent to scrutinize over the executive branches agencies. It is possible that the appropriate infrastructure is created and that oversight powers can be earned but then the chamber begins to blur its intent and organization with that of more conventional republican chambers.

The same limitation applies to a democratic chamber's contributions to taxing and public finance. Future evolutions and improvements to the true democratic chamber can include powers over budgets and taxes but they can produce more disastrous results more quickly where a span of misallocated budgets and ill-conceived taxes cripple a nation or states within just a few years.

    4. Jurisdictions (zones for tallying votes)
        a.   Municipalities
        b. Counties
        c. States

One of the most important properties of the democratic chamber is how the voting jurisdictions are organized. It complements the voting method in almost every respect. The nation is already dissected into discrete parts with each state divided into counties which are further divided into municipalities. In order to have a competitive democratic chamber all state must employ the same system for voter demographics. It is unacceptable for one state to organize around counties and another by municipalities. For this reason, the attribute list was paired down into only states and municipalities. States can be combined into regions of equal size, but consideration must be made on how to apportion the distinct populations among the jurisdictions.

Jurisdictions must satisfy the lowest common denominator in terms of population or size. This is important for alignment between the cities or counties within the participating state. It matters less to maintain an equivalent sized unit between the states, but each jurisdiction should be paired with a legislature or committee that can use the result of the True Democratic institutions vote. Each vote produces recordable data for use in future legislation production and confirmation processes. Even if measures fail on the national level, there may be enough votes to pass in a majority of lower level jurisdictions.

The city or state legislatures can pass legislation using the democratic vote as a triangulation measure. All it needs is an affirmative vote in the majority for the True Democratic chamber to be used as confirmation. Most legislature chambers are bicameral, and this mechanism gives either chamber the opportunity to circumvent the other. This will maximize legislation production within all of the city, state, and federal tiers. This brings an amazing component of popular will and momentum to the legislative process. It allows for parties to expand politics from 2 dimensions to 4 dimensions with leadership declared from within the federal tier. This could be an incredible accelerant to an amendment process with a huge reservoir of votes being accessible to parties seeking reforms within the Constitution or federal system.

xxxxx. Abolished
1. Executive assumes Legislative Powers
   a.President
   b. Treasurer
   c.Attorney General
2. Authoritarian (Unitary)

An important aspect of a government's structure is whether the legislature has been abolished and which institution assumes the responsibilities. Although this stands to be updated, the two current options are assumption are truncated executive officers (tripartite, bipartite, fractal, etc.) or an authoritarian system (unitary). Executives can always legislate through agency law. The more successful variation will be when individual components of the elected executive branch all have their own agency powers with a means to check each other. Executive law is a potent force in most contemporary democracies and it will translate to an acceptable substitution if due process is temporarily interrupted. The worst-case scenario is when only one primary executive has control over agency law. This is far from optimal but for most of human history this was a legitimate form of law.

The powers of the Legislative branch are also enumerated within the attributes list so they can be delegated between the chambers. Many of the powers are self-explanatory. The powers are;

iii. Powers
    1. Laws
    2. Oversight
        a. Unitary
        b. Judicial
        c. Tripartite Presidential
        d. Tripartite Attorney General
        e. Tripartite Treasury
    3. Ratification (Treaties)
    4. Executive
        a. Foreign (President/ Military/
            Intelligence/Alliances)
        b. Domestic (Attorney General/
            Law enforcement/ General
            Administration)
        c. Commerce (Treasurer/Central Bank &
            Banking/Insurance Agencies,
            Commerce).
        d. Fractal (all executive functions assumed by
            separate committees)
    5. Appropriation (Budgets)
    6. Removed
    7. Appointments (confirmations)
        a. Judicial confirmations
        b. Executive confirmations
            i. Unitary
            ii. Presidential
            iii. A.G.
            iv. Treasurer
    8. Direct Democracy Role
        a. Presentation (Filter)
        b. Deliberation only
        c. Ratification (within the same branch)
    9. Triangulation
        a. Stipulated (Powers apportioned to the chamber)

        b. General (Powers apportioned to the other chambers)

10. Taxing
11. Appointments (Direct, by Majority leader)
12. Elections
13 Amendments
      a. Scope
          i.   Unilateral
          ii.   Bicameral
      b. Width
          i.   Simple Majority
          ii.   Supermajority 60%
      c. Depth
          i.   State affirmed
          ii.   Democratic chamber

Enumerating the different powers is really important for all systems that maintain more than one or two chambers. The separation of powers is also necessary when the executive branch is divided into multiple branches or fractal (departmental) structures. Executive powers can easily be assumed by committees within legislatures with the chairperson acting as CEO and the remaining legislators acting as a corporate board. This permits the most interesting and possibly most useful combinations and intersections of power within democratic systems of representation and governance.

In most conventional democratic systems, the majority party automatically receives chairmanship of all committees (and majorities on all committees) while the political parties independently determine members appointed. The current committee allocation system reinforces the majority status of the majority party by imposing its will on all of the chambers committees. In order for a political system to provide opposition parties or minorities parties more influence in or control over legislatures the committee selection process can be better regulated and provide more opportunity for leadership.

Committee selection is more critical in prime ministerial systems where committee chairs have access to executive responsibilities and true power sharing will result from the improved process. By allocating one member at a time in a rotation the parties have to decide which committee is important and which they want to staff in higher numbers. The allocation process can result in unequal or disproportional numbers of staff on each committee and it can result in opposition parties acquiring majority in select committees at the expense of representation on other committees.

    iv. Committee Selection
        1. Composition
            a. Coalition
            b. Independent

2. Order
   a. 3/5ths rule: the majority party and chamber dictate how committees are formed (conventional).
   b. 3/5ths, one for one, rotating
   c. 3/5ths, incremental, rotating
   d. proportional, one for one, rotating
   e. proportional, incremental, rotating

The current committee allocation systems can contribute to sectarian or partisan tension if the proportion of demographics is stable and they are one of the more important factors when determining elections. A minority will feel as though the government isn't favorable to them when most of the federal elections result in majorities favorable to the other demographic groups. When the minority has less faith in the government it can result in obstruction, dysfunction, and worse. The best way to diffuse this is with a more competitive committee selection process.

There are two methods for allocating seats within coalitions. The first is grouping all of the parties forming the coalition together and forcing them to coordinate their appointments as one organization. Order of rotation is still dependent upon size of party. The winning coalition makes the first pick with the largest component getting the first pick, the second largest getting the second pick, and so on and so on. This continues in order until each individual party's runs out of seats or the coalition runs out of seats. The minority party is comprised of all parties not included within the majority coalition.

They apportion their committee seats by size and number as well. Smaller parties are given a slight advantage in that they have access to better committee selection earlier on. Coalitions often form through concessions and minority parties can take committee selection process into account before staking out a claim. Ordinal picks are important, but the size advantage is much more critical. A larger presence on a committee greatly improves chances of the party producing legislation that it supports.

The second method allows each party to be evaluated in terms of its actual size (number of seats won in the election) with the rotation going in order from greatest to least. This might result in the winning coalition having the first two or three seat allocations but that would only allow the minority party to consolidate seats in other committees. The largest party may not be in the majority coalition and this method will allow it to pick first despite not allocating the largest number of seats.

Current committee staffing processes don't permit any order or number variation. They simply permit the majority party to appoint 3/5ths of the committee seats in any manner they wish. This can be improved by establishing an order to the committee selection process. Order can't be equivocated with equality, as the process can result in either under-representation on certain committees and over-representation on other committees. However, establishing a regimented order will provide opposition parties the opportunity to secure majority positions on several committees - an opportunity they would otherwise be excluded from in conventional processes.

The majority party in the legislature will still control the order of voting and be more likely to control the passage of bills but at least the minority party could expect to pass more bills from committee to the general legislature. In executive legislatures (parliamentarian governments) the majority party will have oversight over the committees they staff in minority proportions granting them recourse when minority parties staffing executive committees with majorities.

The 3/5ths rule is meant to maximize cooperation. If there are 20 committees each staffed with 9 members then the chamber will allot 180 members to committees where the 3/5th rule permits the majority party to allocate 108 members (60%) to the minority parties 72 (40%) in a 435-member chamber (can be scaled up or wound down, depending on the number of committees and the size of the chamber). The majority party will have a hefty advantage despite the small margin of seats over the minority.

A proportional system is meant to impose conditions on membership that reflect the actual ratio of seats owned by each party. If the 435 seats of an institution are split 235 to one party and 200 to the opposition party, this ratio is imposed onto the 180 open committee seats so that 54% of the seats will be apportioned to the party with 235 seats and 46% of the seats will be apportioned to the party with 200 seats. The majority party will only have a slight numerical advantage over the minority party.

The five methods of distributing committee membership will provide varying degrees of opportunity to the participating parties. With a one: one rotating appointment process the majority party maintains the most control over the process and the number of party chairs, but minority parties will still have the opportunity to acquire chairmanship of 20% of the committees if they abandon significant representation on the other committees. Most opposition parties will distribute their representatives over the largest number of committees to gain access to the debate and discussions relevant to each committee. However, a small minority of opposition parties will favor a majority position on a few committees at the expense of representation on the other committees.

An incremental selection process starts with one appointment and adds one after every rotation so that it progresses from one, to two, to three, to four, and ongoing until all of the seats are exhausted. An incremental selection process will allow a party more strategic maneuvering with the ability to quickly staff 4/5ths of a committee or as a means to quickly distribute its members to as many committees. In an incremental process, the minority party stands the greatest chance of securing a chair or majority control over a committee they deem more valuable than others. This will be the most successful method in environments charged with sectarian or partisan divide as it produces the most power sharing without seriously compromising the legislature or government. The 3/5ths rule applies to the number of candidates available for appointment to committees.

If a party acquires the opportunity to appoint multiple seats but can't due to limited members, then those additional seats are forfeited with the next party in order assuming the next value in the individual or incremental allotment of seats. This provides smaller parties a modest efficiency in the process for incremental allotments as they will have access to a larger number of allotments earlier on and able to exhaust only after gaining appointment to the committees of their choice. This is a minor check on the power of larger majority parties who will earn earlier appointments at a lower value.

There are fewer options for Executive branches, but most combinations are more potent in regard to changing the function and essence of a government. Most executive branches emphasize top down control which means considerable power is concentrated within a single individual. Executive Branches have direct access to military assets and law enforcement officers which allows them to defend their policies and priorities much better than a legislature which is often divided by party and split into a large number of districts or jurisdictions.

2.) Executive

    i.) Unitary (standard) – Primary determines subordinates

The most common, earliest, and simplest of configurations is the unitary structure where one executive maintains complete and unchallenged command over the entire executive branch. This permutation offers incredible efficiencies regarding coordinating internal policing with external intelligence and actions, especially regarding foreign policy and treaties but also between commerce and economy. Efficiencies come at a cost with no significant internal check on the abuses of power. This can occur within the domain of economy as regulatory agencies and or legal through policing agencies. One of the most frequent abuses is the refusal to enforce regulations and previously enacted laws. This is exacerbated with free market ideologies which in limited party systems produces an environment where regulations are ignored or enforced for periods of equal length resulting in unpredictable markets.

To mitigate this natural flaw in political science Executive branches can be separated into multiple parts to preserve the net advantage of the branch while introducing internal checks on power. The simplest division is into three parts. A President maintains control over foreign policy, militaries, state departments, and intelligence agencies. An Attorney General maintains control over internal domestic law enforcement and regulatory agencies. And finally, a Treasurer General to focus on the Federal Reserve, economic stimulus, permanent funds or sovereign wealth, sciences, R&D, and infrastructure. The divisions mitigate accumulation in powers during states of emergency or in erosions of system balance between the legislature and executive departments.

More complex systems can marry one component with another, so combinations of Presidential/Treasurer, Presidential/Attorney General, or Attorney General/Treasurer occur. These may introduce efficiencies without devolving back into a unitary structure. These combinations can be labeled tripartite, bipartite, or bifurcated and may offer more flexibility when married with more sophisticated legislature or judicial systems. Not only can the powers be assigned on a permanent basis, but more complicated multiple executive systems can manufacture for themselves a system to delegate or auction executive powers between the executives during or between election years, possible as a system of competitive budgeting or corporate governance.

ii.) Divided; all individually elected, primaries determine subordinates
      x.) Compartmentalized
            c.) Treasurer/Central Bank, Science,
                Permanent Funds, Commerce,
            cc.) President/ Military/ Intelligence/ State,
            ccc.) Attorney General/Law enforcement/ Regulatory/
            General Administration
            cccc.) Fractal – each department or agency elected or
                appointed individually
                a. Division
              1. Departments (Secretaries)
              2. Individual (Agency)

The fourth option is a Fractal structure (departmental) which provides an opportunity for the public to elect each agency or department director independently. It should be noted that this differs from an Executive Legislature because the agencies are not governed by committees but rather specific individuals. The Fractal structure eliminates almost all concerns of individuals assuming too much power during states of emergency. A Fractal system permits leadership to be tailored to the agency rather than the party allowing for a more flexible election process. In contemporary liberal versus conservative political divisions, it would permit the electorate to install more conservatives within the military and law enforcement agencies with liberals retaining executive control over the regulatory and economic agencies. This might result in significant advantages for the state or nation.

iii.) Abolished (Congress assumes responsibilities and
        internally determines agency chairs or department
        secretaries)

Executive branches can be abolished with the powers and responsibilities usurped by legislative or judicial branches. The function will be dictated by the powers prescribed to the branch within that section's options. Executive legislatures are just one possible solution with executive powers able to be apportioned to judicial branches or reserve branches as well. Less mature federal systems and economic unions may incorporate legislatures and court systems without an independent executive branch. It would then be the responsibility of the member states and nations to enforce any of the laws and regulations established by the legislature.

Judicial Branches need not necessarily maintain the contemporary structure of interlocked and hierarchical circuits. Instead, Justices can be appointed or elected to Congresses, representative of population or some other criteria, with an annual internal vote determining which judges are appointed to which committee. Committees will replace the different hierarchical circuits within the court system. This permits the Judicial Congress to rotate individuals within committee to minimize abuses of power, be it on an annual basis, a term basis, or life tenure basis (i.e., permanent). It limits the monopolization of a circuit or court by a party due to specific appointments with the new majority granted authority to adjust every year. This can accommodate changes in voting preferences of the public while preserving the inherent stability court systems need.

3.) Judicial
    A. Structure
        i.) Independent Circuits (like family/ criminal/ superior/ supreme)
        ii.) Congressional structure with internal votes forming committees

    B. Powers.
        i.) Judicial
        ii.) Legislative Sub Routine
        iii.) Executive Sub Routine
        iv.) Reserve Sub Routine

The number of justices in a Congress can be determined by population or made representative of some criteria like number of states or counties, GDP, or a jurisdiction's tax liabilities. This is of critical importance as the caseload should normally determine the number of judges. A larger number of justices do not dilute the prestige of the court system. In fact, it makes deliberation more effective and minimizes the impact of outlier verdicts and opinions. It reduces the negative consequences of a bad appointment or an ineffective judge. A Congressional Structure naturally allows for more points of view from more demographic groups, with more research performed, and more facts to be presented. More judges within larger populations will speed up the time it takes for civil and criminal matters to be processed with due diligence. More importantly, a larger number of judges allow more specialization within the courts for more precise and accurate verdicts.

Most judicial branches will be pre-occupied with discharging the typical responsibilities of justice and law but there will be times that they assume individual responsibilities from the other three branches. The attribute matrix provides the flexibility to attach powers through subroutines. This can occur during periods of emergency, the powers can be prescribed at the inception of the institution, or they can be bestowed by some other branch by amendment. Many of the tripartite executive branches assume appointment powers over the Judicial which might legitimize justices assuming more specialized executive functions. In other instances, the judicial department should be granted access to traditional legislative powers like oversight or confirmation as they fall within similar domains of authority

C. Transmission
    i.) Elected
        x. Representative of population (like House)
           tethered to individual jurisdictions
        xx. Unrepresentative (like US Supreme Court,
           or Senate) with a stipulated number of
           justices untethered to jurisdictions

    ii.) Appointed
        x.) By executive
           1. Unitary
           2. Presidential
           3. Attorney General
           4. Treasury
           5. Determined by the committee/ circuit
        xx.) By legislature

After the number of justices is determined, it must be stipulated whether the group is elected or appointed, and if appointed, appointed by whom. With more complicated political systems come more sophisticated appointment powers. Specific circuits and committee can be appointed by specific executive or legislative branches. This is especially useful in Tripartite executive structures where judicial appointment powers can provide a check to domestic policing powers with the President or Treasurer General delegated authority while excluding the Attorney General from the process.

    ii.) Appointed
        x.) By executive
           1. Unitary
           2. Presidential

>   3. Attorney General
>   4. Treasury
>   5. Determined by the committee/
>   circuit (stipulated)
>   xx.) By legislature

Elections for judges do mitigate the threat of conflicts of interests within political appointments. They also guarantee that the court's ideology keeps pace with the general populations ideologies. Both impart a measure of stability that is lost when other elected officials appoint judges for indefinite or permanent terms which causing a dislocation in representation and execution within government institutions.

Reserve branches offer a government the invaluable opportunity to recycle previously elected officials and preserve their years of experience within the government within an institution with abbreviated powers. Reserve branches can be relatively simple with all public officials maintaining eligibility or they can be partitioned into separate parts for different party or branch members. Admitting all retired officials is the easiest method to immediately constitute a Reserve body for a new government institution. A greater number of participants do imbue greater legitimacy as it is harder for one party or one generation of officials to dominant the dialogue or powers of the branch. For maximum utility, the Reserve branch can be composed from previous elected officials from different tiers and branches of government so that more precise checks and balances can be installed.

Even more sophisticated reserve branches can be self-admitting with current members authorizing new memberships based on terms. This better ensures the highest quality of official is admitted within the Reserve branch rather than opening membership up to one term retired officials who demonstrated no particular affinity for politics or integrity. Reserve branch members can even be appointed so that the number is naturally measured, and the participants can be vetted.

4.) Reserves (continuing to use retired political
representatives)
>   i.) members
>   a.) all retired elected officials
>   b.) self-admitting (internal party vote)
>   i. Terms
>   ii. Permanent
>   c.) appointed (determined by previous
>   position, speaker, whip, president)
>   i. Term
>   ii. Permanent

Reserve branches offer an incredible opportunity to continue regulating political officials after their terms expire. With Reserve branch responsibilities come restrictions on employment and permanent salaries. This can mitigate the more corrupting forces within a democratic government where private sector companies can coerce politicians with lucrative positions after they are unelected from office. The Reserve Branch members will continually draw a public salary and be precluded from employment in the private sector. The incentive to forward the agenda of powerful corporations is diminished with the permanent salary and permanent oversight over politician's finances. If there are no elections for Reserve Branch members corporations can't exert pressure through campaign contributions. This will provide an interesting check on the other elected branches of government which might still be influenced by businesses or the wealthy.

There are powers that are indigenous to Reserve Branches and those that can be borrowed from the other branches. The traditional Reserve powers are the power to Repeal, Excision, Excommunication, and Triangulation. With a consensus between a two chambered Reserve branch, a simple majority in a unicameral structure, or most chambers within multi-cameral structures, the Reserves can employ the Repeal, Excise, or Excommunication powers. The Reserve Branch acts as the rear guard and protects the body politic from outlier political maneuvers or unwarranted pieces of legislation. These actions should not occur at a high frequency and will require a bi-partisan effort among different chambers and retired party members, but they can be instrumental in the institutions self-regulating itself. The Reserve Branch should have considerably more experienced career politicians within its ranks which justify their high caliber powers.

If the traditional powers of the Reserve branch are not adequate, new powers can be prescribed to the Reserve branch or it can assume those of other chambers and branches. Most executive and legislative powers can be delegated on an individual basis or in lots of traditional groupings. The Reserve branch can more easily assume legislative powers with the ability to confirm appointments, write and confirm legislation, oversight, ratify treaties, and the other responsibilities ordinarily delegated to similar bodies. Judicial powers aren't transferred too easily but in moments of crisis concessions can include Reserve branches with access to appellate courts or lower level circuits.

ii.) Powers
      a.) Executive (sub routine)
      b.) Legislative (sub routine)
      c.) Judicial (sub routine)
      d.) Exclusive Reserve
            x.) Repealing; Legislation
            xx.) Excising; Executives, Legislators,
               or Judges

xxx.) Excommunication; removing reserve
branch eligibility
xxxx.) Triangulation (can confirm laws from one of
two other chambers but can't write laws).

Repealing legislation is a powerful check on the Legislatures authority. Repeals can occur immediately after the passage of a bill or years later after the consequences have been deemed dangerous or detrimental. This will make the overall political system more conservative with the number of passed bills and legislations subjected to the threat of repeal from both the Reserve chamber and General Legislatures. Executive branches with triangulation powers instead of veto powers would accelerate the rate of passed laws warranting a more mature repeal process and allowing the two to offset each other's advantages.

With a super majority within one chamber or consensus between multiple Reserve chambers the institution can Excise currently elected or appointed legislators, executives, or justices from office. Reserve branches should not agree very often considering the natural split in party or regional affiliation so when consensus is earned it implicitly authorizes the severe actions. Fear of retaliation should limit the number of unjustified excising attempts with the other party or parties likely to gain consensus in a counter-movement and orchestrate similarly aggressive maneuvers.

According to a sum over histories explanation of history for prediction of behavior, these episodes will be unavoidable but that doesn't mean they can't be checked by a Veto by the Executive. The instances where an opposition party maintains a supermajority in the Reserve branch will be small and the frequency will be even less when the Executive branch won't be able to defend against these episodes with a Veto. Most excised legislators will immediately gain access to voting within the Reserve branch which inherently diminishes the majority abusing the excise power. There are many self-limiting attributes which make the Excising powers more acceptable than first impressions typically impart.

Excommunication is a similar power to Excision although it only concerns members of the Reserve branch. This allows the chamber to self-regulate and disjoin members guilty of crimes or misdemeanors that embarrass or threaten the body politic. This power must be restrained to super-majority proportions as well to help ensure that one dominant party does not overwhelm a smaller less relevant party and exclude them unjustly from the Reserve system. This is true even in cases where one political party has been relegated to history with no active members in the General Legislature or Executive branches to defend them.

Triangulation is a power that permits one branch to confirm the actions of another branch but where there are multiple chambers or branches each vying for confirmation in competition with the others. The institution with triangulation powers will usually be the odd member so that it can select legislation from multiple sources to confirm. Generally, this pertains to legislation with an executive branch or reserve branch confirming legislation passed by one chamber of a multi-chamber legislative branch at the expense of dissent from the other chamber or branch. Repeal powers might slow the pace of legislation, but Triangulation powers will accelerate the number of passed bills.

iii.) Structure
      a. Bifurcated by party (multi-Cameral);
      b. Unicameral (indiscriminate)
      c. Fractal; organized by decade (or increments that
           produce odd numbers, singularly or in tandem
           by position within boards and legislatures (with a delay in
           activation of the reserve body politic until the imbalance is
           achieved if necessary to perpetuate the ordinary progression
           of politics).

Consensus is necessary to deploy any of these powers and that completely depends on the structure of the Reserve branch. Unicameral systems allow for a more dynamic interface between retired politicians and currently elected government with less of a check on the powers of the Reserve Branch. Unicameral structures should be used more often when the Reserve branch assumes those powers of other conventional branches of government and less often when apportioned the special Repeal, Excise, and Excommunication powers.

Multiple chambers for Reserve Branches provide innate checks on the powers of the branch by making it much less likely that consensus is reached. The Reserve branch should be an auxiliary part of the government with its most important powers used during crises or where most retired officials agree they should be used. Chambers of Reserve branches can be dedicated to individual parties (or coalitions of parties) so that its members with self-admitting or appointment powers primarily influence their own parties Reserve powers.

Fractal organizations allow for multiple chambers to be engineered around decades, parties, branches, or other indices to produce an odd number for convenience in authorizing Reserve powers or for a more precise control over the Reserve Boards. Increasing the number of Reserve components might improve the likelihood of achieving the consensus necessary to implement any of the powers. Different generations of the same party may have different intentions or preferences imparting some predictability or flexibility within the branch. Peer pressure is always a factor and a majority should be easier to earn with smaller and more distinct groups of retired politicians.

It is very important to stipulate the exact pool of retired officials eligible for election or appointment to the Reserve branch. The specific branch and tier of official can be determined in accord with the apportioned powers so that a pool of retired state level governors acquire powers to check an executive branch or a pool of state legislators can apply continual oversight over the currently elected federal Congress. Retired officials need not be constrained to the same branch they served in.

iv.) Pool
    1. Tier
        a.) National
        b.) State
        c.) Local (county + municipal)
    2. Branches
        a.) Executive
        b.) Legislative
        c.) Judicial

When necessary, the Reserve Branches can be engineered with a parameter or time frame requiring a confirmation from the legislature for continued use; this would permit governments to experiment with different combinations of Reserve branches knowing they are temporary in nature unless re-confirmed. This allows for older nations to introduce the Reserve Boards within the framework of its constitution or government without disrupting the current checks and balances within the system. A system of temporary authorizations will increase the number of different Reserve Boards created within the Reserve Branch maximizing the likelihood of successfully integration and minimizing the occurrences of failures due to abuses in powers.

Term lengths are one of the most important attributes for Reserve members. Reserve members aren't elected. When legislators lose an election or are forced to retire, they earn a term in the Reserve chamber. These terms are of variable lengths determined by the length of service of the legislator in their primary chamber. The term length for Reserve members can be set at single equivalency allowing the member to serve a term equal to that of one normal term in the legislature. Double and triple equivalency is acceptable too. The Reserve chamber can have a total equivalency so that legislators who serve multiple terms capture the entire length of service in the new Reserve chamber term. A legislator who served for 18 years in the upper chamber would gain 18 more years in the Reserve chamber. If a half total equivalency term is used, the legislator would earn only half of their total service in the other legislature. A Permanent term allows the former legislator to serve out their life in the Reserve chamber, unless they are disqualified by criminal conviction.

v.) Terms
        a.) single equivalent

     b.) double
     c.) triple
     d.) total equivalent
     d.) Permanent
     e.) Half total equivalent

The attribute matrix allows for separate tiers to be engineered independently of each other. Most governments are composed of municipal tiers, state or regional tiers, and then federal tiers. More complicated systems of government now include economic unions. Economic Unions are meta governments that extend some regulator powers and some taxing powers to a group of participating states but where the members retaining significant independence from each other for other matters.

Many federal systems start off as economic unions and over time consolidate regulatory powers, taxing powers, and law enforcement powers. A supremacy clause is usually necessary for an economic union to transform into a more mature political union. There should be no doubt that larger single currency and single language markets are a major accelerant to economy when a universal regulatory system is applied.

5.) Tier
    A. National
    B. State
    C. Municipal (and County)
    D. Corporate
          1. Industrial Nonprofit Regulators
          2. Employee Owned (Resident Owned, Socialist)
          3. (Permanent Funds) C-G/ Private Finance
    D. Economic Unions

Contemporary innovations in public finance allow corporations to receive the classification of government tier. Industrial nonprofit regulators are a critically important aspect of government. It permits professional with the expertise to regulate an industry the legal authority to regulate it. This is typically accomplished through licensing or some other mechanism. It is not the most effective means of regulation. The regulators will have the same education and fail in the same judgment as the members. However, it can function during periods of relative dysfunction within the Congress or legislature.

Another fulcrum for representation will be local communes with resident owned enterprises. These are less common in capitalist states but open societies should invite more diverse ownership systems which will include employee owned or resident owned companies. A larger system of representation can be extrapolated out from this organizational hierarchy. If industries can self-regulate with nonprofit associations, then the cooperatives owned locally will also be permitted to organize themselves into an institution that regulates itself. It may not be optimal but a mixed market economy should accommodate all forms of economic and political organization.

It is intended that permanent fund eventually acquire representation within the government system. The managers will be political appointments by Governors but they will be constrained by fiduciary laws and a profit incentive. This makes them an effective locus for political representation. Permanent Fund managers can be given an institution that operates as some capacity of the legislature, to confirm laws or write laws, which captures the interests of both the citizenry and industry. The permanent fund managers will also self-regulate industry through shareholder activism. The permanent fund managers can organize their ownership shares and push through reforms that benefit employees, consumers, and government stakeholders, despite losses in revenue or depreciation of assets. This should mitigate concerns that industry is unfairly represented within the institution.

Term limits are often a necessary component of all functional democracies. Term limits comes in two varieties. The length of the term is often determined independently for every institution. The total number of terms a candidate can earn office is also determined for each elected office. However, one constraint is often enough, with certain offices limited by either length or number, but not both.

6.) Term limits
    a.) max length of term
        i.) 2
        ii.) 4
        iii.) 6
        iv.) unlimited

Term limits can be too constraining and have a counter-productive result. The deleterious effect of the abbreviated length of terms for U.S. Representatives is evidence that terms should be longer than 2 years, especially in competitive election systems that require significant effort for re-election and involve deregulated campaign finance. The short term predisposes members to way too much undue influence from wealthy contributors and corporations. It has an incredibly corrupting force on contemporary politics with members often required or incentivized to neglect voting constituency interests in favor of corporate or wealthy donors.

Shorter terms favor corporations who can entice representatives with high salaries after public service ends. The shorter terms with more frequent elections make it much more likely that a politician's career ends earlier making them aware of the opportunities available in the private sector. The high salary and low effort company positions are repayment for the unprofessional and untrustworthy representation provided to constituents during the short term.

Terms of only 2 years also depreciate the labor involved in performing the public service as half of their appointment is spent campaigning for the next election which imposes serious constraints on time and effort. Candidates and officers don't develop the intellectual capital to discharge their duties until much later in their careers. However, this is made far less likely with shorter terms and more frequent elections.

Terms of six years are more adequate for managing the time and effort constraints installed within election based systems of representation. They also mitigate some of the undue influence corporations have over the chamber by making the election more infrequent. More importantly, public policy requires time to be expressed in economic terms and longer terms allow for more accurate evaluations of efforts. A public won't be as susceptible to the animal spirits when terms are generally longer than the medias' short attention span.

Those national representatives sitting on intelligence committees or armed services committees should have years of dedicated experience to maximize benefits to the country in regards to national security and oversight. A nation certainly wants their politicians to develop the necessary political or intellectual capital to discharge their duties. However, establishing a maximum number of terms makes it harder and more costly for corporation to unduly influence politicians with lucrative post career positions for large sums of money. Corporations will have to make more investments into new campaigns for more members unlike successful career politicians who can leverage institutional election advantages to minimize corporate campaign donations by attracting a larger number of donors.

Legislators should not have unrestricted access to terms as it predisposes the nation to terrible generational imbalances in cultural and ideology. Labor environments change, demographic environments change, and economic environments change. All of which makes one representative more qualified and more useful than another. This exposes the nation to imbalances in representation despite numerical parity or accuracy. Instead, a system should be developed to encourage politicians whose careers end due to limits to pursue other chambers or offices within the federal, state, or local tiers. Reserve Branches adequately conserve the political capital (experience) while enforcing the pertinent restraint on accumulated power.

b.) max number of terms
     i.) 2
     ii.) 4
     iii.) 6
     iv.) unlimited

It is possible for a politician to acquire significant expertise over the course of 8 - 16 years or longer with moderate term lengths and term number limits. The typical length of service for a working adult from age 25 to retirement is only 40 years which sets an ordinary ceiling or threshold for maximum term length and numbers. Most citizens are only eligible for election at a more advanced age, which is appropriate considering the maturity or experience necessary to author legislation, and provide oversight on executive functions. This gives legitimacy to the argument that shorter terms and fewer consecutive terms are more appropriate. It is also precedent for establishing a ceiling or retirement age for politicians. Senior representatives don't have the same sympathies or interests as younger generations, and this could contribute to a serious imbalance in representation.

c.) constraints on number of terms
       i.) Lifetime Maximum (sum)
       ii.) Intermittent (reset after absence)
       iii.) Unlimited

There is an important distinction between consecutive terms and total terms. Consecutive terms are only those where re-election is earned immediately after the preceding term. This usually determines institutional advantages, which makes a lower number of consecutive terms safer regarding maintaining accurate representation between demographics and generations. Establishing a threshold for total terms allows an elected official to leave office after defeat or a switch between government roles and then return but with an extension of maximum number of terms. Establishing controls on both consecutive terms and total terms so that officials can be forced out of office for a few terms to return with only a slightly higher threshold of remaining terms of eligibility is appropriate to conserve political capital and expertise while mitigating the threat of excessive accumulation of institutional power.

d.) restraints on terms
       i.) Sum of both elected and appointed
       ii.) Sum of all elected
       iii.) Per individual office/region

The structure of the election is incredibly important for determining how the government is modeled. Democratic elections involve many variables including campaign donation regulations, election coordination (Presidential or Prime Ministerial), and whether they are popular elections, or are more insulated with electoral colleges or appointed representatives. Most elections involve competitive campaigns with multiple opponents pitted against each other in public debates and T.V. advertisements. Whether these contests are funded by public sources with prescribed tax contributions or by private more competitive sources determines how susceptible the system is to corruption.

These attributes can make one system magnitudes more conservative than other systems. They affect how quickly the government apparatus adapts to crises and circumstances, how fast it progresses towards labor rights, and how likely it is to adopt civil rights protections and Universal Suffrage. They can also dictate how susceptible they are to corporate money, government money, or foreign money. Most citizens make policy choices based exclusively on how popular the options are in their immediate vicinity and culture. They are in fact mirrors of either restrictive or progressive policies meaning that they conditioned by exposure to favor either political inclination.

7.) Elections
    a.) Campaign Donations
        x. Publicly Funding
        xx. Privately Funded
            i.) citizen only
            ii.) citizen and corporate
            iii.) government (corporate equivalency)
            iv.) open (citizen, corporate, and foreign entity)

The soundest way to organize democratic elections is through public campaign finance. It helps the nation to develop diversity in candidates that might otherwise be compromised in a private campaign finance system. Many of the best examples of democracies all employ public campaign finance and it is arguable that their citizens enjoy more equitable economies with stronger labor protections, more civil liberties, with higher voter turnout, and less institutional corruption.

Corruption is less of an issue when corporations can't use their incredible economic power to win themselves less regulated labor markets and lower taxes to earn more profits and distribute more campaign donations to protect those privileges. When economic conditions deteriorate the enticements by corporations appear larger and become more effective. Moneyed politics is a "Might Makes Right" system where poorer citizens are less represented and therefore are less likely to acquire the economic opportunities and capital in the future. It's a vicious cycle that leads to wealth inequality, political instability, and eventual decline. However, there are democracies that choose to open their elections to private campaign contributions.

No doubt there will still be examples of democratic governments that accept the risks of private campaign finance. If this is the case the estate or nation must first decide whether its independent citizens can participate. Then it must decide whether corporations can. If Corporations can make campaign contributions, there should be discussion of what boundaries and conditions exist for the entitlement. The last possible source for political donations is governments. They too should be constrained by reasonable laws to protect the integrity of elections.

Corporations can be both privately owned or publicly owned and those that are listed on the stock exchanges or have multiple owners should take the diversity of those owners' political beliefs into question prior to donating to a party or candidate. It should be unlawful for management to transfer corporate dollars to political candidates unless they are in proportion to the listed affiliations of stock holders with management shares redistributed by the same proportion a second time. There should be no concessions made on this issue as executive's incentives aren't completely aligned with shareholder preferences especially if they come from different demographics, income brackets, and where a nearly half of all securities are typically owned by pension funds including public pensions.

Politicians construct tax policies, trade policies, and regulatory systems which make any political donation by the corporation more potent than the initial intent. The use of shareholder equity to forward the designs and ambitions of company executives is unwarranted and closer to theft than any legitimate representation of interests. The best examples of this are public and private pension fund investments into companies favor candidates that don't synch up with pensioner beliefs. Most pensioners are not aligned with management regarding the labor policies they enforce, the fiscal policies they advocate for, and the misuse of natural resources, and especially the forceful deregulation stance posited. When political contributions are involved, the fiduciary duty encompasses more than profits as the costs include tax penalties, subsidies, or remediation and often accumulate in amounts greater than the original investment.

Unrestrained corporate campaign donations set precedents for state governments and local governments also making campaign donations. Corporate charters should be given no powers that municipal charters and state charters don't have. Other governments are actually more responsible political donors than corporations which are far from representative of the populations employed by them or which purchase their products.

Government campaign donations may be one of the only ways a democracy can protect itself from the coercive effects corporate access to political contribution. A party pledging better labor rights, unionization, more regulations, and progressive taxes would improve its chances for beating a party espousing pro-corporate policies including deregulation and regressive taxes, despite their advantage in corporation donation, when they can distribute state or city tax revenues through the various allied Governors offices and Mayoral offices. It is a source of political contributions that can rival corporate donations when combined with donations from employees and consumers.

b.) Structure
      i. System
            x. Presidential (antagonistic or
               unsynchronized with legislature)

xx. Parliamentarian (majority
in legislature determines executive
officer)

Many citizens don't recognize the difference between Presidential Elections and those with Prime Ministers. Presidents are typically elected independently from their legislatures resulting in scenarios where the President can win office but then face a Congress where the Opposition Party is a majority. When Prime Ministers are elected, they implicitly have the support of the political party winning most seats in the primary legislature. Prime Ministers can enact reforms more easily and have the political power to enact laws that coincide with campaign promises and agendas. Parliamentarian governments are much more efficient passing laws more quickly and in greater numbers.

Presidents can sit idle for years prior to earning the political support for a mandate. Inefficiencies in the system of representation are abused more easily as it is far easier to limit the rate of progress or reform simply by refusing to enact new legislation. Take for example a bicameral legislature in combination with a Presidential Veto. The likelihood of successfully passing reforms is minimal with a split congress occurring half the time, an antagonistic congress occurring one in four times, and majorities in both chambers having a frequency of only one in four instances. This contributes to a 25% chance to pass legislation before the Presidential Veto is taken into consideration. A Veto changes the frequency of passing laws to 1 in 8 or approximately 15%. During crises, this could spell doom for the nation. Worse, is that this innate inefficiency causes parties to seek compromises and to give concessions that seriously undermine the strength of all regulations and tax systems. The low legislative production rate results in a lower number of lower quality laws rather than a moderate number of more reasonable laws.

Coalition governments improve this ratio to nearly 1 in 1 with only one chamber of congress and no self-limiting Veto power necessary. With a 100% success rate the quality of regulations improve as well as increasing the frequency of passed laws. There is no evidence that suggests that these systems are prone to frequent and disruptive repeals which would be the single best argument for maintaining an antagonistic bicameral legislature. There is also no evidence that Parliamentarian systems are more prone to despotism or political fanaticism which was the philosophical underpinning for a bicameral process with presidential veto. More representative governments are sounder governments with more equitable economies and more moderate populations.

Universal Suffrage is an ideal. Voting systems need not be relegated to one vote for every eligible person. Instead, votes can be distributed according to the value of asset, number of stocks, number of acres, or in relationship of part to whole, or some other pre-set calculation. As previously discussed, many of the more successful democracies formed as the result of hundreds of years of reform. These nations started with land based or wealth based systems of representation and only recently required Universal Suffrage.

        ii. Vote
            x. Number (One stock or One Acre = One vote or Ratio)
            xx. Part: Whole (Asset Value = Number of Votes, coefficient)
            xxx. Combinational (Weighted Part: Whole)
            xxxx. One Citizen = One Vote

Although not always a political reality, Democracy is premised on one vote per citizen. It is an exceptionally good measurement for a legitimate and efficient government. However, more complicated governments with more branches and departments might actually gain efficiencies by introducing variations in voting systems for those particular parts. It might be more convenient to permit one chamber of a bicameral legislature to be determined by stock ownership and the value of bond assets in order to introduce significant corporate and economic interests into government while simultaneously eliminating private campaign finance and maintaining the standard one person one vote mechanism for the executive branch and second legislative chamber. It might even be more appropriate for new institutions to be incorporated with the enhanced voting entitlements so that older power bases remain intact. A third legislative chamber with triangulation powers and premised on wealth representation might be a serious improvement to a bicameral process, as long as those wealth based entitlements distribute voting rights to a diverse cross section of citizens or residents.

All senate structures are direct arguments and contradictions of the primary premise of democracy as majority rule. Senates aren't representational of populations as each city or state is afforded and equal number of senators regardless of population. Obviously, the one person one vote rule is violated when comparisons are made in regard to ratio of senators to represented citizens. However, senates can be an effective hedge against abuses levied by a majority but are more easily abused by minorities gaining a disproportionate amount of influence in the nation or union. Minorities can be extremely effective at obstructing government and the progress of civil rights, economic rights, and developing well-funded and strong public sectors. Political Systems with too many protections against majority rule are prone to extreme periods of dysfunction and susceptible to instability.

If one readily accepts the deficiencies involved in Senatorial representation, then one must as earnestly consent to the deficiencies of wealth based representation. Wealth based representation can be manipulated to a greater extent than Senatorial representation providing some meaningful improvements. One such method for voter representation is value voting. Value voting assigns votes in accord with some other factor, like income or income tax. The amount of income tax paid translates to a raw figure used in tabulating elections or legislative votes. Make no mistake, might makes right with this method but most of the political force of a democracy will continue to be found in the middle class who will combine average individual values with staggering numbers of instances within the group.

Value voting can be reformed by introducing a scale of representation with brackets reflecting a static amount of representation. The premise is similar to how tax brackets are formed except that rather than producing a percentage of taxes owed an integer is substituted for vote representation. This figure conveys a numerical value for voting. Those in the lowest voting bracket would maintain a one to one ratio for votes per person, those in the middle bracket would gain a two to one ratio of votes per person, while the top income bracket would confer a vote multiplier of 3:1. Note that this ratio translates to 1 voter per person, 2 votes per person, or 3 votes per person. In other value voting systems, a larger proportion of the total vote might go to the top 10% of income earners who pay a much larger proportion of taxes in terms of the total number of payers. In effect, this would constrain the top 1% of income earners to a total of 3% of the vote where they might otherwise capture 10% or 20% with more liberal voting entitlements.

A value voting bracket should skew voting powers to the middle classes with the raw voting power of the first three income quartiles continuing to outnumber the voting power of the 4th income quartile. The middle class tend to be more representative of the whole population anyway. It includes professionals, union members, public sector employees, and small business owners. A large proportion of the 4th quartile is still considered middle income, especially by standards set by the top 1% of income earners, which will bolster the raw voting power of the middle class in the middle two income quartiles.

Combinational value is similar to value voting, but it provides individuals with a number of votes equal to the number of persons living within the jurisdiction they are in charge of, under their direct command, or within the same department or agency. In a combinational voting system citizens would be afforded one vote apiece, their mayor would gain access to a number of votes equal to that of the town, a county executive would earn an equivalent number of votes as the number of residents in all of the participating towns, while the Governor would leverage a number of votes equal to the entire population of the state. The method is reminiscent of feudalism and can be applied to corporate, military, or governmental elections and appointments (confirmations). This is intended to be less democratic and more authoritarian in nature.

If the state had 1 million residents split into 10 counties with 100,000 residents each, for a total of 100 cities of 10,000 residents, then the Governor would have 1 million votes, the 10 county commissioners would each have 100,000 votes, each of the 100 mayors would have 10,000 votes, and all 1,000,000 residents would each have a vote. The total number of votes in the system is 4 million with the Governor only capturing 25%, the 10 County

Commissioners capturing 25%, the 100 Mayors capturing 25%, and the residents capturing 25%. However, there are other constraints to this voting mechanism.

Politicians can't participate in their own election, but they can leverage their votes in elections for executives in higher echelons. For example, a mayor couldn't vote for himself in his own election, but he could vote in a county commissioner election with the full number of residents of his city. This allows executives to elect other electives in a similar fashion that parliamentarian governments allow the majorities of representatives to appoint their own Prime Minister and government. The residents can participate by electing the executives wielding the combinational vote while also leveraging their own individual votes in economies of scale.

In state elections Governors couldn't participate so 1/3rd of the vote would be earned by the county commissioners, 1/3rd earned by the mayors, and 1/3rd by the residents. If one examined national elections through this prism, it would work out that the Governors would have 1/4th of the total vote, county commissioners would have 1/4th of the total vote, Mayors would have 1/4th of the total vote, and the residents would have 1/4th of the total vote. Obviously, the President would be excluded from all combinational votes by virtue of his apex position. Not all states are equal and those states with larger populations will have proportionally lager voter entitlements. Previous elections would have tremendous impact on future elections with the leverage of populations up through the ranks of executives within the state or nation.

At some future point, combinational value voting representation can be used in true democratic chambers. This will reign in some of the animal spirits that might make the institution less predictable or management than the other institutions. Combinational representation goes against the main premise of true democracy so the attributes are not currently available but that doesn't mean future evolutions can't include more executive control over the chambers. In these instances, all executive would participate allowing them to moderate the results of the democratic votes. In this respect, they could prime the legislative body with affirmative votes to confirm laws with other parts of the legislature.

Each system will have to determine how to structure its own elections. The two most common methods are direct through popular voting and indirect through systems like the Electoral College. A 3rd option is one that insulates elections from the public by relegating voting to the domain of the legislatures. This is the same mechanism by which a parliamentarian system elects their prime minister. A fourth option exists where the President is elected by a consensus of Governors. The State level executives determine the candidates from their ranks and they vote in accord to the number of votes earned by their representatives and/or senators in the federal legislature.

By far the most appropriate and effective method for voting is the most direct through popular voting. It enfranchises the entire population with majority rule which should be checked by a strong alternating binary party system or a more functional rotation in a multiparty system. There is a more practical reason for permitting majority rule to govern a nation – the people must take responsibility for the actions of the nation unlike situations where minorities are vested with the principal political power. This implied responsibility is a burden to all descendants and all voters; it persists even in cases where a minority establishes political control and usurps all the benefits of the state or wages war in the name of the state. Maintaining the integrity of majority rule is extremely important as current administrations and cultures create legacy and history with mistakes often reverberating through history for the length of the state's survival.

c.) Intimacy
      x. Direct (Popular)
      xx. Indirect (Electoral College)
      xxx. Insulated (Legislative dictates)
            i. Upper chamber – majority appoints from their own ranks
            ii. Lower chamber - majority appoints from their own ranks
          iii. Reserves - majority appoints from their own
            ranks
      xxxx. Coalition (a majority of Governors determine executive from their own ranks)
            i. vote equals number or representatives in Upper chamber
            ii. vote equals number of senators in Lower chamber
            iii. each governor is afforded a single vote regardless of population.

Electoral College is an indirect method that produces inconsistent results for popular representation in elections which contributes to political instability and long-lasting feuds. Electoral Colleges are scandalous affairs in democratic countries as they remove the executive branches from popular control. Even inefficiencies as small as 4% differentials between electoral votes and popular votes between states will produce extremely divergent results in political economy over extended periods of time. As the sample size increases so do the outliers and deviance from normalized results. That figure of 4% represents an outcome of 4 times in 100 elections where the imbalance in representation likely results in an unpopular election of a politician to office.

That poor statistic is only in best case scenarios within unadulterated system where party interference isn't an obstacle. Examples of bad behavior that can exacerbate these conditions include voter suppression efforts or manipulating campaign finance laws to dilute representation. Stability is engendered by votes wholly dependent on accurate and popular elections. This does not mean there won't be failures in public finance or governance when majorities can self-regulate and self-govern themselves, but it does mean that more of the population can expect to be held responsible for their errors and mismanagement during office. Where there is inaccurate representation and excessive amounts of waste in the political markets there is less culpability and a greater likelihood of secession, insurrection, civil war, or occupation. At the very least, inefficiencies in the political market produce imbalanced wealth concentrations and poverty which can't be cured as power accumulates within the institutionally wealthy.

Insulated elections occur when democratically elected legislators hold a quorum and reach consensus on electing the chief executive officer for that tier. It's not a direct election but it's not an indirect system like an electoral college either. It is very like how parliamentarian systems elect their prime ministers except that the legislators are already elected, and the election pertains to a branch external from their own. The transitive property transfers legitimacy by prior democratic election for the legislators holding the quorum.

Likewise, a coalition of governors can be bestowed election powers over the chief executive of a federal tier in the same respect legislators can be given the power to appoint an executive. The Governors hold a quorum and the majority verdict determines the outcome of the presidential election. Each Governor can be given a number of votes equal to the number of representatives they have in the chamber that is more representative of population. This will ensure that more numerous but less populous states can dominate elections unfairly. If a nation wants rural communities or minorities to exert more political control over the government, they can elect to have the Governors leverage senatorial votes or individual votes. This is another form of insulated election that is neither direct nor indirect, but which must be considered as valid as the elections held for those individuals participating in the insulated election.

Appointment powers have been enjoyed by executive branches since they were first authorized through popular elections. A legislature typically maintains traditional oversight with all appointments conditional on a confirmation process. In more complicated systems of government, more precise declarations must be made regarding which executive branch is permitted to exercise the appointment power. This book deal primarily in Tripartite and Bipartite structures which divide the executive branch within two or three principal branches which is the main reason why three options are offered.

        d.) Appointed
              x. Tyrannical
                1. Executive
                    a. Presidential
                    b. Attorney General
                    c. Treasury General
                    d. Unitary

2. Legislatures Majority Party
3. Judicial

Appointment powers can be wielded by legislatures just as effectively as executives with a majority leader allowed to install the directors of their choice. When Executive Legislatures usurp all of the previous responsibilities and charges of a unitary executive branch it will obviously need to delegate authority over the apparatus of government. In other instances, a judicial branch might have domain over an agency requiring appointment with confirmation from another branch. The delegation of appointment and confirmation powers are necessary for checks and balances between the various branches or chambers. A government can fall into complete dysfunction with the abuse or neglect of either appointment or confirmation powers. All efforts must be made to ensure they are accessible during even the most dire or stressful of circumstances.

xxx. Eligibility
1. Individual
        A. Citizen
        B. Resident
        C. Alien

On the individual basis eligibility can be made more exclusive by citizenship constraints, residency requirements, or alien entitlements. The alien entitlement can be combined with the citizenship option so that nonresident citizens can hold office. None of the attributes are exclusive and from these three options come an almost infinite number of combinations when systems are engineered with the access provided for specific tiers and branches. Resident aliens might gain representation on the local tier but be prohibited from voting or holding office in state and federal tiers. Nonresident citizens could be an instrumental resource for governing reconstruction or occupation efforts. Other combinations might aid in imperialism and other efforts to engineer empires between otherwise disparate jurisdictions.

By designating difference between citizenship requirements, residency requirements, and alien entitlements one system can coerce compatibility with other foreign systems and larger economic unions. All of these attributes can be toggled independently to manufacture different variations of democratic governments. Governmental tiers can be dissected into city, county, state, and federal with the domains restricted by executive, representative (legislature or reserve), judicial, or by agency in either domestic or foreign jurisdictions.

2. Governmental
        A. Tier
                i. city

      ii. county
      iii. state
      iv. Federal
      v. Union
     B. Domain
      i. Office
        x. Executive
        xx. Representative
        xxx. Judicial
      ii. Agency (Fractal)
    C. Jurisdiction
      i. Domestic
      ii. Foreign
  4. Any

If any specific quality defines a democratic nation, it will be the eligibility requirements for voting. The very fabric of the society and soul of the nation is found in which demographic groups are empowered with representation, in what proportion, and combinations. Most modern democracies don't discriminate between criteria when it comes to administering a popular vote for elections but with more refined and exact systems of representation, stricter regulation of voting hierarchies can produce more efficient systems.

Certain governmental powers can be exercised with more precision and expertise from legislatures exacted from more practiced and knowledgeable legislators and voting constituents. Manipulating voting rights is a treacherously dangerous power to exercise but political engineers can ensure that privileges are delegated responsibly with adequate checks and balances. Voter rights and eligibility criteria can be re-organized according to contemporary social and economic pressures. More sophisticated governments with multiple executive branches and multiple legislative chambers will accommodate the extra specialization necessary to administer larger economic unions and empires.

8.) Eligibility Constraints
  a.) Criteria
     i.) removed
     ii.) removed
     iii.) removed

For centuries land barons dominated medieval Europe and although there was no voting with ballots, the aristocracy voted with pledged soldiers and promised military support in exchange for maintaining titles and access to taxes and income from the land. The Magna Carta was an important development towards Democracy and it was a revolt staged by the landed aristocracy within England that demanded representation in the Monarchy through a Legislature. This would be the basis of future democratic reforms despite the fact it was not a popular form of representation. The United States premised its initial democratic representation on land requirements. It was an aristocratic republic for the first few decades until protesting veterans earned universal suffrage for Caucasian adult males. Wealth based representation is a major improvement to these classical examples of democracy. Wealth based representation are high quality entitlements that protect universal suffrage and majority rule.

Wealth offers the greatest opportunity to enact voter eligibility criteria as a huge variety of different indices can be used which accommodate most citizens of the nation. Representation can be conserved within the system which makes it the perfect substitute for universal suffrage contributing to the specialization in both governmental branches and tiers. Most of the wealth based representation relies on divisions between above median and below median so that the entire public is included within the electorate. Zero values are factored into the below median group to ensure that all citizens have an opportunity to vote. The most applicable wealth based attributes are personal incomes, tax liabilities, and gross domestic product. Each one can be dissected into above median and below median groups. These attributes are not to be confused with representational coefficients which determine the number of representatives per district or jurisdiction, rather than participation in an electorate, despite the similarities in the values used (GDP, population, Tax liabilities, etc.).

iv.) Wealth
    A. removed

    B. Income or Liability based
        i. Source
            a. Income (household and family)
            b. Tax liabilities
            c. removed
            d. removed
            e. removed
            f. Gross Domestic Product

All natural persons in a nation have an income, even if it is a zero value. This makes personal income an adequate attribute to split an electorate. A personal income can be compared to a national median, a state median, or a district median, and the population can be split into two parts. These parts may be equal in size depending on the jurisdiction, but two unequal parts is an acceptable outcome. Ultimately, the population will be split into two (nearly) equal parts when all of the districts or jurisdictions are tallied, depending on the median value used. Class divisions are exception themes in politics and they can improve the quality of representation with role identity and more accurate self-interests.

Tax Liabilities can apply to individuals, corporations, or governments. Individuals can be split into above median and below median groups as easily as income earners. This includes non-tax payers who will be allocated within the below median group. Citizens may pay different amounts of taxes depending on the instrument used and this may differ from the group they would be normally allocated when income is used. When governments pay taxes, it is usually to a higher organizational tier. A municipal government would pay taxes to a state by virtue of its residents paying taxes to the state. A state would pay taxes to a federal tier by virtue of its residents paying taxes to the federal tier. The total tax liability of a jurisdiction or district can be tallied and then separated into above median and below median.

Correlating representation to GDP captures a fair proportion of representation by population but has extracurricular benefits by exporting the region's more successful economic policies through the increased political influence. Large population bases can have lower GDP than small efficiently managed population bases. GDP representation is a measure of the differential and a way to distribute the efficiency across jurisdictional borders. There is the danger that a jurisdiction will vote in accord to its own self-interest and take advantage of other cities, counties, or states but that gross behavior already occurs in most contemporary political systems. Senatorial representation has propagated within most democratic systems and is predicated on disrupting majority rule and providing inaccurate representation.

The term political-economy predates both modern democracy and modern global economy and was used specifically to illustrate the very intimate and intricate relationship economy has with politics; Modern states should employ more precision in defining the roles and powers of the different facets of government in accord with the powers and privileges of the classes of individuals working as legislators or voting for representation within the chamber or branch. The species entertains most ideologies in binary opposition with unchecked capitalism rivaled by ominous communism where both are extremes within one spectrum of political economy. Generally, neither satisfies all that the citizenry require. However, they still introduce significant themes that ultimately benefit the growth of theory and practice which will help leaders and voters navigate the tumultuous exchange of sacrifice and service across generations and national borders. The dynamism between the owner class and the labor class has entertained the race for hundreds of years and more specialized systems of political economy will empower both segments with democratic franchise through the refinement of government institutions and the reinforcing of roles.

Imagine the potential of an entire chamber representative of only employees and laborers offset by another chamber dedicated to the interests of the owners' class and leisure class (institutional wealthy and investors). Normally labor and the owners' class represent opposite positions and it would be easy to predict non-cooperation between two specialized chambers acting in opposition but if both chambers also included the professional class or middle class as a bridge in interests it increases the likelihood that moderate policies will be passed by both chambers. One chamber will admit only below median income earners and the other will admit only above median income earners; this prevents cross corruption from intermingling of campaign donations or other means of influence. The middle class typically votes in larger numbers (with a component unionized) which will be competitive with the upper class which has the capital advantage but not the advantage in votes.

When the legislators more readily recognize the class, they represent and suffer the same economic stressors they will be better advocates for their constituencies. There will be more transparency when everybody appreciates their designated roles. There will be less incentive and less opportunity for ambitious legislators to leverage their votes for another income or asset class without the camouflage of one or two ambiguous national parties with ideologies based on coalition rather than specific interests in economy or society. Multi-party systems can accommodate income based representation better especially in cases where multiple chambers are employed as the parties can specialize their platforms within a chamber devoted to a specific economic class and their associated legislative powers.

Bifurcating the measure into above median and below median segments is one of the most effective means to create distinct populations from one pool of eligible voters. It ensures that all segments of a population are represented and share economic interests and pressures. The more egregious forms of economic oppression through wage suppression and duress modeling must be more forcibly argued in the prism of wealth and class differences. The differentiation of population based on economic criteria will provide the specialization the chambers need to focus more intently on their own economic interests.

ii. Attribute
    z. Value Index
           a. removed
           b. removed
           c. removed
           d. Below Median
           e. Above Median
           f. removed
      g. removed
      h. removed
    zz. District Index

a. Independent
b. aggregate
zzz. Threshold
    i. national median
    ii. state median
    iii. district median

When districts are separated into above median and below median groups, the value can be based on the districts independent value or the states aggregate value. For an example in GDP based representation, if an independent value is used, the district calculates its own GDP. If an aggregate value is used the same district would use the states GDP value to calculate its position in the sequence to determine the median value. Aggregate values will generally separate districts from the same states into the same above median or below median group. Independent values will dissect a state into separate districts, part of which may be in the above median group and the others in the below median group.

zzzz. Instrument
    a.) sales
    b.) property
    c.) income
    d.) capital gains
    e.) payroll
    f.) Total (Combined)

The representation is dependent on the type of instrument being measured. Most states use sales taxes, property taxes, income taxes, and capital gains taxes. There are plenty of other taxes not represented in this matrix and they can all be fairly easily introduced or substituted. The point is more that the representation can be tailored to a specific instrument. Many governmental tiers specialize in a tax and it would be more appropriate for the jurisdiction to utilize only that measure. Any number of instruments can be listed with the values averaged or tallied. Sometimes it is more appropriate for a jurisdiction or tier to tally all applicable tax liabilities. All of the public records and prior histories should be available to aid in organizing the voter entitlement.

Most nations do not control their borders with enough precision to only grant access to approved individuals. Therefore, the nation would be in a position to establish a tiered citizenship system. Resident Aliens could acquire certain rights or privileges over unauthorized aliens. Still unauthorized aliens could gain work permits for certain industries and protections for transit or healthcare.

v.) Domicile

    a. Resident Alien
    b. Citizen
    c. Unauthorized Alien

Voting rights can be relegated to certain lower tiers or specific agency representation. Obviously, states participating in an economic union with other states could elect to empower resident aliens with special suffrage while the other states in the Union are protected by continuing to exclude the alien from federal elections or their own state votes.

b.) Action
    i.) to vote
      ii.) to hold office

Eligibility requirements can be independent, or they can be accumulative. Independent attributes are non-exclusive which means permits citizens satisfying one component of the eligibility criteria to vote or hold office when multiple attributes are listed. Exclusive domains require voters or candidates to maintain all eligibility criteria listed making the population of possible voters or candidates much smaller. More complicated systems of representation will attempt to index divergent qualities to hedge or check the influence or power of any single segment of the population. An example of this would be maintaining a domicile requirement with an income requirement. Neither are related but in exclusive systems both must be satisfied in order to qualify.

c.) domain
    i. exclusive
    ii. non-exclusive

An example of non-exclusive attributes would be indexing one legislative chamber to income earners within the lowest bracket along with income earners from the highest bracket. Obviously one resident couldn't possibly satisfy both requirements. This has an important effect on representation because it conjoins the political power of the lowest income earners who occur in large numbers with the highest income earners which occur infrequently. By offsetting this chamber with another devoted exclusively to middle class income earners it dilutes the richest segment and emphasizes the middle class without mitigating the poorest. This might be an effective check to the corrupting power of private campaign finance which overwhelmingly benefits the highest income earners.

    There will definitely be times when it is appropriate for legislators or executives from different tiers of government to appoint the officers of other branches. This is true in instances of colonial or imperial rulership but also has uses for integrating more efficient command hierarchies between federal and state tiers or within local jurisdictions. Appointed officers can occur within the same jurisdiction which has the potential to maximize efficiencies in governance without depreciating the franchise of democratic rule within the jurisdiction. Political engineers should consider both top down control and bottom up control where elected municipal officers appoint state officials or where state officials appoint federal civil servants. Appointments can occur through the consensus of legislators which would imitate a parliamentarian mode of elections or an executive from lower jurisdictions can vote to install the executives within higher jurisdictions. There is a myriad of different combinations that can be explored in theory prior to implementing for self-governance or union management.

9.) Appointed by
    a.) region
                ii) municipal
      ii.) county
      iii) state
    b.) branch
   ' i. legislature
      ii. executive
      iii.. judicial
      iv.. reserve

Voting isn't a right it's a duty and a responsibility. Advocating for mandatory or compulsory voting for citizens is an appropriate response to the expected malaise that typically overtakes democratic societies and governments. The danger in contemporary governments is that special interest groups and other outlier populations are more likely to vote than average or lower-class citizens. This pressures government engineers into satisfying the demands of minorities rather than the base and contributes to the polarization of political-economy. The product is an unstable government, dangerous to itself as well as its neighbors and others community members.

10.) Voting
    a.) compulsory
    b.) voluntary
      c.) automated

Making voting mandatory is complementary when specializing eligibility criteria for voting and holding office; with greater privileges come greater responsibility. Voluntary voting is the standard for contemporary democracies, but the mode of representation and political governance is relatively new and it can be expected that as political systems evolve more will demand compulsory voting from their eligible citizens.

Mandatory voting presents an excellent opportunity for the state to enact automated voting although it can be used for voluntary systems as well. In automated voting, an individual registers as an affiliate of a political party and all votes occurring within that jurisdiction are allotted towards the predetermined candidate. This will have no effect on primaries with the voter still required to make a selection unless a more exact preference based on ideology can be selected. The individual registers once and doesn't need to personally cast a vote until he elects to suspend the automated voting at some future point.

This should improve voting turnout a great deal by eliminating the effort needed to vote. Voters can be registered upon the age of majority and enrolled within automated voting system that allows the individual to vote regardless of economic or other stressors that generally inhibit voting during elections.

Democracies can suffer from periods of low voter turnout which expose the nation to extreme amounts of danger. When popular will isn't translated into political will the public will be susceptible to fundamentalist ideologies and vote against their interests. This is exacerbated when a strict voting system excludes a large number of poorer citizens. Automated voting will make these populations less susceptible to voter suppression efforts and exploitation that prevents them from voting.

Examine the United States where 75% of the citizens don't vote in 75% of the elections. A minority of 18% dictates most off year elections with off year elections describing 3 of the 4 election seasons. Even in Presidential election years only 76% of the population votes. An automated voting system wouldn't result in a 100% voter turnout, but it could double the number of off cycle voters. The US is critically sensitive to voter suppression movements with access to voting sites regularly obstructed and all efforts are at inhibiting new voter registration and prohibiting voters who actually make it to the sites. An automated voter system will make it virtually impossible for opposition parties to obstruct voting attempts for general elections although primaries will still be vulnerable.

Automated voting coordinates with value voting systems in that voting already requires for labor to be exerted on determining the number of votes cast. At the time of registration an eligible voter can select automated voting preferences and from that period on all of their re-ported tax data will translate into value voting for candidates within the appropriate jurisdiction. It will be far easier to tabulate value voting systems with the use of automated voting as the time required to process the tax information can be distributed more easily during an election period. Mandatory voting and automated voting will make election prediction much easier with turnout almost guaranteed and where prior year econometrics and tax data is available for analysis.

Most democracies won't function correctly if an oligarchy of political parties constricts the political choices voters can make. Every opportunity must be taken advantage of to ensure that binary political systems do not dominate the political markets. Multi-party systems promote more cooperation and coalition building and reduce the deleterious byproducts from peer pressure and lack of diversity. Political Parties can be regulated by size so that smaller units of similar parties exist, but their leadership is individually determined with bureaucracy limiting how efficiently they can market and organize their efforts.

If size is not an adequate limit, then each state or provincial jurisdiction must organize its own party with its own leadership and work to negotiate the regulations governing the marketing of the individual parties so that one brand name does not exist, and a national initiative is harder to organize. Most state representatives and parties have wildly different and often antagonistic interests that compete for funding and legislative priority. Requiring different party names will help identify reoccurring patterns in power distributions and profit sharing. Political parties vary within distant regions with their own conservative and liberal spectrum differentiating the members from one state and another.

11.) Political Parties
    a.) Primaries
        i.) closed
        ii.) Open
    b.) Endorsements
        i.) Two Party System
        ii.) Multiple Party Endorsements
        iii.) Endorsement Parties

A more interesting structure for forming political parties is enfranchising the special interest groups by patenting the issues and permitting those groups to extend or retract endorsements based upon performance. The special interest group can then dictate how all endorsed politicians vote on any measure tabled regarding their interest. This will disrupt the any command hierarchies within a two party or multi-party structure while infusing more integrity within the legislature by limiting politician's abilities to claim endorsement while bargaining votes on that issue for other issues.

Endorsement party structures enables open primaries with multiple candidates to satisfy more individualized constituent groups with more specialized representation. The endorsements are individually tailored and demand performance which means voters will have more accurate representation on the issues the care most about. The endorsement parties themselves should be able to dedicate more resources to debating and deliberating the issues voted on by the professional politicians with less conflict in policy. More sophisticated endorsement systems will permit the endorsed politicians to hold a practice vote prior to the real vote with the result dictating the endorsements party formal and public position on the issue. The era of computer technologies will grant the access needed for more highly organized voting.

Jurisdictions or districts typically define a legislator's constituency. Jurisdictions tend to encompass a whole state, city, or county. For example, if a state is permitted two senators all of the resident citizens are permitted to vote for both offices. The senators are both responsible for representing the same constituency. Districts reduce the State or city into distinct regions with a dedicated constituency. If the state has three districts and three assembly members each is only responsible for representing only one jurisdiction.

The difference is access with jurisdiction wide candidates required to satisfy a larger cross section of interests and district wide candidates allowed to specialize within a smaller cross section of interest. One produces a regression to the mean (or average) while has polarizing tendencies. Both have their individual merits; however, the two methods are not equal; jurisdictions tend to promote more cooperation within a state or city while districts tend to invite political abuses like Gerrymandering.

Although contrary to most critical beliefs, a smaller number of representatives should be accorded to district representation with a greater number allotted to jurisdiction representation; this will permit faster and easier political reorganizations with more binary or symmetrical areas of representation while also dedicating more resources to the representation attempting to satisfy the averaged interests within the jurisdiction.

More complex forms of representation including Legislative Broker and Executive Representation are more accessible with jurisdictional organization which must be considered when engineering a political system. A third qualifier is presented as a means to integrate commercial interests and accommodate corporate statehood if it ever applies. When and if corporations are granted suffrage, they may need more specialized representation which does not necessarily correlate to either Jurisdiction or District but rather Industrial sector or market.

12.) Jurisdiction;
      a. Jurisdiction wide (Senators)
      b. Districts (Representatives)
      c. Sector (Commercial)

After the criteria is established to determine eligible voters and candidates each system of representation must have a method to determine the number of representatives provided to each jurisdiction. Most Democracies correlate representation to population as it is the reasonable and balanced way to organize democratic government. The number of representatives can be correlated to other measures that have important functions within the nation state. For instance, representation based on GDP typically aggregates population with productivity producing a more practical form of representation because it can help transmit the economic ideologies that contributed to the higher economic product. Correlating representation to taxes is an even more sophisticated measure for representation because it combines population, with economic productivity, and fiscal policy. It can help ensure that one subset of the population does not exploit another through unfair gradients in tax policies or exploitative economic policies. It also positive reinforces tax collection by associating political power with the surrendered moneys.

13. Determining the Number of Representatives
      a. Population
            i. Jurisdiction

Most democracies are built around the concept of proportional votes between jurisdictions which are based upon the size of the population in each. The premise of democracy is inextricably associated with popular representation. A least common denominator is calculated and then each population is divided by the figure to produce the representational coefficient. The coefficient equals the number of politicians prescribed to that region or state. This process results in representative government with all citizens earning an equal ratio of representatives: residents. It is by far the fairest and most accurate way to structure representation. Population naturally accounts for economic figures, demographic figures, and civil figures and is the basis for majority rule.

b. GDP
        i. Straight
        ii. Per capita

GDP and similar economic indicators are substitutes to population when establishing the ratio of representatives distributed among the various jurisdictions. There are two variants in the way GDP can be used in calculating the Representational Coefficient. The first is a straight calculation using a least common denominator. The raw GDP figure is divided by the LCD to determine the exact representative coefficient for each jurisdiction. GDP can vary from jurisdiction to jurisdiction with some states being much richer and earning much more direct influence within the system. Exceptions and outliers gain proportionally more or less representation. With the straight calculation of representation, the wealthier jurisdictions can export their economic and political ideologies through the efficiency gained in representation. These are absolute terms which don't take population into account.

The second method is to average the value by dividing GDP by the population. The LCD is determined and divided into each result to calculate coefficient for representation. This is a Per Capita value. When using the Per Capita calculation, there will always be differences in the representation earned by each individual and each jurisdiction, but the variance should be much smaller than the result of the straight calculation. A Per Capita calculation will result in a more equal distribution of representation between jurisdictions. A larger component of the population may be willing to accept this form of wealth representation making it more practical for all intents and purposes.

c. Federalist Tax Policy (Macro Tax Liabilities)
    i. Gross
    ii. Net
        x. Surrendered
        xx. Minimum

Tax representation for jurisdictions can be a convenient means to establish tighter controls on federal or state budgets and check other imbalances within the system of representation. A nation that rewards tax liabilities with increased representation will be stronger and more influential than other nations. They will have better funded militaries and more equitable economies. These are huge advantages for nations over with nations that favor austerity and deregulated economies. Countries that develop cultures that resist tax policies will find their governments under siege with debt defaults and government shutdowns. Wealth inequality will grow along with political corruption, and eventually the people will sow discord and consider rebellion. A nation with more equitable economies with better funded governments with access to healthcare and education are less likely to favor regime change. Tax based representation make it far more likely that nations perform better at economic engineering and wealth control.

Tax representation can be based on net taxes paid or gross taxes paid. Net taxes paid are calculated from the previous year with the total federal or state rebates subtracted from the total remitted. This figure is not proportional representation and it is more than likely that certain jurisdictions will lose their representation due to receiving more federalist tax rebates than contributions. Gross tax representation is based on the total amount of taxes remitted to the tier of government where the representation is earned. The amounts assessed to each region are compared to each other to determine the proportional number of seats earned. The primary mechanism for establishing the comparative values is a ratio of taxes remitted: number of representatives. Each increment produces another representative. Each of the states or regions will be in ratio or proportion to one another

Federalist tax policy is necessary for stimulating lower GDP jurisdictions and should be a major component of fiscal policy. The idea is exceptional, but its application is generally flawed. It is too easy to exploit wealthier jurisdictions where there is an imbalance in representation favoring the poorer and less populous states. A political union's measure of inefficiency is huge differences within taxes paid into a federal system and rebates received. Economic Unions and most Federal governments are based on cooperation and mutual consent; these extreme differentials can exacerbate over extended periods of neglect and can precipitate premature dissolution of the organization or entity.

Tax exploitation can be compensated for by introducing representation based on net taxes paid so that those jurisdictions acting as net donors of federal taxes can leverage more political power within the system than the net welfare recipients. This will discourage the net welfare jurisdictions from perfecting their exploitative practices. It should condition them to think of the nation as a whole rather than focusing on their short term self- interests, and develop macro-economic strategies based more on competition than federal government subsidy by reducing their net political influence and likelihood of earning future federalist government subsidies. Due to the representational deductions due to tax rebates, those states that are welfare recipients won't have any representation in that specific chamber, branch, or tier of government which should be an extremely potent and effective means to discourage tax exploitation.

In both methods, larger jurisdictions with more mature economies will have access to much more representation which is correlated to their extra contributions to federalist taxes. This will benefit the nation as population with the more specialized labor and more experienced professionals will have more representation. The regions with higher GDP and stronger economies will be able to export their economic practices and government theories. The net result of enfranchising those regions which pay more taxes should be faster economic growth and more competitive markets for export.

There is an option for regions or states with negative federalist tax contributions to continue receiving representation. It would be a bare minimum, a lowest common denominator set by the constitution that would apply every time a state would normally lose representation in the chamber due to federalist tax policy. States with positive contributions to federalist tax policy will earn that minimum representation in addition to number if seats earned by proportional positive contributions to federalist tax policy. The representation gained by positive federalist tax contributions are still based on a value equal to an LCD in ratio to itself with the coefficients then added to the primary (minimum) coefficient.

This is a significant concession, but it will improve the chances of states agreeing to representational coefficients based on net taxes. Surrendering representation in exchange for increased federalist tax contributions might be too extreme a consequence for a conventional public policy intended to build market economies and strengthen the public sector within poorer, smaller, or less capable regions.

f. Executive Representation
    i. Registered Voters
    ii. Allied Voters
    iii. Total Voters

Executive Representation concentrates the amount of influence awarded from proportional representation within one elected office. If the popular representation would have produced 11 senators for the jurisdiction the single Executive Representative would wield the equivalent of 11 votes within the legislature. It combines the best attributes of representational government with focus. Leadership is concentrated onto a smaller number of representatives without diminishing the proportional influence the jurisdiction should have. The administrative staff of an executive representatives within the legislatures will have to bulk up to accommodate the larger number of committees they must participate in and the executive representative appoints their surrogates on any committee they sit on. Executive representation can use any representational coefficient based on population, GDP, or taxes, and any variant thereof.

Even more complicated systems of Executive Representation can predicate the votes leveraged by the position on the number of votes the individual received during election to the office, the number of registered voters in the jurisdiction, or the number of total voters in the jurisdiction. The variable figure will introduce some uncertainty in votes from year to year. This is especially true when Presidential elections affect voter turnout making those executive representatives elected during that year much more powerful. Results will be less predictable over any length term adding impetus and emergency to passing laws when the opportunity presents itself. It should make the political more responsive to popular movements and much harder to obstruct.

Executive Representation based on voter turnout requires the election system to be engineered so that the states coinciding with Presidential election and increased turnout is on a rotation that grants the extra advantage to all Executive Representatives in a cyclical manner. This can be accomplished with making sure the Presidential term is one step or two steps longer than the executive representatives terms allowing the constellation of states affected by the increased voter turnout to change every full term.

If the Presidential term and Executive Representative's terms were equal the same states would always benefit from the improved turnout making their Executive Representatives more potent. This could be purposefully engineered into the election cycle to create a two-tiered state system (imperial) where certain states had institutional advantages. Take the United States as an example with Presidential voter turnout at 70% and off years at only 30%. Those executive representatives elected during those years would have more than double the representation. The states or party with elections during the Presidential election would dominate for the next few years. This can simulate the same mechanism that provides a Prime Minister is guaranteed a majority in the Parliament.

This system of Executive Representation can be used to form empires. Instead of a rotation a pre-selected number of states would always gain the advantage of stronger presidential turnout and thus more legislative power. This would allow a democratic nation to actively seek or coerce more membership through war or negotiation with new states provided clearly stipulated but abbreviated representation in the political union. It would still qualify as democratic with each citizen gaining one voter. Contemporary democracies have many representational deficiencies that are ruthlessly exploited by opposition parties rendering any formal criticism of an imperial presidency less accurate or meaningful.

Executive Representation follows the traditional method for allocating committee representation. If an executive representative earns a total of 10 votes this translates to the equivalent to 10 separate representatives when allocating the committee seats. If the executive representation uses registered voters, raw, population, or recorded votes the process is slightly different. The total number of votes earned by each executive representative is divided by the number of committee seats available. This simulates an LCD where each Executive Representative then takes turns appointing themselves to committees until their personal store of votes is exhausted.

If there are 1 million votes in a system and only 100 committee seats each seat is worth 1000 votes. Seats can be purchased for less votes than the LCD if it represents the last of the executive representative's appointments. Any votes remaining after all seats are filled are lost. This should favor minority parties just enough to ensure that popular movements in the electorate are checked by a slight decrease in committee seats for the majority. The majority party will still own a majority of the votes in the legislature and can pass all measures escaping committees.

Representatives install themselves on committees in the order of most votes or least votes, one at a time or according to the various committee staffing procedures. It is also possible for the political parties to dictate the order of seat selection instead of individual members. Leadership will decide the candidate and the committee in the order prescribed to the system.

g. Combinational (Scale)

Scaled representation is an abridged form of democracy that can be used in occupations, empires, or for feudal variations. The population would continue to vote on a proportional basis with the majority of participants receiving a single vote. However, a coefficient is introduced to provide management representation equal to that of the number of employees or enlisted under their command. Authoritarian control is avoided by distributing votes among all levels of leaders so that the bulk of the votes remain with the lower level managers when combined with the free vote of all enlisted or employed. The top commander would have the most individual votes, but the combined total of all votes including subordinates always maintains a majority requiring all legislators to seek out coalitions within the institution or company and rule through consensus.

h. Legislative Brokers

Legislative broker powers allow currently elected politicians to consolidate power by winning elections in other chambers of the legislature or by earning multiple seats in the same chamber. Each position permits an additional vote and access to more committees. Legislative brokers are paid for each position and can use that salary to hire the staff they need to administer to the new duties and powers. When necessary, a legislative broker should be permitted to authorize a surrogate to vote in his stead if the multiple chambers are operating simultaneously.

Successful legislative brokers are more likely to win other seats adding value to the set of appointments and making the candidate more attractive for campaign donations. In most political systems, the total number of eligible seats will still be restricted by location ensuring that the integrity is protected as one broker will typically only represent one state. Legislative brokers will vary in size, power, and party contributing to the overall competitiveness of the system.

J. Senatorial
      i. 1
      ii. 2

Senatorial Representation is capped at either 1 Senator per state or 2 Senators per state, but this is purely arbitrary. The ratio between states and senators should remain fixed regardless of the number of senators. For example, if there are 50 states and they are split into two groups, with one group maintain control over 20 states and the other group maintaining control over 30 states, it doesn't matter which representational coefficient is used the ratio will remain about 66% each time. If there are 1 Senator per state, it would result in 20 Senators from one group and 30 Senators from the other group. This has the same ratio of senators when there are 40 Senators in one group and 60 in the other. No matter how many Senators are apportioned to each state, the ratio remains the same.

14. Macro-political (Executive, Legislative)
    1.) Class
        a. alpha (primary executive or legislator)
        b. agency heads, committee heads (Fractal)
        c. proportional (Governors and Mayors)

2.) Power
  a. Veto
  b. Confirmation (triangulation)
  c. both.

When an Executive branch is split in multiple parts each one can be empowered with a macro-political vote for use in negotiating with legislators. Each Executive branch or agency would have a vote in whether or not legislation passes, with each institution maintaining one vote equivalent with the final vote of the legislation. It is a more productive form of a veto requiring legislation passes by a Legislature to be confirmed by the majority of institutions including the executive branch prior to being made into law. This is a progressive reform to the contemporary single executive veto power. Increasing the number of intuitional parties with a macro-political vote actually increases the likelihood of more legislation passing.

For example, in a bicameral legislature with unitary executive, there would be 3 total votes, with each institution gaining 1 vote, and where only a 2/3rds majority is needed to pass a law. The two institutions contributing to the passage could be both the lower chamber and the higher chamber of the legislature, or the lower chamber and the executive branch, or the higher chamber and the executive. The three permutations increase the chances of laws passing with both chambers acting more aggressively to author laws the executive agrees with.

When the voting franchise is extended to cabinet members and agency directors it greatly increases the likelihood of a diverse response which is appropriate provided the many intricate ways even minor laws can impact the socio-economic fabric of the nation. In order for macro-political votes based on large numbers of competitive positions it should occur where the directors and managers have the most discretion and independence. Fractal organizations will benefit most from this power.

History demonstrates that Inefficiencies in a political system are often ruthlessly exploited for personal gain and profits. Imbalanced wealth concentrations and political representation produce an environment of instability and danger. The usual symptoms are present; extreme budgetary problems resulting from low taxes and sustained government expenditures in excess of revenues, and excessive corruption in the election cycles from lack of access or excessive moneyed interests.

More obvious imbalances are evident when public sector institutions like penitentiaries and security services are privatized, and where labor protections remain diluted and ineffective. Decay occurs over the span of years and decades and is often irreversible when the population accepts and even advocates for their degraded environment – the result is always the same in that it ends in rebellion, revolt, or war as body politics suffer the same threats of injury and death as its citizens due but in economies of scale.

Political systems that resist change or impede the rate of change are subject to more threats of insolvency and dissolution. It's only a matter of time until excessively complex or rigid systems of political governance are exposed to crises which require quick decisive action but where the awkward interaction of antagonistic legislative chambers or executive branches fail to resolve a critical issue and precipitate a system ending event. More cumbersome systems, requiring more dedicated cooperation, are the easiest to exploit economically as regulations will be irregular and infrequent with institutional powers protecting current market share and monopolies rather than producing economic opportunity and fair exchanges.

Under-regulated political markets also subjected to moneyed representation based on campaign contributions rather than fixed proportions of asset or income representation is the quickest way to destroy integrity and faith in the system. Most economies have steep natural gradients towards monopolistic market share and dangerous wealth concentrations. Moneyed influence accelerates this trend and makes it more resistant to reform. Within decades, a nation could be rendered noncompetitive and irrelevant within the global theatre of political-economy.

All of these deficits present opportunities for insurrection, rebellion, and reformation. Stability is the most valuable currency in political economy, but when a nation or state is in decline maintaining the current trajectory is not productive. Order can be achieved by diluting civil liberties, inhibiting organization, and enforcing property laws but this is hardly sufficient in dispelling the potential instability. Nations can continue to suppress opportunities for self-determination, but it will be a persistent ambition and goal for the population, especially when the premise of democracy exists elsewhere, and the ideas can be communicated through trade or example. Democratic societies should thrive more often simply because the communities can provide for themselves with political and economic reforms. They will naturally seek out more stability and more productivity.

Notes

Chapter One

Investopedia http ://www.investopedia.com/ask/answers/199.asp
[2] Investopedia http://www.investopedia.com/terms/g/gross-national-income-gni.asp
[3] Przeworski, A. (1999) "Minimalist Conception of Democracy: A Defense."
In Democracy's Value edited by Shapiro, I. and Hacker-Cordon, C.
Cambridge: Cambridge University Press.
[4] Accessed on 4/2/2018 at http://statisticstimes.com/economy/gdp-capita-of-india.php
[5] derived from state GDP and median income accessed on 4/2/2018 at
https://www.worldatlas.com/articles/indian-states-by-gdp.html,
http://statisticstimes.com/economy/gdp-capita-of-indian-states.php
[6] This is an imperfect translation. It does not include the 12 nominated
representatives in the lower house. The GDP-based representational
coefficient produced 228 base representatives rather than the current 233
without the nominated representatives
[7] Przeworski, A. (1999) "Minimalist Conception of Democracy: A Defense."
In Democracy's Value edited by Shapiro, I. and Hacker-Cordon, C.
Cambridge: Cambridge University Press.
[8] Accessed on 4/2/2-018 from https://tradingeconomics.com/iraq/gdp-per-capita
[9] Accessed on 4/2/2018 at https://www.worldatlas.com/finance/
Afghanistan/gdp.html
[10] Accessed on 4/4/2018 from http://abcnews.go.com/Politics/afghanistan-americas-longest-war/story?id=10770029

Chapter 2

[11] Accessed on June 24, 2017 and retrieved from http://www.politico.com
/magazine/story/ 2014/08/the-sad-end-of-the-british-empire-110362
[12] Accessed on June 24, 2017 and retrieved form
http://www.pbs.org/battlefieldvietnam/ history/
[13] Retrieved from 2010 US Census Wyoming 2015 ACS 5-year Population
estimate on 7.1.2017
https://factfinder.census.gov/faces/nav/jsf/pages/community _facts.xhtml
[14] Retrieved from retrieved from 2010 US Census California 2015 ACS 5-year Population estimate on 7.1.2017 from https://factfinder.census.gov/faces/
nav/jsf/pages/commu-nity_facts.xhtml
[15] Derivative of California 2015 population estimate / Wyoming 2015
population estimate

[16] Retrieved from 2010 US Census New York 2015 ACS 5-year Population estimate on July 1st, 2017

https://factfinder.census.gov/faces/nav/jsf/pages/commu-nity_facts.xhtml

[17] Retrieved from 2010 US Census Florida 2015 ACS 5-year Population estimate on July 1st, 2017

https://factfinder.census.gov/faces/nav/jsf/pages/commu-nity_facts.xhtml

[18] Derivative of New York and Florida 2015 population estimates / Wyoming 2015 population estimate (individual)

[19] Retrieved from 2010 US Census Texas 2015 ACS 5-year Population estimate on 7.1.2017

https://factfinder.census.gov/faces/nav/jsf/pages/commu-nity_facts.xhtml

[20] Derivative of Texas 2015 population estimates / Wyoming 2015 population estimate

[21] Retrieved from World Bank on 7.1.2017

http://data.worldbank.org/indicator/NY. GDP.MKTP.CD?locations=MX

[22] Retrieved from World Bank on 7.1.2017

http://data.worldbank.org/indicator/NY. GDP.MKTP.CD?locations=US&view=chart

[23] Derivative of US 2015 GDP estimates / Mexico 2015 GDP estimate

[24] Representational ratio of Texas/Wyoming and US/Mexico, or 46/16 = 2.875

[25] Retrieved from World Bank on 7.1.2017,

http://data.worldbank.org/indicator/NY.GDP. MKTP.CD?locations=CA

[26] Derivative of GDP estimate for Canada/ GDP estimate of U.S.

[27] Derivative of California 2015 population estimate / Wyoming 2015 population estimate

[28] Derivative of California's 2015 GDP estimate / Wyoming's GDP estimate, retrieved from the BEA on July 1st 2017 from

https://bea.gov/newsreleases/regional/gdp_state/qgsp_ newsrelease.htm

[29] Retrieved from BEA on July 1st 2017 through

https://bea.gov/newsreleases/regional/ gdp_state/qgsp_newsrelease.htm

[30] Retrieved from World Bank on July 1st 2017 at

http://data.worldbank.org/indicator/SP.POP.TOTL?locations=MX

[31] Retrieved from World Bank on July 1st 2017 at http://data.worldbank.org/ indicator/SP.POP.TOTL?locations=CA

[32] Retrieved from 2010 US Census California 2015 ACS 5-year Population estimate on July 1st, 2017

https://factfinder.census.gov/faces/nav/jsf/pages/commu-nity_facts.xhtml

[33] Retrieved from 2010 US Census Texas 2015 ACS 5-year Population estimate on July 1st, 2017

https://factfinder.census.gov/faces/nav/jsf/pages/commu-nity_facts.xhtml

[34] Retrieved from 2010 US Census Florida 2015 ACS 5-year Population estimate on July 1st, 2017

https://factfinder.census.gov/faces/nav/jsf/pages/commu-nity_facts.xhtml

[35] Retrieved from 2010 US Census New York 2015 ACS 5-year Population estimate on July 1st, 2017 https://factfinder.census.gov/faces/nav/jsf/pages/commu-nity_facts.xhtml

[36] Derivative of Mexico's population of 125.9m / California's population of 38.42m

[37] Derivative of Mexico's population of 125.9m / Texas' population of 26.54m

[38] Derivative of state revenue data from the IRS for tax year 2015 accessed on July 2nd 2017 at https://www.irs.gov/pub/irs-soi/15databk.pdf

[39] Derivative of state expenditures from US Census for year 2015 accessed on July 2nd 2017 at https://www.usaspending.gov/transparency/Pages/StateSummaries.aspx

[40] The revenues and expenditures from states were assigned between party affiliation on page 42

[41] Derivative of state expenditures from US Census for year 2015 accessed on July 2nd 2017 at https://www.usaspending.gov/transparency/Pages/StateSummaries.aspx

[42] Accessed article in New York Times on July 3rd, 2017, written by Richard Florida, Jan 3rd, 2015 and retrieved from https://www.nytimes.com/2015/01/04/opinion/sunday/is-life-better-in-americas-red-states.html

[43] Multiplied 2015 US Census data on government spending by 57% for blue states and 43% for red states.

[44] Derivative of state expenditures from US Census for year 2015 accessed on July 7th 2017 at https://www.usaspending.gov/transparency/Pages/StateSummaries.aspx

[45] Derivative of state revenue data from the IRS for tax year 2015 accessed on July 2nd 2017 at https://www.irs.gov/pub/irs-soi/15databk.pdf

[46] Derivative of U.S. 2015 GDP estimate by estimated party preference of state, retrieved from the BEA on July 7th, 2017 from https://bea.gov/newsreleases/regional/gdp_state/qgsp_ newsrelease.htm in terms of state revenue data by estimated party preference of state, retrieved from the IRS for tax year 2015 accessed on July 7th 2017 at https://www.irs.gov/pub/irs-soi/15databk.pdf

[47] Estimate of Federal Expenditures in ratio of GDP, p. 14, Gruber, J. (2013). Public finance and public policy. New York, NY: Worth Publishers.

[48] Derivative of U.S. 2015 GDP estimate by estimated party preference of state, retrieved from the BEA on July 7th, 2017 from https://bea.gov/newsreleases/regional/gdp_state/qgsp_ newsrelease.htm

[49] Derivative of U.S. 2015 SIC GDP estimate by estimated party preference of state, retrieved from the BEA on July 7th, 2017 from https://bea.gov/newsreleases/regional/ gdp_state/qgsp_newsrelease.htm

[50] Derivative of U.S. 2015 SIC GDP estimate by estimated party preference of state, retrieved from the BEA on July 7th, 2017 from https://bea.gov/newsreleases/regional/ gdp_state/qgsp_newsrelease.htm

[51] Derivative of U.S. 2015 NAIC GDP estimate by estimated party preference of state, retrieved from the BEA on July 7th, 2017 from https://bea.gov/newsreleases/regional/ gdp_state/qgsp_newsrelease.htm

[52] Derivative of the difference in total proportion of NIAC GDP estimates for 1997-2015 and SIC GDP estimates for 1963-1997, by state party preference.

[53] Derivative of the net difference between of NIAC GDP estimates for 1997-2015 and SIC GDP estimates for 1963-1997, by state party preference.

[54] Derived from state party preferences demonstrated on page 42

[55] Derived from state party preferences demonstrated on page 42

[56] Derivative of 2015 population data retrieved from the US Census on July 3rd, 2017 at https://www.census.gov/data/tables/2016/demo/popest/nation-total.html

[57] Comparing California to Wyoming by population constrained by terms of Senate representation.

Chapter 3

[58] Divided number of times 60 seat margin in Senate overcome since 1933, where the House and President were all of the same party. Accessed on 7.8.2017 and retrieved from http://wiredpen.com/resources/political-commentary-and-analysis/a-visual-guide-balance-of-power-congress-presidency/

[59] History of filibuster provided by Donnelly, T., And Rosen, J. (2017, April 8th). Political polarization killed the filibuster. The Atlantic. Accessed on 7.8.2017 and retrieved from https://www.theatlantic.com/politics/archive/2017/04/ political-polarization-killed-the-filibuster/522360/

[60] Monaghan, A., (2014, Nov 13). Wealth inequality top 01 worth as much as bottom 90. The Guardian. Accessed on July 8th, 2017 and retrieved from https://www.theguardian.com /business/2014/nov/13/us-wealth-inequality-top-01-worth-as-much-as-the-bottom-90

[61] Mishel, L., Gould, W., Bivens, J. (2015, January 6th). Wage stagnation in nine charts. Economic Policy Institute. Report. Accessed on July 8th, 2017 and retrieved from http://www.epi.org/publication/charting-wage-stagnation/

[62] Accessed on 7.10.2017 and retrieved from https://www.thoughtco.com/european-wars-and-battles-4133312

[63] Accessed on 7.12.2017 and retrieved from https://www.thoughtco.com/major-wars-and-conflicts-20th-century-1779967

[64] Accessed on 7.12.2017 and retrieved from http://genocidewatch.net/genocide-2/genocide-and-politicide/

[65] Accessed on 7.10.2017 and retrieved from https://www.forbes.com/sites/singularity/ 2012/07/19/could-automation-lead-to-chronic-unemployment-andrew-mcafee-sounds-the-alarm/#60603fda1a31

[66] Accessed on 7.10.2017 and retrieved from http://www.economist.com/node/18558041

[67] Access on 7.12.2017 and retrieved from https://www.thoughtco.com/major-wars-and-conflicts-20th-century-1779967

Chapter 4

[68] Accessed on 7.14.2017 and retrieved at
http://data.worldbank.org/indicator/NY.GDP. MKTP.CD?locations=IQ
[69] Accessed on 7.14.2017 and retrieved at http://data.worldbank.org/indicator/
SP.POP.TOTL ?locations=IQ
[70] Accessed on 7.14.2017 and retrieved at http://data.worldbank.org/indicator/
SP.POP.TOTL ?locations=IQ
[71] Accessed on 7.14.2017 and retrieved at
http://data.worldbank.org/indicator/NY.GDP. MKTP.CD?locations=IQ
[72] Accessed on 7.14.2017 and retrieved at
http://data.worldbank.org/indicator/ SP.POP.TOTL ?locations=IQ
[73] Accessed on 7.14.2017 and retrieved at
http://data.worldbank.org/indicator/NY.GDP. MKTP.CD?locations=IQ
[74] Accessed on 7.14.2017 and retrieved at http://data.worldbank.org/indicator/
SP.POP.TOTL?locations=AF
[75] Accessed on 7.14.2017 and retrieved at
http://data.worldbank.org/indicator/NY. GDP.MKTP.CD?locations=AF
[76] Accessed on 7.14.2017 and retrieved at http://data.worldbank.org/indicator/
SP.POP.TOTL?locations=AF
[77] Accessed on 7.14.2017 and retrieved at
http://data.worldbank.org/indicator/NY. GDP.MKTP.CD?locations=AF
[78] Accessed on 7.14.2017 and retrieved http://data.worldbank.org/indicator/
SP.POP.TOTL?locations=AF
[79] Accessed on 7.14.2017 and retrieved
http://data.worldbank.org/indicator/NY. GDP.MKTP.CD?locations=AF
[80] Accessed on 7.14.2017 and retrieved at http://data.worldbank.org/indicator
/SP.POP.TOTL?locations=US
[81] Accessed on 7.14.2017 and retrieved by http://data.worldbank.org
/indicator/ NY.GDP.MKTP.CD?locations= US&view=chart
[82] Accessed on 7.14.2017 and retrieved at http://data.worldbank.org/indicator
/SP.POP.TOTL?locations=US
[83] Accessed on 7.14.2017 and retrieved by http://data.worldbank.org
/indicator/ NY.GDP.MKTP.CD?locations= US&view=chart
[84] Derivative of GDP data from http://data.worldbank.org/
[85] Derivative of GDP data from http://data.worldbank.org/
[86] Accessed on Retrieved from
https://www.census.gov/population/apportionment/about /computing.html
[87] Accessed on 7.14.2017 and retrieved from
http://www.house.gov/representatives/
[88] Derivative of the demographic data on U.S., Afghanistan, and Iraq from
http://data.worldbank.org/

[89] Derivative of the demographic data on U.S., Afghanistan, and Iraq from http://data.worldbank.org/
[90] Derivative of the demographic data on U.S., Afghanistan, and Iraq from http://data.worldbank.org/
[91] Derivative of the GDP data on U.S., Afghanistan, and Iraq from http://data.worldbank.org/
[92] Derivative of the GDP data on U.S., Afghanistan, and Iraq from http://data.worldbank.org/
[93] Comparison of demographic data and GDP data for U.S., Afghanistan, and Iraq from http://data.worldbank.org/
[94] Comparison of demographic data and GDP data for U.S., Afghanistan, and Iraq from http://data.worldbank.org/
[95] Comparison of demographic data and GDP data for U.S., Afghanistan, and Iraq from http://data.worldbank.org/
[96] Comparison of demographic data and GDP data for U.S., Afghanistan, and Iraq from http://data.worldbank.org/
[97] Accessed on 7.15.2017 and retrieved from https://www.opendemocracy.net/zana-khasraw-gul/who-is-responsible-for-iraq%e2%80%99s-sectarian-violence
[98] Accessed on 7.15.2017 and retrieved from http://data.worldbank.org/indicator/ SP.POP.TOTL?locations=MX
[99] Accessed on 7.15.2017 and retrieved http://data.worldbank.org/indicator/NY. GDP.MKTP.CD?locations=MX
[100] Accessed on 7.15.2017 and retrieved from http://data.worldbank.org/indicator/ SP.POP.TOTL?locations=MX
[101] Accessed on 7.15.2017 and retrieved http://data.worldbank.org/indicator/NY. GDP.MKTP.CD?locations=MX
[102] Derivative of demographic data on Mexico from http://data.worldbank.org/
[103] Derivative of GDP data on Mexico from http://data.worldbank.org/
[104] Accessed on 7.15.2017 and retrieved from http://data.worldbank.org/indicator/ SP.POP.TOTL?locations=CA
[105] Accessed on 7.15.2017 and retrieved from http://data.worldbank.org/ indicator/NY.GDP.MKTP.CD?locations=CA
[106] Accessed on 7.15.2017 and retrieved from http://data.worldbank.org/indicator/ SP.POP.TOTL?locations=CA
[107] Accessed on 7.15.2017 and retrieved from http://data.worldbank.org/ indicator/NY.GDP.MKTP.CD?locations=CA
[108] Derivative of demographic data on Canada from http://data.worldbank.org/
[109] Derivative of GDP data on Canada from http://data.worldbank.org/
[110] Accessed on 7.15.2017 and retrieved from http://data.worldbank.org/indicator/ SP.POP.TOTL?locations=CA
[111] Accessed on 7.15.2017 and retrieved from http://data.worldbank.org/ indicator/NY.GDP.MKTP.CD?locations=CA
[112] Accessed on 7.15.2017 and retrieved from http://data.worldbank.org/indicator/ SP.POP.TOTL?locations=CA

[113] Derivative of demographic data on Canada from http://data.worldbank.org/
[114] Accessed on 7.15.2017 and retrieved from http://data.worldbank.org/ indicator/NY.GDP.MKTP.CD?locations=CA
[115] Derivative of GDP data on Canada from http://data.worldbank.org/
[116] Accessed on 7.15.2017 and retrieved from http://data.worldbank.org/ indicator/SP.POP.TOTL?locations=US
[117] Accessed on 7.15.2015 and retrieved from http://data.worldbank.org/indicator/ SP.POP.TOTL?locations=EU
[118] Accessed on 7.15.2017 http://data.worldbank.org/indicator/ NY.GDP.MKTP.CD?locations=EU
[119] Comparison of demographic data and GDP data for U.S., Canada, and Mexico from http://data.worldbank.org/
[120] Comparison of demographic data and GDP data for U.S., Canada, and Mexico from http://data.worldbank.org/
[121] Accessed on 7.15.2017 and retrieved from http://financial-dictionary. thefreedictionary.com/Mature+economy
[122] Comparison of GDP data for U.S., Canada, and Mexico from http://data.worldbank.org/
[123] Comparison of GDP data for U.S., Canada, and Mexico from http://data.worldbank.org/
[124] Comparison of GDP data for U.S., Canada, and Mexico from http://data.worldbank.org/
[125] Comparison of GDP data for U.S., Canada, and Mexico from http://data.worldbank.org/
[126] Comparison of demographic data for U.S., Canada, and Mexico from http://data.worldbank.org/
[127] Comparison of demographic data for U.S., Canada, and Mexico from http://data.worldbank.org/
[128] Comparison of population date from US Census accessed on 7.15.2017 and retrieved from https://factfinder.census.gov/faces/nav/jsf/pages/index.xhtml
[129] Comparison of population date from US Census accessed on 7.15.2017 and retrieved from https://factfinder.census.gov/faces/nav/jsf/pages/index.xhtml
[130] Comparison of demographic data for U.S., Canada, and Mexico from http://data.worldbank.org/
[131] Comparison of demographic data for U.S., Canada, and Mexico from http://data.worldbank.org/
[132] Comparison of population date from US Census accessed on 7.15.2017 and retrieved from https://factfinder.census.gov/faces/nav/jsf/pages/index.xhtml
[133] Comparison of population date from US Census accessed on 7.15.2017 and retrieved from https://factfinder.census.gov/faces/nav/jsf/pages/index.xhtml

[134] Comparison of population date from US Census accessed on 7.15.2017 and retrieved from
https://factfinder.census.gov/faces/nav/jsf/pages/index.xhtml
[135] Comparison of population date from US Census accessed on 7.15.2017 and retrieved from https://factfinder.census.gov/faces/nav/jsf/pages/index.xhtml
[136] Comparison of demographic data for U.S., Canada, and Mexico from http://data.worldbank.org/
[137] Comparison of GDP data for U.S., Canada, and Mexico from http://data.worldbank.org/
[138] Comparison of GDP data for U.S., Canada, and Mexico from http://data.worldbank.org/
[139] Comparison of GDP data for U.S., Canada, and Mexico from http://data.worldbank.org/
[140] Accessed on 7.15.2017 and retrieved from http://data.worldbank.org/indicator/SP.POP.TOTL?locations=AU
[141] Accessed on 7.15.2017 and retrieved from http://data.worldbank.org/indicator/SP.POP.TOTL?locations=CA
[142] Accessed on 7.15.2017 and retrieved from http://data.worldbank.org/indicator/SP.POP.TOTL?locations=GB
[143] Comparison of population data for Australia, Canada, United Kingdom from http://data.worldbank.org/
[144] Comparison of population data for Australia, Canada, United Kingdom from http://data.worldbank.org/
[145] Accessed on 7.15.2017 and retrieved from http://data.worldbank.org/indicator/NY.GDP.MKTP.CD?locations=AU
[146] Accessed on 7.15.2017 and retrieved from http://data.worldbank.org/indicator/NY.GDP.MKTP.CD?locations=CA
[147] Accessed on 7.15.2017 and retrieved from http://data.worldbank.org/indicator/NY.GDP.MKTP.CD?locations=GB
[148] Comparison of GDP data for Australia, Canada, United Kingdom from http://data.worldbank.org/
[149] Comparison of GDP data for Australia, Canada, United Kingdom from http://data.worldbank.org/
[150] Comparison of GDP data for U.K., Canada, and Australia from http://data.worldbank.org/
[151] Comparison of GDP data for U.K., Canada, and Australia from http://data.worldbank.org/
[152] Comparison of GDP data for U.K., Canada, and Australia from http://data.worldbank.org/
[153] Comparison of GDP data for U.K., Canada, and Australia from http://data.worldbank.org/
[154] Comparison of population date from US Census accessed on 7.15.2017 and retrieved from
https://factfinder.census.gov/faces/nav/jsf/pages/index.xhtml

[155] Comparison of population date from US Census accessed on 7.15.2017 and retrieved from
https://factfinder.census.gov/faces/nav/jsf/pages/index.xhtml
[156] Summation of GDP data for U.S., Canada, Australia, and U.K. from
http://data.worldbank.org/
[157] Summation of population data for U.S., Canada, Australia, and U.K. from
http://data.worldbank.org/
[158] Accessed on 7.15.2017 and retrieved from http://data.worldbank.org/
indicator/SP.POP.TOTL?locations=EU
[159] Comparison of population data for U.S., U.K., Canada, and Australia from
http://data.worldbank.org/
[160] Comparison of population data for U.S., U.K., Canada, and Australia from
http://data.worldbank.org/
[161] Comparison of GDP data for U.S., U.K., Canada, and Australia from
http://data.worldbank.org/
[162] Comparison of GDP data for U.S., U.K., Canada, and Australia from
http://data.worldbank.org/
[163] Comparison of GDP data for U.S., U.K., Canada, and Australia from
http://data.worldbank.org/
[164] Comparison of Population data for U.S., U.K., Canada, and Australia from
http://data.worldbank.org/
[165] Comparison of GDP data for U.S., U.K., Canada, and Australia from
http://data.worldbank.org/
[166] Summation of GDP data for U.K., Canada, and Australia from
http://data.worldbank.org/
[167] Accessed on 7.16.2017 and retrieved from http://www.bbc.com
/news/politics/eu_referendum/results
[168] Accessed on 7.16.2017 and retrieved from
https://factfinder.census.gov/faces/tableservices/jsf/pages/productview.xhtml?
src=bkmk
[169] Derivative of GDP data by state on https://bea.gov (interactive data,
regional data) – only "Red States"
[170] Accessed on 7.16.2017 and retrieved from
https://factfinder.census.gov/faces/tableservices/jsf/pages/productview.xhtml?
src=bkmk
[171] Accessed on 7.16.2017 and Derivative of GDP data by state on
https://bea.gov (interactive data, regional data) – only "Red States"
[172] Comparison of 2015 GDP for Red Stats and Blue States
[173] Accessed on 9.19.2017, Janice Beaver, CRS Report for Congress, U.S.
International Borders: Brief facts, retrieved from
https://fas.org/sgp/crs/misc/RS21729.pdf
[174] Accessed on 9.19.2017, Archibald, R. (2013, April 26), New York Times,
In Trek North, First Lure is Mexico's Other Line, retrieved from
http://www.nytimes.com/ 2013/04/27 /world/americas/central-americans-
pour-into-mexico-bound-for-us.html

[175] Accessed on 7.18.2017 and retrieved from
https://factfinder.census.gov/faces/
tableservices/jsf/pages/productview.xhtml?src=bkmk
[176] Accessed on 7.18.2017 and retrieved from https://bea.gov (interactive data,
regional data) – only "Red States"
[177] Accessed on 7.18.2017 and retrieved from http://data.worldbank.org/
indicator/SP.POP.TOTL?locations=MX
[178] Accessed on 7.18.2017 and retrieved from
http://data.worldbank.org/indicator/ NY.GDP.MKTP.CD?locations=MX
[179] Accessed on 7.18.2017 and retrieved from
https://factfinder.census.gov/faces/
tableservices/jsf/pages/productview.xhtml?src=bkmk
[180] Accessed on 7.18.2017 and retrieved from https://bea.gov (interactive data,
regional data) – only "Red States"
[181] Accessed on 7.18.2017 and retrieved from http://data.worldbank.org/
indicator/SP.POP.TOTL?locations=MX
[182] Accessed on 7.18.2017 and retrieved from
http://data.worldbank.org/indicator/ NY.GDP.MKTP.CD?locations=MX
[183] Summation of Mexico and Red States' population 2015 estimates.
[184] Accessed on 7.18.2017 and retrieved from
https://factfinder.census.gov/faces/
tableservices/jsf/pages/productview.xhtml?src=bkmk
[185] Summation of Mexico and Red States' GDP 2015 estimates
[186] Accessed on 7.18.2017 and retrieved from
http://data.worldbank.org/indicator/ NY.GDP.MKTP.CD?locations=MX
[187] Accessed on 7.18.2017 and retrieved from http://data.worldbank.org/
indicator/SP.POP.TOTL?locations=MX
[188] Accessed on 7.18.2017 and retrieved from https://bea.gov (interactive data,
regional data) – only the Central and Southern States
[189] Comparison of 2015 populations in Mexico and the Central and Southern
States.
[190] Comparison of 2015 population for Mexico and the Central and Southern
States
[191] Comparison of 2015 population for Mexico and the Central and Southern
States
[192] Comparison of 2015 GDP for Mexico and Red States
[193] Comparison of 2015 GDP between Mexico and the Central and Southern
States
[194] Comparison of 2015 population between Mexico and the Central and
Southern States
[195] Accessed on 7.18.2017 and retrieved from
http://data.worldbank.org/indicator /SP.POP.TOTL?locations=CU
[196] Comparison of Mexico, Cuba, and U.S. 2015 populations
[197] Comparison of Mexico, Cuba, and U.S. 2015 populations
[198] Comparison of Mexico, Cuba, and U.S. 2015 populations

[199] Accessed on 7.18.2017 and retrieved from http://data.worldbank.org/ indicator/NY.GDP.MKTP.CD?locations=CU

[200] Comparison of Mexico, Cuba, and U.S. GDP

[201] Accessed on 8.9.2017 and retrieved from https://factfinder.census.gov/ faces/ tableservices/jsf/pages/ productview.xhtml?src=bkmk

[202] Accessed on 8.9..2017 and retrieved from https://bea.gov (interactive data, regional data)

[203] Accessed on 8.9.2017 and retrieved from https://factfinder.census.gov /faces/ tableservices/jsf/pages/productview.xhtml?src=bkmk

[204] Accessed on 8.9.2017 and retrieved from US Census data and World Bank data (Multiple sources)

[205] Accessed on 8.9.2017 and retrieved from http://data.worldbank.org/indicator/NY.GDP.MKTP.CD?locations=US&view =chart

[206] $12.5T/$18T Accessed on 8.9.2017 and retrieved from http://data.worldbank.org/indicator/NY.GDP.MKTP.CD?locations=US&view =chart

[207] Accessed on 8.9.2017 and retrieved from http://data.worldbank.org/indicator/NY.GDP.MKTP.CD?locations=US&view =chart

[208] Derivative of demographic data from US Census and World Bank

[209] Derivative of demographic data from US Census and World Bank

[210] Derivative of demographic data from US Census and World Bank

[211] Derivative of demographic data from US Census and World Bank

[212] Derivative of BEA data and World Bank data

[213] Derivative of BEA data and World Bank data

[214] Derivative of BEA data and World Bank data

[215] Derivative of World Bank data and US Census data

[216] Derivative of World Bank data and BEA Data

[217] Derivative of World Bank data and US Census data

[218] Derivative of World Bank data and BEA Data

[219] Accessed on 8.9.2017 and retrieved from http://data.worldbank.org/indicator/NY.GDP.MKTP.CD?locations=EU&view =chart

[220] Derivative of World Bank data and US Census Data

[221] Derivative of World Bank data and US Census data

[222] Derivative of World Bank data and US Census data

[223] Derivative of World Bank data and US Census data

[224] Derivative of World Bank data and US Census data

[225] Derivative of World Bank data and BEA data

[226] Derivative of World Bank data and BEA data

[227] Derivative of World Bank data and BEA data

[228] Accessed on 8.9.2017 and retrieved from https://www.nytimes.com/2017/03/28/world/europe/scotland-britain-brexit-european-union.html?_r=0

[229] Accessed on 8.9.2017 and retrieved from
http://www.newstatesman.com/politics/uk/2016/06/what-does-brexit-mean-northern-ireland
[230] Accessed on 8.9.2017 and retrieved from Retrieved from
http://www.newstatesman.com/politics/uk/2016/06/what-does-brexit-mean-northern-ireland
[231] Derivative of World Bank and US Census data
[232] Derivative of World Bank and US Census
[232] Accessed on 8.9.2017 and retrieved from
http://data.worldbank.org/indicator/NY.GDP.MKTP.CD?locations=CN&view=chart
[234] Accessed on 8.9.2017 and retrieved from https://bea.gov (interactive data, regional data) – "Red state GDP" compared to "Blue State GDP" in proportion.
[235] Derivative of state revenue data from the IRS for tax year 2015 accessed on July 2nd 2017 at https://www.irs.gov/pub/irs-soi/15databk.pdf
[236] Accessed on 8.9.2017 and retrieved from http://www.governing.com/gov-data/military-civilian-active-duty-employee-workforce-numbers-by-state.html
[237] Derivative of BEA data and IRS data – comparing differences in state revenues with contributions made.
[238] Derivative of state revenue data from the IRS for tax year 2015 accessed on 8.9.2017 at https://www.irs.gov/pub/irs-soi/15databk.pdf
[239] Derivative of state revenue data from the IRS for tax year 2015 accessed on 8.9.2017 2017 at https://www.irs.gov/pub/irs-soi/15databk.pdf
[240] Derivative of World Bank data and US Census data
[241] Derivative of World Bank data and BEA data
[242] Derivative of World Bank data and US Census data
[243] Derivative of World Bank data and BEA data
[244] Derivative of World Bank data and US Census data
[245] Derivative of World Bank data and US Census data
[246] Derivative of World Bank data and BEA data
[247] Derivative of World Bank data and BEA data
[248] Accessed on 8.9.2017 and retrieved from https://bea.gov (interactive data, regional data) – "Central and Southern state GDP" compared to "Northern and West Coast State GDP" in proportion.

Chapter 6

[249] Brenner, N. and Keil, R. (2006). *The Global Cities Reader*. New York, NY. Routledge.
[250] Brenner, N. and Keil, R. (2006). *The Global Cities Reader*. New York, NY. Routledge.
[251] Sassen, S., (2012). *Cities in a World Economy*. Thousand Oaks, California: Pine Forge Press

Imperial Union

Executive:

- 2.iii (Abolished Executive), 5.a. (National)

Legislative:

- **1.i.x (Unicameral legislature),** ii.x (Representative), iii.1.2.a.3.4.a.5.7.10.13.a.i.b.ii.c.i (Laws, Oversight, Ratification, Unitary Executive Powers, Appropriations, Appointments, Taxing, Unilateral Amendments with supermajority), **iv.1.b.2.a (Independent, 3/5ths rule, majority party),** 5.a (National), 6.a.iii (6 year terms), b.iv (Unlimited), c.iii (Unlimited), d.iv (no restraints), **7.a.i (Publicly Funded),** b.i.xx (parliamentary), **ii.xxxx (Universal Suffrage),** c.x (direct elections), 8.a.v.b (Citizen), b.i.ii (to vote and to hold office), c.ii (non -exclusive), 10.b (voluntary), 12.b (Districts), **13.b.i (Representative of GDP Straight)**

Judicial:

- 3.A.i (Judicial, Hierarchical), b.i. (Judicial powers only), c.ii.x.1 **(appointed by the Prime Minister),** 5.a.(National), 6.a.iv (Unlimited), b.iv (unlimited), c.iii (Unlimited), d.ii (sum of elected), 8.a.v.b, b.ii (citizen to hold office)

The Economy Union

Executive;

- 2.i (Unitary Presidential), 5.a (National), 6.a.ii (6 year terms), b.i (1 term maximum), c.i (lifetime maximum), d.ii (sum of elected), **7.a.i (publicly funded, citizens),** b.i.x (Presidential), **ii.xxxx (Universal Suffrage),** c.x (direct elections), 8.a.v.b (Citizen), b.i.ii (eligibility for voting and holding office), c.i (exclusive), 10.b (voluntary voting), 14.1.a.2.a (Executive, Veto)

Legislative:

- 1.i.xx.z (Bicameral legislature, House), ii.x (Representative), **iii.1.2.a.5.10.13.a.ii.b.ii.c.i (Laws, Oversight over Unitary, Appropriations, Taxes, Amendments),** iv.1.b.2.a (Independent,

3/5th rule, majority party), 5.a (National), 6.a.iii (6 year terms), b.iv (unlimited terms), c.iii (unlimited); d.iv (no restraints), **7.a.i (publicly funded, citizens),** b.i.x (Presidential), **ii.xxxx (Universal Suffrage),** c.x (direct elections), 8.a.v.b (Citizen), b.i.ii (to vote and hold office), c.i (exclusive), 10.b (voluntary), 12.b (Districts), **13.b.i (Representative of GDP Straight)**

- 1.i.xx.zz (Bicameral legislature, Senate), ii.x (Representative), **iii.1.2.3.7.13.a.ii.b.ii.c.i (Laws, Oversight, Ratification, Appointments),** iv.1.b.2.a (Independent, 3/5th rule, majority party), 5.a (National), 6.a.iii (6 year terms), b.iv (unlimited terms), c.iii (unlimited); d.iv (no restraints), **7.a.i (publicly funded, citizens),** b.i.x (Presidential), **ii.xxxx (Universal Suffrage),** c.x (direct elections), 8.a.v.b (Citizen), b.i.ii (to vote and hold office), c.i (exclusive), 10.b (voluntary), 12.a (Jurisdictions), **13.j.ii (Senatorial, two)**

Judicial:

- 3.a.i (Judicial, Hierarchical), b.i.a (Judicial powers only, general), c.ii.x.2 **(appointed by the President),** 5.a.(National), 6.a.iv (Unlimited), b.iv (unlimited), c.iii (Unlimited), d.ii (sum of elected), 8.a.v.b, b.ii (citizen to hold office)

Econometric Democracy

Executive;

- 2.i (Unitary Presidential), 5.a (National), 6.a.ii (6 year terms), b.i (1 term maximum), c.i (lifetime maximum), d.ii (sum of elected), **7.a.i (publicly funded, citizens),** b.i.x (Presidential), **ii.xxxx (Universal Suffrage),** c.x (direct elections), 8.a.v.b (Citizen) b.i. (eligibility for voting), c.i (exclusive), 10.b (voluntary voting),

Legislative:

- 1.i.xx.z (Bicameral legislature, House), ii.x (Representative), **iii.1.2.3.5.7.a.b.10.13.a.i.b.ii.c.ii (Laws, Oversight, Treaties, Appropriations, Confirmations for judicial and executive, Taxes, Unilateral Amendments with supermajority),** iv.1.b.2.d (Independent, proportional, one for one, rotating), 5.a (National), 6.a.iii (6 year terms), b.iv (unlimited terms), c.iii (unlimited); d.iv (no restraints), **7.a.i (publicly funded, citizens),** b.i.x (Presidential),

ii.xxxx (Universal Suffrage), c.x (direct elections), 8.a.v.b (Citizen), b.i.ii (to vote and hold office), c.i (exclusive), 10.b (voluntary), 12.b (Districts), **13.b.i (Representative of GDP Straight)**

- 1.i.xx.zz (Democratic chamber, 2nd house) ii.ixxxx (True Democratic), 1.a.i (Mono-chamber, straight), **2.b.ii.x (Executive Filter),** iii.xxx (federal), 2.a.iii (Referendum monthly), 3 b.ii (confirm laws bicameral), c (Repeal legislation), 4.a (municipal jurisdictions), 8.a.v.b (Citizen), b.i (to vote), 10.b (voluntary)

Judicial:

- 3.a.i (Judicial, Hierarchical), b.i. Judicial powers only), c.ii.x.2 **(appointed by the President),** 5.a.(National), 6.a.iv (Unlimited), b.iv (unlimited), c.iii (Unlimited), d.ii (sum of elected), 8.a.v.b, b.ii (citizen to hold office)

Unity Parliament

Executive:

- 2.iii (Abolished Executive), 5.a. (National)

Legislative:

- **1.i.xx.z (Bicameral legislature,** 1st House) , ii.x (Representative), iii.1.2.d.e.4.a.5.7.b.iii.iv.13.a.ii.b.ii.c.i (Laws, Oversight over A.G./Treasurer, Unitary Executive Powers, Appropriations, Appointment over A.G./Treasurer, Amendments bicameral and supermajority), **iv.1.b.2.b (Independent, 3/5ths rule, one by one, rotating),** 5.a (National), 6.a.ii (4 year terms), b.iv (Unlimited), c.iii (Unlimited), d.iv (no restraints), **7.a.i (Publicly Funded)** b.i.xx (parliamentary), c.x (direct elections), 8.a.v.b (Citizen), b.i.ii (to vote and to hold office), c.ii (non -exclusive), 10.b (voluntary), 12.a (jurisdictions), **13.a.i (Representative of Population), 13.h (Legislative Broker)**

- **1.i.xx.zz (Bicameral legislature,** 2nd House), ii.x (Representative), iii.1.2.c.3.7.a.ii.10.13.a.ii.b.ii.c.i (Laws, Oversight over foreign executive, Ratification, Appointment over judicial and foreign executive, Taxes, Amendments bicameral and supermajority), **iv.1.b.2.c (Independent, 3/5ths rule, incremental, rotating),** 5.a (National), 6.a.ii (4 year terms), b.iv (Unlimited), c.iii (Unlimited), d.iv (no restraints), **7.a.i (Publicly Funded),** b.i.xx (non-parliamentary), c.x (direct elections), 8.a.v.b (Citizen), b.i.ii (to vote and to hold office), c.ii (non -exclusive), 10.b (voluntary), 12.a (jurisdictions), **13.b.i (Representative of GDP Straight),**

Judicial:

- 3.a.i (Judicial, Hierarchical), b.i. (Judicial powers only), c.ii.x.2 **(appointed by the President),** 5.a.(National), 6.a.iv (Unlimited), b.iv (unlimited), c.iii (Unlimited), d.ii (sum of elected), 8.a.v.b, b.ii (citizen to hold office)

Executive Union

Executive:

- 2.iii (Abolished Executive), 5.a. (National)

Legislative:

- **1.i.xx.z (Bicameral legislature,** 1st House) , ii.x (Representative), iii.1.2.d.e.4.b.f.5.7.iii.iv.10.13.a.i.b.ii.c.i (Laws, Oversight over A.G/Treasurer, Foreign Executive Powers, Appropriations, Appointments over A.G./Treasurer, Taxes, and unilateral amendments with supermajority), **iv.1.b.2.d (proportional, one by one, rotating),** 5.a (National), 6.a.iii (6 year terms), b.ii (2 terms), c.iii (Unlimited), d.iv (no restraints), **7.a.i (Publicly Funded)** b.i.xx (parliamentary), c.x (direct elections), 8.a.v.b (Citizen), b.i.ii (to vote and to hold office), c.ii (non -exclusive), 10.b (voluntary), 12.a (jurisdictions), **13.a.i (Representative of Population), 13.f (Executive Representation)**

- **1.i.xx.zz (Bicameral legislature,** 2nd House), ii.x (Representative), iii.1.2.c.3.4.c.d.5.7.a.b.ii (Laws, Oversight over Foreign Executive, Ratification, Domestic Executive Powers, Central Banking/Treasury Executive, Appropriations, Appointment confirmation over judicial and foreign executive), **iv.1.b.2.d (proportional, one by one, rotating),** 5.a (National), 6.a.iii (6 year terms), b.iii (3 terms), c.iii (Unlimited), d.iv (no restraints), **7.a.i (Publicly Funded),** b.i.xx (non-parliamentary), c.x (direct elections), 8.a.v.b (Citizen), b.i.ii (to vote and to hold office), c.ii (non -exclusive), 10.b (voluntary), 12.a (jurisdictions), **13.b.i (Representative of GDP Straight), 13.f (Executive Representation)**

Judicial:

- 3.a.i (Judicial, Hierarchical), b.i. (Judicial powers only), c.ii.x.2 **(appointed by the President),** 5.a.(National), 6.a.iv (Unlimited), b.iv (unlimited), c.iii (Unlimited), d.ii (sum of elected), 8.a.v.b, b.ii (citizen to hold office)

Presidential Median Partition

Executive;

- **2.i (Unitary Presidential),** 5.a (National), 6.a.ii (4 year terms), b.ii (2 terms maximum), c.i (lifetime maximum, d.ii (sum of elected), 7.a.i (publicly funded), b.ii.xxxx (One citizen = One vote), c.x (direct elections), 8.a.v.b (Citizen), b.i.ii (to vote and hold office) c.i (exclusive), 10.b (voluntary voting), 14.1.a.2.a **(Macro-political vote, Veto)**

Legislative:

- 1.i.xx.z (Bicameral legislature, 1st House), ii.x (Representative), iii.1.2.3.7.13.a.ii.b.ii.c.i (Laws, Oversight over unitary, Ratification, Appointments, and Amendments), iv.1.b.2.b (Independent, 3/5ths rule, one by one, rotating), 5.a (National), **6.a.iii (4 year terms), b.i iv (unlimited terms),** c.i (lifetime maximum, d.ii (sum of elected), 7.a.i (publicly funded), b.ii.xxxx (One citizen = One vote), c.x (direct elections), **8.a.iv.b.i.f.ii.z.d.zz.a.zzz.i (GDP, below median, independent, national median),** v.b (Citizen), b.i.ii (to vote and hold office), c.i (exclusive), 10.b (voluntary), 12.b (Districts), **13.a.i (Representative of Population, by jurisdiction)**

- 1.i.xx.zz (Bicameral legislature, 2nd Chamber), ii.x (Representative), iii.1.2.a.3.5.10.13.a.ii.b.ii.c.i (Laws, Oversight over unitary, Appropriations, Taxes, and Amendments), iv.3 (majority rule, one for one rotation), 5.a (National), **6.a.iii (4 year terms), b.i iv (unlimited terms),** c.i (lifetime maximum, d.ii (sum of elected 7.a.i (publicly funded), b.ii.xxxx (One citizen = One vote), c.x (direct elections), **8.a.iv.b.i.f.ii.z.d.zz.a.zzz.i (GDP, below median, independent, national median),** v.b (Citizen), b.i.ii (to vote and hold office), 10.b (voluntary), 12.b (Districts), **13.a.i (Representative of Population , by jurisdiction)**

Judicial:

- 3.A.i (Judicial, Hierarchical), b.i.a (Judicial powers only, general), c.ii.x.2 **(appointed by the President),** 5.a.(National), 6.a.iv (Unlimited), b.iv (unlimited), c.iii (Unlimited), d.ii (sum of elected), 8.a.v.b, b.ii (citizen to hold office)

Bipartite Median Partition

Executive;

- 2.ii.x.c. **(Executive Presidential**), 5.a (National), 6.a.iii (6 year terms), b.i (1 terms maximum), c.i (lifetime maximum), d.ii (sum of elected), **7.a.i, b.i., ii.xxxx, c.x (publicly funded, presidential, one person = one vote, direct elections),** b.i.ii (eligibility for voting and holding office), 10.b (voluntary voting), 14.1.a.2.b (Executive, Confirmation)

- 2.ii.x.cc.ccc **(Executive Attorney General and Treasury),** 5.a (National), 6.a.iii (6 year terms), b.ii (2 terms maximum), c.i (lifetime maximum), d.ii (sum of elected), **7.a.i, b.i., ii.xxxx, c.x (publicly funded, presidential, one person = one vote, direct elections),** 8.a.v.b (Citizen), b.i.ii (eligibility for voting and holding office), 10.b (voluntary voting), 14.1.a.2.b (Executive, Confirmation)

Legislative:

- 1.i.xx.z (Bicameral legislature, 1st House), ii.x (Representative), **iii.1.2.3.5.7.a.b..ii.10.13.a.ii.b.ii.c.i (Laws, Oversight, Treaties, Appropriations, Appointments Judicial & Presidential, Taxing, and Amendments),** iv.1.b.2.b (Independent, 3/5ths rule, one by one, rotating), 5.a (National), 6.a.iv (6 year terms), b.i iv (unlimited terms**),** c.i (lifetime maximum, d.ii (sum of elected), 7.a.i (publicly funded), b.ii.xxxx (One citizen = One vote), c.x (direct elections), **8.a.iv.b.i.f.ii.z.d.zz.a.zzz.i (GDP, below median, independent, national median),** v.b (Citizen), b.i.ii (to vote and hold office), c.i (exclusive), 10.b (voluntary), 12.b (Districts), **13.a.i (Representative of Population, by jurisdiction)**

- 1.i.xx.zz (Bicameral legislature, 2nd Chamber), ii.x (Representative), **iii.1.2.5.7.b..iii.iv.13.a.ii.b.ii.c.i (Laws, Oversight, Appropriations. Appointments Executive – Attorney General & Treasurer,**

Amendments), iv.1.b.2.b (Independent, 3/5ths rule, one by one, rotating), 5.a (National), **6.a.iv (6 year terms), b.i iv (unlimited terms),** c.i (lifetime maximum, d.ii (sum of elected 7.a.i (publicly funded), b.ii.xxxx (One citizen = One vote), c.x (direct elections), **8.a.iv.b.i.f.ii.z.d.zz.a.zzz.i (GDP, below median, independent, national median),** v.b (Citizen), b.i.ii (to vote and hold office), 10.b (voluntary), 12.b (Districts), **13.a.i (Representative of Population , by jurisdiction)**

Judicial:

- 3.A.i (Judicial, Hierarchical), b.i. (Judicial powers) c.ii.x.2 **(appointed by the President),** 5.a.(National), 6.a.iv (Unlimited), b.iv (unlimited), c.iii (Unlimited), d.ii (sum of elected), 8.a.v.b, b.ii (citizen to hold office)

Parliamentary Median Partition

Executive;

- 2.iii (Abolished Executive), 5.a (National)

Legislative:

- 1.i.xx.z (Bicameral legislature, 1st House), ii.x (Representative), iii.1.2.c.d.4.b.f.5.7..iii.iv.10 (Laws, Oversight over Domestic and Commerce Executive, **Foreign Executive Powers, Executive Judicial Powers, Appropriations, Appointment powers over A.G./Treasurer, and Taxes**), iv.1.b.2.c (Independent, 3/5ths rule, incremental, rotating), 5.a (National), 6.a.iii (4 year terms), b.i iv (unlimited terms), c.i (lifetime maximum, d.ii (sum of elected), 7.a.i (publicly funded), b.ii.xxxx (One citizen = One vote), c.x (direct elections), **8.a.iv.b.i.f.ii.z.d.zz.a.zzz.i (GDP, below median, independent, national median),** v.b (Citizen), b.i.ii (to vote and hold office), c.i (exclusive), 10.b (voluntary), 12.b (Districts), **13.a.i (Representative of Population, by jurisdiction)**

- 1.i.xx.zz (Bicameral legislature, 2nd Chamber), ii.x (Representative), iii.1.2.b.3.4.c.d..5.7.10.13.a.i.b.i.c.i (Laws, **Ratification,** Oversight over Foreign Executive, **Domestic Executive Powers, Central Banking/Treasury Executive, Appropriations, Appointment confirmation powers over judicial and foreign, Amendments),** iv.1.b.2.c (Independent, 3/5ths rule, incremental, rotating), 5.a

(National), **6.a.iii (4 year terms), b.i iv (unlimited terms),** c.i (lifetime maximum, d.ii (sum of elected 7.a.i (publicly funded), b.ii.xxxx (One citizen = One vote), c.x (direct elections), **8.a.iv.b.i.f.ii.z.d.zz.a.zzz.i (GDP, below median, independent, national median),** v.b (Citizen), b.i.ii (to vote and hold office), 10.b (voluntary), 12.b (Districts), **13.a.i (Representative of Population , by jurisdiction)**

Judicial:

- 3.A.i (Judicial, Hierarchical), b.i. (Judicial powers only), c.ii.x.2 **(appointed by the President),** 5.a.(National), 6.a.iv (Unlimited), b.iv (unlimited), c.iii (Unlimited), d.ii (sum of elected), 8.a.v.b, b.ii (citizen to hold office)

Bipartite Presidential Partitioned Senate

Executive;

- 2.ii.x.c. **(Executive Presidential)**, 5.a (National), 6.a.ii (4 year terms), b.ii (2 terms maximum), c.i (lifetime maximum), d.ii (sum of elected), **7.a.i, b.i., ii.xxxx, c.x (publicly funded, presidential, one person = one vote, direct elections),** b.i.ii (eligibility for voting and holding office), 10.b (voluntary voting), 14.1.a.2.a.b (Macro-political vote, Veto and Confirmation)

- 2.ii.x.cc.ccc **(Executive Attorney General and Treasury)**, 5.a (National), 6.a.ii (4 year terms), b.ii (2 terms maximum), c.i (lifetime maximum), d.ii (sum of elected), **7.a.i, b.i., ii.xxxx, c.x (publicly funded, presidential, one person = one vote, direct elections),** 8.a.v.b (Citizen), b.i.ii (eligibility for voting and holding office), 10.b (voluntary voting), 14.1.a.2.a.b (Macro-political vote, Veto and Confirmation)

Legislative

- 1.i.xxx.z (Multi-cameral legislature, 1st House), ii.x (Representative), iii.1.2.b.5.7.a.b.13.a.ii.b.i.c.i (Laws, Oversight over foreign executive, Appropriations Appointment Confirmation powers over judicial and foreign executive, Amendments), iv.1.b.2.a (Independent, 3/5th rule, majority party), 5.a (National), 6.a.iii (4 year terms), b.i iv (unlimited terms), c.i (lifetime maximum, d.ii (sum of elected), 7.a.i (publicly funded), b.ii.xxxx (One citizen = One vote), c.x (direct elections), **8.a.iv.b.i.f.ii.z.d.zz.b.zzz.i (GDP, below median, aggregate, national median),** v.b (Citizen), b.i.ii (to vote and hold office), c.i (exclusive), 10.b (voluntary), 12.a (Jurisdictions), **13.a.i (Representative of Population, by jurisdiction)**

- 1.i.xxx.zz (Multi-cameral legislature, 2nd Chamber), ii.x (Representative), iii.1.2.c.d.3.5.7.a.b.10.13.a.ii.b.i.c.i (Laws, Oversight over A.G./Treasurer, Treatise, Appointment Confirmation over judicial and domestic executive, Appropriations, Taxes, and Amendments), iv.1.b.2.a (Independent, 3/5th rule, majority party), 5.a (National), **6.a.iii (4 year terms), b.i iv (unlimited terms),** c.i (lifetime maximum, d.ii (sum of elected 7.a.i (publicly funded), b.ii.xxxx (One citizen = One vote), c.x (direct elections), **8.a.iv.b.i.f.ii.z.d.zz.b.zzz.i (GDP, below median, aggregate, national median),** v.b (Citizen), b.i.ii (to vote and hold office), 10.b (voluntary), 12.a (Jurisdictions), **13.a.i (Representative of Population , by jurisdiction)**

Judicial:

- 3.A.i (Judicial, Hierarchical), b.i.a (Judicial powers only, general), c.ii.x.2 **(appointed by the President),** 5.a.(National), 6.a.iv (Unlimited), b.iv (unlimited), c.iii (Unlimited), d.ii (sum of elected), 8.a.v.b, b.ii (citizen to hold office)

Democratic Reserve Partition

Executive:

- 2.iii (Abolished Executive), 5.a. (National)

Legislative:

- 1.i.xxx.z (Multi-cameral legislature, 1st House), ii.x (Representative), iii.1.2.a3..5.7.10.13.a.ii.b.ii.c.ii (Laws, Oversight over Unitary, Treatise, Appropriations Appointments, Taxes, and Bicameral Amendments with supermajority), iv.1.b.2.b (Independent, 3/5ths rule, one by one, rotating), 5.a (National), 6.a.iii (4 year terms), b.i iv (unlimited terms), c.i (lifetime maximum, d.ii (sum of elected), 7.a.i (publicly funded), b.ii.xxxx (One citizen = One vote), c.x (direct elections), **8.a.iv.b.i.f.ii.z.d.zz.b.zzz.i (GDP, below median, aggregate, national median),** v.b (Citizen), b.i.ii (to vote and hold office), c.i (exclusive), 10.b (voluntary), 12.a (Jurisdictions), **13.a.i (Representative of Population, by jurisdiction)**

- 1.i.xxx.zz (Multi-cameral legislature, 2nd Chamber), ii.x (Representative), iii.1.2.a.5.10.13.a.ii.b.ii.c.ii (Laws, Oversight over Unitary, Appropriations, Taxes), iv.1.b.2.b (Independent, 3/5ths rule, one by one, rotating), 5.a (National), **6.a.iii (4 year terms), b.i iv (unlimited terms),** c.i (lifetime maximum, d.ii (sum of elected 7.a.i (publicly funded), b.ii.xxxx (One citizen = One vote), c.x (direct elections), **8.a.iv.b.i.f.ii.z.d.zz.b.zzz.i (GDP, below median, aggregate, national median),** v.b (Citizen), b.i.ii (to vote and hold office), 10.b (voluntary), 12.a (Jurisdictions), **13.a.i (Representative of Population , by jurisdiction)**

- 1.i.xxx.zzz (Multicamera legislature, 3rd chamber), ii.ixxxx (Direct Democracy), 1.a.ii (Mono-chamber, Leveraged), 2.a.iii (Referendum monthly), **2b.ii.x.iii.xxx (Unitary filter, Federal tier, Reserve) 3.b.i, (confirm laws triangulation),** 4.a (municipal jurisdictions), 8.a.v.b (Citizen), b.i (to vote), 10.b (voluntary)

Reserve:

- 4.i.a (Reserves, admitting all retired members), ii.a..**2.i (Unitary President sub routine), ii.d.x (repealing legislation with supermajority),** iii.b (Unicameral), iv.1.a.2.b (Pool of retired national legislators), v.e (half total equivalent terms)

Judicial:

- 3.A.i (Judicial, Hierarchical), b.i.a (Judicial powers only, general), c.ii.x.2 **(appointed by the President),** 5.a.(National), 6.a.iv (Unlimited), b.iv (unlimited), c.iii (Unlimited), d.ii (sum of elected), 8.a.v.b, b.ii (citizen to hold office)

Presidential Biaxial Median Partition

Executive;

- **2.i (Unitary Presidential),** 5.a (National), 6.a.iii (6 year terms), b.i (1 terms maximum), c.i (lifetime maximum, d.ii (sum of elected), 7.a.i (publicly funded), **b.ii.xxxx (One citizen = One** vote), c.x (direct elections), 8.a.v.b (Citizen), bi.ii (to vote and hold office) c.i (exclusive), 10.b (voluntary voting), 14.1.a.2.a (Macro-political vote, Veto)

Legislative:

- 1.i.xx.z (Bicameral legislature, 1st House), ii.x (Representative), iii.1.2.a.3.5.7.a.b.i (Laws, Oversight over Unitary, Ratification, Appropriations, and Appointments), iv.1.b.2.d (Independent, proportional, one for one, rotating), 5.a (National), **6.a.iii (6 year terms), b.i iv (unlimited terms),** c.i (lifetime maximum, d.ii (sum of elected), 7.a.i (publicly funded), b.ii.xxxx (One citizen = One vote), c.x (direct elections), **8.a.iv.b.i.f.ii.z.d.zz.b.zzz.i (GDP, below median, aggregate, national median),** v.b (Citizen), b.i.ii (to vote and hold office), c.i (exclusive), 10.b (voluntary), 12.b (Districts), **13.a.i (Representative of Population, by jurisdiction)**

- 1.i.xx.zz (Bicameral legislature, 2nd Chamber), ii.x (Representative), iii.1.2.5.10. 13.a.ii.b.i.c.i (Laws, Oversight over Unitary, Appropriations, Taxes, and Amendments), iv.1.b.2.d (Independent, proportional, one for one, rotating), 5.a (National), **6.a.iii (6 year terms), b.i iv (unlimited terms),** c.i (lifetime maximum, d.ii (sum of elected), 7.a.i (publicly funded), b.ii.xxxx (One citizen = One vote), c.x (direct elections), **8.a.iv.b.i.f.ii.z.d.zz.b.zzz.i (GDP, below median, aggregate, national median),** v.b (Citizen), b.i.ii (to vote and hold office), 10.b (voluntary), 12.b (Districts), **13.a.i (Representative of Population, by jurisdiction)**

Judicial:

- 3.A.i (Judicial, Hierarchical), b.i. (Judicial powers), c.ii.x.2 **(appointed by the President),** 5.a.(National), 6.a.iv (Unlimited), b.iv (unlimited), c.iii (Unlimited), d.ii (sum of elected), 8.a.v.b, b.ii (citizen to hold office)

**Master List of
System Attributes**

1.) Legislative
    i. Organization
        x) uni-cameral
        xx.) Bi-cameral
          z. 1st camera
          zz. 2nd camera
        xxx.) Multicameral
          z. 1st camera
          zz. 2nd Camera
          zzz. 3rd Camera
          Zzzz 4th Camera
        xxxx.) Abolished (usurped by executive,
             administrative laws only)

    ii. Attributes
        x. Representative
        xx. Tyrannical
          a.   Appointing Tier
            a.   Same Tier
            b.   Lower Tier
          b.   Appointing Agent
            z. Appointed by Exec
              1. Unitary Executive
              2. Presidential
              3. Attorney General
              4. Treasurer General
            zz. Appointed by legislators
            zzz. Appointed by judicial
            zzzz. Appointed by Reserve Chamber
          c. Proportion (remaining are elected)
            z. minimal 3%
            zz. Optimal 10%
            zzz. Total 100%
        xxx. Atomized (lower tier governments dictate
representatives in higher tier, lowest tier elected by
popular vote)
            1. Council members appoint
            representative
            2. Executives (mayor) appoint
            representative

xxxx. Direct Democracy (non-republican)
   1. Structure
        i. Straight
           1. Representational
           2. Winner Takes All
        ii. Leverage
        iii. Cumulative
        iv. Registered
        v. Senatorial
           1. Arbitrary
           2. Average

   2. Components
        a. Echo-chamber (all functions usurped by referendum)
           i. Referendum weekly
           ii. Referendum biweekly
           iii. Referendum monthly
        b. Auxiliary Chamber
           i. Legislators charged with presentation/filter (veto & Schedule)
              x. Elected advocates (by popular vote)
              xx. Appointed (by Chamber leadership)
           ii. Executives act as filter (veto & Schedule), appoints advocate for presentation
              x. Unitary
              xx. Presidential
              xxx. Attorney General
              xxxx. Treasurer.
       iii. Auxiliary Executives Tier
       x. municipal
       xx. state
       xxx. federal
      iv. Number of Auxiliary Representatives
      x. senatorial – one per jurisdiction
      xx. Representative – ratio coupled to
              population (or GDP, taxes, etc)
  3. Powers
  a. Excising
     i. Appointments
     ii. Legislators
     iii. Executives
     iv. Judicial
  b. Confirms Legislation
      i. Triangulation

ii. Bicameral
c. Repeals Legislation
d. Confirms Appointments (Circuits)
i. Exclusive
ii. Bicameral
e. Confirms Treaties
i. Triangulation
ii. Bicameral

4. Jurisdictions (zones for tallying votes)
a. Municipalities
b. Counties
c. States
d. Federal (single market)

xxxxx. Abolished
1. Executive assumes Legislative Powers
a. President
b. Treasurer
c. Attorney General
2. Authoritarian (Unitary)

iii. Powers
1. Laws
2. Oversight
a. Unitary
b. Judicial
c. Tripartite Presidential
d. Tripartite Attorney General
e. Tripartite Treasury
3. Ratification (Treaties)
4. Executive
a. Unitary
b. Foreign (President/ Military/ Intelligence/ Alliances)
c. Domestic (Attorney General/ Law enforcement/ General
Administration)
d. Commerce (Treasurer/Central Bank & Banking/ Insurance
Agencies, Commerce)
e. Fractal (all executive functions assumed by separate committees)
5. Appropriation (Budgets)
6. Judicial
7. Appointments (confirmations)
a. Judicial confirmations
b. Executive confirmations
i. Unitary

ii. Presidential
iii. A.G.
iv. Treasurer
8. True Democratic Role
9. Triangulation
    a. Stipulated (Sub routine, Powers apportioned to the chamber)
    b. General (Sub routine, Powers apportioned to the other chambers)
10. Taxing
11. Appointments (direct, by majority leader)
12. Elections
13. Amendments
    a.Scope
        i.Unilateral
        ii.Bicameral
        iii. State Affirmed
    b.Width
        i. Simple Majority
        ii.   Supermajority 60%
    c.Depth
        i. States
        ii. Democratic chamber

iv. Committee Selection
    1. Composition
        a. Coalition
        b. Independent
    2.Order
        a. 3/5ths rule: the majority party and chamber dictate how committees are formed (conventional).
        b.   3/5ths, one for one, rotating
        c.   3/5ths, incremental, rotating
        d.   proportional, one for one, rotating
        e.   proportional, incremental, rotating

2.) Executive
    i.) Unitary (standard) – Primary determines subordinates
    ii.) Divided; all individually elected, primaries determine subordinates
        c.) President/ Military/ Intelligence/ Alliances,
        cc.) Treasurer/Central Bank & Banking/ Insurance Agencies,
        Commerce,

ccc.) Attorney General/Law Enforcement/
Administration)
cccc.) Fractal – each department elected or
appointed individually
1. Departments (Cabinet)
2. Individuals (Agency)

iii.) Abolished (Congress assumes responsibilities
and internally determines agency chairs or
department secretaries)

3.) Judicial
A. Structure
i.) Independent Circuits (like family /criminal/
superior/ supreme)
ii.) Congressional structure with internal votes forming
committees subject to
yearly rotations

B.) Powers
i. Judicial
ii.) Legislative Sub Routine
iii.) Executive Sub Routine
iv.) Reserve Sub Routine
C. Access
i.) Elected
x. Representative of population (like
House) tethered to individual
jurisdictions
xx. Unrepresentative (like US
Supreme Court, or Senate)
with a stipulated number of
justices untethered to
jurisdictions
ii.) Appointed
x.) By executive
1. Unitary
2. Presidential
3. Attorney General
4. Treasury
5. Determined by the committee/ circuit
xx.) By legislature
a.Terms Limits
x. Terms
a. 4 years

      b. 6 years

      c. 10 years

    xx. Permanent (life tenure)

4.) Reserves (continuing to use retired political representatives)

    i.) members

        a.) all retired elected officials

        b.) self-admitting (internal party vote)

            i. Terms

            ii. Permanent

        c.) appointed (determined by previous position, speaker, whip, president)

            i. Term

            ii. Permanent

    ii.) Powers

        a.) Executive (sub routine)

        b.) Legislative (sub routine)

        c.) Judicial (sub routine)

        d.) Exclusive Reserve (supermajority)

            x.) Repealing; Legislation

            xx.) Excising;

                i. Executives

                ii. Legislators

                iii. Judges

            xxx.) Excommunication; removing reserve branch eligibility eligibility)

            xxxx.) Triangulation (in Bicameral Legislations); can confirm laws from one of two other chambers but can't write laws

    iii.) Structure

        a.) Bifurcated by party (multi-Cameral);

        b.) Unicameral (in discriminant)

        c.) Fractal; organized by decade (or increments that produce odd numbers, singularly or in tandem by position within boards and legislatures (with a delay in activation of the reserve body politic until the imbalance is achieved if necessary to perpetuate the ordinary progression of politics)

    iv.) Pool

      1.) Tier

        a.) National

        b.) State

        c.) Local (county + municipal

        2.) Branches
                a.) Executive
                b.) Legislative
                c.) Judicial
    v.) Terms
        a.) single equivalent
        b.) double
        c.) triple
        d.) total equivalent
        d.) Permanent
        e.) Half total equivalent

5.) Tier
    a. National
    b. State
    c. Municipal (and County)
    d. Removed
    e. Economic Union

6.) Term limits
    a.) max length of term
        i.) 2
        ii.) 4
        iii.) 6
        iv.) unlimited
    b.) max number of terms
        i.) 1
        ii.) 2
        iii.) 3
        iv.) unlimited
    c.) constraints on number of terms
        i.) Lifetime Maximum (sum)
        ii.) Intermittent (reset after absence)
        iii.) Unlimited
    d.) restraints on terms
        i.) Sum of both elected and appointed
        ii.) Sum of all elected
        iii.) Per individual office/region
        iv.) None

7.) Elections
    a.) Campaign Donations
        i. Publicly Funding
        ii. Privately Funded
            x.) citizen only

xx.) corporate
 c. domestic corporations
 cc.. foreign corporations
xxx.) government (corporate)
 c. constrained to jurisdiction (county, state)
 cc. constrained to nation
 ccc. no restraint (foreign government access)
xxxx.) open (citizen, corporate, and foreign entity)
b.) Structure
 i. System
  x. Presidential (antagonistic or unsynchronized with legislature)
  xx. Parliamentarian (majority in legislature determines executive officer)
 ii. Vote
  x. Number (One stock or One Acre = One vote)
  xx. Value Voting (Asset Value = Number of Votes, stipulated ratio)
   c. .straight
   cc. ratio
   ccc. bracket
 xxx. Combinational (Weighted Part:Whole)
 xxxx. One Citizen = One Vote

c.) Intimacy
 x. Direct (Popular)
 xx. Indirect (Electoral College)
 xxx. Insulated (Legislative dictates)
  i. Majority of seats in unicameral or multi-cameral
  ii. Majority of chambers in multi-cameral (Macro-political Vote, lower tiers)
 xxxx. Coalition (majority of lower tier executives determine higher executive officer)

d.) Appointed
 x. Tyrannical
  1. Executive
   a. Presidential
   b. Attorney General
   c. Treasury General
  2. Legislatures Majority Party
  3. Judicial
 xx. Eligibility
  1. Individual
   A. Citizen

B. Resident
C. Alien
2. Governmental
  A. Tier
    i. city
    ii. county
    iii. state
    iv. Federal
    v. Union
  B. Domain
    i. Office
      x. Executive
      xx. Representative
      xxx. Judicial
    ii. Agency (Fractal)
  C. Jurisdiction
    i. Domestic
    ii. Foreign
4. Any

8.) Eligibility Constraints
  a.) Criteria
    i.) removed
    ii.) removed
    iii.) removed
    iv.) Wealth (employee/employer, aristocratic
      A. Removed
      B. Income based (regionally adjusted)
        i. Source
          a. Income (household and family)
          b. Tax liabilities
          c. removed
          d. removed
          e. removed
          f. Gross Domestic Product
        ii. Attributes
          z. value Index
            a.) removed
            b.) removed
            c.) removed
            d.) below median
          e.) above median
         zz. District Index

                                      a.) Individual
                                        b.) aggregate
                              zzz. Threshold
                                        i. national median
                                        ii. state median
                                        iii. district median
                              zzzz. Instrument
                                        a.) sales
                                        b.) property
                                        c.) income
                                        d.) capital gains
                                        e.) Payroll
                                        f.) Total

                  v.) Domicile
                        a. Resident Alien
                        b. Citizen
                        c. Nonresident Alien

           b.) Action
              i. to vote
              ii. to hold office
          c.) domain
              i. exclusive
              ii. non-exclusive

9.) Appointed by
      a.) region
           i) municipal
           ii.) county
           iii) state
      b.) branch
       ‘ i. legislature
          ii. executive
          iii.. judicial
          iv. reserve

10.) Voting
      a.) mandatory
      b.) voluntary
      c.) automated

11.) Political Parties
      a.) Primaries
          i.) closed

      ii.) Open

   b.) Endorsements

      i.) Two party system

      ii.) Multiple party endorsements

      iii.) Endorsement parties

12. Jurisdiction;

      a. Jurisdiction wide (Senators)

      b. Districts (Representatives)

      c. Sectors (Private or Public)

13. Number of Representatives

      a. Population

         i. Jurisdiction

      b. GDP

         i. Straight

         ii. Per Capita

      c. Taxes

         i. Gross

         ii. Net

            x. Surrendered

            xx. Minimum

      d. Removed

      e. removed

     f. Executive Representation

      i. Active voters

      ii. Registered voters

      iii. Total Population

      iv. Removed

     g. Combinational (Scale)

     h. Legislative Brokers

     i. removed

     j. Arbitrary (Senatorial)

      i. 1

      ii. 2

14. Macro Political Votes

   1.) Class

      a. Alpha (primary executive, speaker)

      b. Agency director (committee chairs)

      c. Proportional (Governors and Mayors)

   2.) Power

      a. Veto

      b. Confirmation (Triangulation)

      c. Both

ABOUT THE AUTHOR

Jordan David Weisinger is currently enrolled at Johns Hopkins University for an M.S. in Government Analytics. He previously graduated from the Northwestern University with an M.A. in Public Policy and Administration (2017) and the University of Massachusetts Amherst with a M.B.A. in General Management (2015). His undergraduate degree is in Literature from the University of Delaware (2000). Jordan Weisinger's books series concentrates on democratic systems of representation, paying close attention to representational coefficients modeled through fiscal policy and econometrics. He emphasizes high quality democratic entitlements that favor universal suffrage and majority rule despite a focus on wealth-based or class-based representation.